Why Crime Rates Fell

John E. Conklin
Tufts University

Boston   New York   San Francisco
Mexico City   Montreal   Toronto   London   Madrid   Munich   Paris
Hong Kong   Singapore   Tokyo   Cape Town   Sydney

Series Editor: *Jennifer Jacobson*
Editorial Assistant: *Elizabeth Lee*
Marketing Manager: *Krista Groshong*
Manufacturing Buyer: *Andrew Turso*
Composition Buyer: *Linda Cox*
Cover Administrator: *Kristina Mose-Libon*
Editorial-Production Service: *Omegatype Typography, Inc.*
Electronic Composition: *Omegatype Typography, Inc.*

For related titles and support materials, visit our online catalog at
www.ablongman.com.

Between the time Website information is gathered and published, some sites
may have closed. Also, the transcription of URLs can result in unintentional
typographical errors. The publisher would appreciate notification where these
errors occur so that they may be corrected in subsequent editions.

Library of Congress Cataloging-in-Publication Data

Conklin, John E.
     Why crime rates fell / John E. Conklin.
          p.   cm.
     Includes bibliographical references and index.
     ISBN 0-205-38157-X
     1. Crime—New York (State)—New York.   2. Crime prevention—New York
(State)—New York.   3. Crime—United States.   4. Crime.   5. Criminal
statistics.   I. Title.

     HV6795.N5 C665 2003
     364.9747'1'09049—dc21

                                                                        2002027758

Printed in the United States of America

10   9   8   7   6   5   4   3   2   1   07   06   05   04   03   02

CONTENTS

PREFACE

Something extraordinary happened in the 1990s: The rate at which Americans were killing, assaulting, and stealing dropped dramatically. This rapid and sustained decline in crime was unprecedented, yet it attracted much less attention than the increase in crime in the 1960s. There was surprisingly little public discourse on the reasons for the shrinking crime problem. This book explores those reasons by examining the way the crime issue was presented in the *New York Times* from 1990 through 1999, then assesses the validity of the explanations offered in the paper for the decline in crime rates. Hypotheses put forth by political leaders, law-enforcement officials, and criminologists are assessed using published research and available data. My hope is that a better understanding of why crime rates fell will point the way to measures that can save more lives and property.

Acknowledgments

I am deeply grateful for the support and advice provided by Allyn and Bacon's Jennifer Jacobson, series editor, and Tom Jefferies, editorial assistant. Expert editorial and production work was done by the team at Omegatype Typography. I want to thank the following people for their helpful suggestions for revising earlier versions of the manuscript: Katherine A. Culotta, Indiana State University; James Ennis, Tufts University; Clayton Steenberg, Arkansas State University; and Gregory B. Talley, Broome Community College. Finally, I want to thank the Trustees of Tufts University for the sabbatic leave that allowed me to complete this book.

CHAPTER

1 Introduction

During the 1990s, the United States experienced a dramatic decline in crime rates. In fact, if the rates that prevailed in 1990 had remained the same throughout the decade, there would have been 34,000 more murders, 6,715,000 more robberies, 5,547,000 more burglaries, and 2,569,000 more motor vehicle thefts than there were.* Whatever forces caused crime rates to fall thus prevented tens of thousands of deaths and millions of thefts.

Mark H. Moore advises against making too much of a decline in crime statistics that is not accompanied by a decline in fear: "The important story is that any movement in reported crime rates fails to capture what are the real aims of any anti-crime effort, namely reducing fear and helping create an environment where a sense of solidarity can be fostered in a neighborhood or city" (January 1, 1995: 36).† I disagree. The consequences of crime—heightened fear, weakened solidarity, limited mobility, and depressed real-estate prices, among others—are certainly important, but even more important are the lives and property lost by the victims of crime. These losses would be incurred even if people were not fearful because they erroneously believed that crime was not a problem.

Little research has been done to figure out why crime rates increase and decrease, so many of the explanations offered by criminologists for the decline in rates in the 1990s were based more on opinion than evidence. Some criminologists remained skeptical that anything had really changed for several years after rates had begun their descent.

---

*These figures were calculated by applying 1990 FBI crime rates to annual U.S. populations for 1990 through 1999, then subtracting the actual number of crimes recorded from 1990 to 1999 from the number that would have been recorded had 1990's rates prevailed throughout the decade (Federal Bureau of Investigation, 1991–2000).

†References throughout this book to *New York Times* articles, editorials, op-ed pieces, and letters to the editor include only the date, section (where relevant), and page number.

A few insisted that people should really be worrying about an imminent increase in crime.

Law-enforcement officials, politicians, community leaders, and news reporters were not shy about offering their own explanations for the decline in rates. In his memoir, *Turnaround: How America's Top Cop Reversed the Crime Epidemic*, New York Police Department Commissioner William Bratton (1998) asserted that his corporate-style management and systematic use of computerized crime statistics to redeploy officers were responsible for the unprecedented reduction in the city's crime rate, and that criminologists who said otherwise were simply wrong. Bratton ignored two facts: New York's crime rate had started to drop several years before he became commissioner, and other large cities also experienced big reductions in rates.

During the 1990s, national attention to the crime issue often focused on New York City. New York is the nation's largest city, and it is widely but incorrectly seen as a dangerous place to live or visit. This misperception is reinforced by the popular television show *NYPD Blue* and other fictional portrayals of the city. New York also garnered national attention because its crime rates fell sooner and more rapidly than rates elsewhere in the country. Influential national news media headquartered in the city, such as television networks and weekly news magazines, brought the story of falling crime rates to the country's attention. The city also had two media-savvy advocates for their own success in reducing crime: Mayor Rudolph Giuliani, a former federal prosecutor who first won office in 1993 on the basis of his promise to make the city safer, and Police Commissioner Bratton, a former New York Transit Police chief who applied the methods he had used to curb subway crime to the city as a whole.

To learn how criminologists, political leaders, law-enforcement officials, and the news media were explaining the decline in crime rates in New York City and in the nation as a whole, I gathered all relevant articles, editorials, op-ed pieces, and letters to the editor that appeared in the *New York Times* during the 1990s. A somewhat different picture might have emerged had I relied on national news magazines, television news programs, or different newspapers. I chose the *Times* because it is readily available on microfilm and it publishes an index for locating articles. According to Todd Gitlin (1980: 299), the *Times* has "the best claim to be called *the* national newspaper and *the* newspaper of record" because it is widely read by powerful and influential people who live far from New York; it is highly regarded by journalists everywhere; it is the source of many stories presented by other newspapers, television and radio news programs, and national news magazines; and it "sets agendas, generating and certifying issues in government, business, intellectual, professional, and academic circles throughout the country." Police Commissioner Bratton (1998: 280) has made the following observation on the importance of the *Times* in discussing his strategy for reducing crime:

> Because the reporting on crime shapes fear, from day one I had intended to marry *The New York Times*. I wanted the paper of record to tell our story, and I went out of my way to make the *Times* understand what we were doing. . . . Unlike the tabloids, which would generate great headlines and public support, the *Times* would reach the decision and influence shapers, nationally and internationally.

The *Times* covered the decline in crime rates in depth. Three items on this topic appeared in 1990. Five items appeared in 1991 and six appeared in 1992, the years when New York's rates were just beginning to fall. Coverage grew steadily, with the exception of a dip in 1998, to fifty-four items in 1999. Many of the 204 items published during the decade focused on crime in New York, but the explanations offered for the decline were usually more broadly applicable. Over the course of the decade, the paper gave increasing attention to the drop in the nation's crime rates.

Just before the prolonged decline in nation's crime rates began, Christopher Jencks (1991: 99) wrote that the news media "have a very selective approach to crime statistics. When crime declines, as it did in the early 1980s, editors assume the decline is only temporary and give it very little air time. When crime increases, as it did in the late 1980s, both journalists and editors see the increase as a portent of things to come and give it a lot of play." Jencks was wrong in his belief that declining crime rates are largely ignored by the media, but he was correct that the press prefers bad news about crime to good news: The number of articles in the *New York Times Index* on the rising crime rates of the 1963–1972 period is more than double the number of items on the falling crime rates of the 1990–1999 period.

From their content analysis of feature articles published in the *New York Times*, the *Washington Post*, and the *Los Angeles Times* between 1992 and 1995, Welch, Fenwick, and Roberts (1997, 1998) concluded that the news media's frame of reference for presenting the crime issue is set by law-enforcement officials and political leaders. Their views are cited more often than those of professors and nonacademic researchers. Sixty-three percent of the experts quoted in the articles were "state managers" (mostly law-enforcement officials and politicians), and 37 percent were "intellectuals" (mostly professors, but a few nonacademic researchers as well). The papers tended to quote the state managers as primary, official sources of information about crime, and to present the views of the intellectuals as secondary, nonofficial interpretations. According to Welch, Fenwick, and Roberts, intellectuals' theories of crime causation are slighted by the press in favor of the crime-control model preferred by state managers. Therefore, public discourse focuses on incapacitation and deterrence rather than on rehabilitation and root causes of crime, such as unemployment, poverty, and racial discrimination.

Welch, Fenwick, and Roberts's finding that one-third of the experts quoted in the feature articles were professors and researchers shows that newspapers provide an important forum for criminologists to interpret changes in crime rates. In addition, they can do so in more timely fashion than they can in scholarly books and professional journals, which present research that takes years to propose, fund, conduct, interpret, review, and publish. Consequently, this book uses the *Times* as a source of information about how criminologists made sense of the falling crime rates of the 1990s. Early in the decade, many of those cited in the paper were skeptics, cautioning that it was too early to tell if the small dip in crime rates signaled a meaningful long-term decline. They also noted that because many crimes are not reported, the dip could have been due to reduced crime reporting by citizens. Even by mid-decade, when it was clear that the decline was substantial, some criminologists warned that rates would soon rise again because of an impending growth in the number of crime-prone 15- to 24-year-olds in the population.

As rates continued to drop, most criminologists accepted that the trend was real, though they seemed puzzled as to exactly why rates had fallen. FBI crime statistics for the first half of 1996 were greeted with applause from some criminologists who had previously questioned the reality of the decline. Franklin E. Zimring remarked, "I have been a skeptic. But now, because of the length of the decline, its magnitude and the number of places it is occurring, I think I am experiencing a foxhole conversion" (cited in January 5, 1997: 10). Jeffrey Fagan agreed that the decline was meaningful, noting that because both the FBI's police statistics and the Bureau of Justice Statistics's victimization survey data had shown steady and sizeable reductions for several years, as had hospital data on injuries and deaths, "we can now have more confidence that we are in the midst of a trend, not simply a short-term or random fluctuation" (cited in November 16, 1997: 18).

Once the decline in crime was accepted as significant, the *Times* sought explanations for the change. There was no shortage of people willing to offer ideas about why rates had dropped, but there was little consensus among them. According to one editorial, "Criminologists offer many guesses for why crime is dropping, but in this field where sociology, economics, community attitudes and policing strategies all come into play, few agree on which factors have the biggest impact or how long the trend can last" (October 14, 1997: A26). Some criminologists even questioned their ability to explain the decline. According to Zimring, "When push comes to shove, nobody has an ability to explain the increases any better than the decreases. Criminologists are like weathermen without a satellite. We can only tell you about yesterday's crime rates" (cited in May 6, 1996: B8). Erik Monkkonen expressed his doubts as follows: "The closer we look at the drop in crime, the more complex it gets. . . . It's like cancer. The more we know, the more what looks like one problem becomes a series of problems" (cited in March 29, 1998, sec. 1: 16).

Subsequent chapters use published research and available evidence to assess the accuracy of the explanations for falling crime rates offered in the *Times*. These explanations propose that the decline in rates was the result of

- Less reporting of crime to the police, or less recording of crime by the police (Chapter 2)
- A natural cycle in crime rates (Chapter 2)
- More effective policing (Chapter 4)
- More use of incarceration (Chapter 5)
- Changes in the market for illegal drugs, especially crack (Chapter 6)
- Changes in the attitudes of young people (Chapter 6)
- Reduced access to, or use of, firearms (Chapter 7)
- Changes in the age distribution of the population (Chapter 8)
- Improved economic conditions (Chapter 9)
- Increased participation in community organizations (Chapter 9)

Also examined are two possible factors that the *Times* ignored: increased legitimacy of the family and the political and economic systems (Chapter 9) and increased religiosity (Chapter 9).

In contrast to the *Times*'s usual approach of listing a series of influences on crime rates, criminology can provide (1) an analysis of how changes in those factors cause crime rates to drop, (2) research to determine the relative contribution of each factor to the decline in rates, and (3) an understanding of how the different factors interact with one another to affect crime rates. For example, increased incarceration of offenders might reduce crime rates, perhaps most dramatically when unemployment rates are low. Changes in youths' attitudes might also lead to lower crime rates, though to a lesser degree. In addition, increased incarceration might indirectly reduce crime rates by changing the attitudes of youths in ways that deter them from crime. Research by criminologists almost always shows that the causes of changing crime rates are more complex than suggested by the news media.

Rarely mentioned in the *Times*'s investigation of why crime rates fell in the 1990s were two issues that are critical to assessing the cause-and-effect relationship between crime rates and possible influences on those rates. One issue is the problem of simultaneity or reciprocal causation: Factors that might cause crime rates to fall, such as an increase in the use of incarceration, can also be affected by falling crime rates. For instance, a decline in crime rates could lead to the imprisonment of fewer offenders. The second issue is time-lags in causation; for example, how soon after the prison population increases will crime rates fall? Some factors might have nearly immediate effects. An example of this might be a police tactic of stopping and searching all minor offenders in an attempt to deter gun carrying. Other factors, such as changes in child-rearing methods, might not have an impact on crime rates for years. In evaluating the various explanations for the decline in crime rates in the 1990s, this book relies as much as possible on studies that have addressed these two issues in an effort to separate cause from effect and determine when the impact of various influences on crime rates occurs.

Before evaluating the competing explanations for the decline in crime rates, Chapter 2 offers a rationale for using four crime indicators: the per capita rates of homicide, robbery, burglary, and motor vehicle theft. Changes in these indicators since 1960 are examined for the nation as a whole, for large cities, and for New York City, with emphasis on the declines that occurred in the 1990s. Hypotheses about why crime rates fell can be evaluated with these four indicators. For example, if innovations in policing curbed crime in New York City, why did crime rates also fall in Los Angeles, where no such innovations were introduced?

CHAPTER

2 The Decline in Crime Rates in the 1990s

Any analysis of why crime rates fell during the 1990s requires valid and reliable measures of crime and a method for using these measures to gauge changes in rates. This chapter describes four crime indicators and the rationale for selecting them, then employs them to document changes in rates since 1960. The possibility that changes in the reporting or recording of crime might account for the dramatic decline in rates in the 1990s is investigated, as is the suggestion that rates rise and fall in natural cycles.

Measuring Crime

Since 1930, the Federal Bureau of Investigation has published its *Uniform Crime Reports: Crime in the United States,* an annual volume that summarizes information on crimes recorded by local and state police departments. Criminologists have criticized the UCR crime statistics for being incomplete because citizens fail to report many crimes to the police and because the police do not record all crimes reported to them. They are also criticized for being unreliable because crime data have sometimes been manipulated for political purposes. Despite their shortcomings, UCR statistics are routinely used by criminologists because there are no other national crime statistics that span so many years and contain so much detail. The only other available measure of long-term national trends is the Bureau of Justice Statistics's National Crime Victimization Survey (NCVS). Administered annually since 1973, this survey asks samples of Americans about their experiences as crime victims. This chapter uses both UCR and NCVS data to describe changes in crime rates.

Changes in rates are examined for the nation as a whole, for New York City, and for a composite category of cities other than New York that have populations of more than one million. Focusing on New York provides a richly detailed example of how the decline in crime in one large city was interpreted; looking at other large cities and at the nation as a whole makes it possible to determine if the explanations offered for New York's decline in crime rates are specific to that city or apply more generally. Crime rates began to fall in New York after 1990, and after 1991 in the nation as a whole, so 1990 is used as the starting point in the analysis. Rates changed very little from 1999 to 2000, suggesting that the decline was coming to an end. Therefore, 1999 marks the end of the period under consideration.

Crime Indicators

The FBI's Uniform Crime Reports provide detailed information on the following Part I or index crimes because they are regarded by the public as serious, because they occur relatively often, and because they are likely to be reported to the police:

1. Murder and nonnegligent manslaughter: the willful killing of another human being
2. Forcible rape: carnal knowledge of a female forcibly and against her will, including assaults and attempts to commit rape
3. Robbery: the taking of anything of value from a person by force or threat of force, including attempts
4. Aggravated assault: an unlawful attack on another person for the purpose of inflicting severe bodily injury, usually with a weapon or by other means likely to produce great bodily harm
5. Burglary: unlawful entry of a structure to commit a felony or theft
6. Larceny-theft: the unlawful taking, carrying, leading, or riding away of property from the possession of another
7. Motor vehicle theft: the theft or attempted theft of an automobile, truck, bus, motorcycle, or other vehicle
8. Arson: the willful or malicious burning of any personal property of another, including attempts

The FBI calculates rates for the first seven crimes in terms of numbers of offenses per 100,000 people. It gives no rate for arson because of incomplete data. The UCR also includes three summary rates: a violent crime rate (the total number of recorded cases of murder and nonnegligent manslaughter, forcible rape, robbery, and aggravated assault per

100,000 people); a property crime rate (the total number of recorded cases of burglary, larceny, and motor vehicle theft per 100,000 people); and a crime index rate (the total number of index crimes, exclusive of arson, per 100,000 people).

Some of these ten crime rates have deficiencies that undermine their usefulness for assessing crime trends. Before 1973, the FBI included in its crime index only larcenies in which the stolen property was worth more than $50. Since then, however, the larceny rate, as well as the summary rates of all property crimes and all index crimes, have included all larcenies. This inclusion means that pre-1973 larceny rates cannot be compared with those since 1973. Even before the 1973 revision, larceny rates were problematic because the $50 cutoff was difficult to apply to many thefts. For example, should the theft of a five-year-old bicycle that originally cost $100 be classified as a larceny over $50 or a larceny under $50? Because of the difficulty of establishing the actual value of stolen property, and because of the change in the way that larceny rates are calculated, the FBI's larceny rate is a poor indicator of how larceny has changed over time. The overall property crime rate and the crime index rate are also problematic because larcenies make up the majority of all crimes included in both of these summary rates.

Questions are also raised about the usefulness of the UCR forcible rape rate, which measures the number of actual and attempted incidents of sex forced on women without their consent. Rape is probably the most undercounted of all index crimes, with only 10 to 50 percent of all rapes being reported to and recorded by the police (Skorneck, 1992; Rennison, 2001). Because of the large number of uncounted sexual assaults, increases in police rape statistics might reflect improved reporting and recording practices rather than actual increases in the crime. Other difficulties with rape statistics include uncertainty over what proportion of all recorded cases are completed rapes and what proportion are attempts, and the exclusion of male victims from the FBI's definition of rape.

In contrast to the Part I crime of aggravated assault, the FBI defines the Part II offense of simple assault as an unlawful attack or attempted attack in which no weapon is used and no serious bodily injury occurs. Police classification of an assault as aggravated or simple can be an arbitrary decision that varies from officer to officer, from one department to another, and over time. For example, assaults once classified as simple might now be more likely to be categorized as aggravated because of an increase in public condemnation of domestic violence (Blumstein and Beck, 1999). The problems involved in accurately measuring aggravated assault and forcible rape rule out use of the FBI's rates of those crimes, as well as its summary rates of violent and index crimes.

Although they are not without problems, the following four crime indicators, each expressed in number of recorded offenses per 100,000 people, are the best ones available for measuring crime trends (Gove, Hughes, and Geerken, 1985; O'Brien, 1985). These will be used to evaluate the reasons for the decline in crime rates in the 1990s.

1. The *murder rate* measures the most serious offense recorded by the FBI. Zimring and Hawkins (1997) persuasively argue that it is lethal violence of this sort that most clearly distinguishes crime in the United States from crime in other industrial nations. Murder is also the crime that attracts the most public attention. It is the offense most likely to be recorded by the police, with the possible exception of motor vehicle theft. Therefore, changes in murder rates are not likely to be due to variations in citizen reporting or police recording practices.

2. The *robbery rate* measures the prototypical street crime, one that involves both violence and theft. Because robbery is often committed by strangers without warning in public places, it elicits great fear and leads to self-protective changes in daily behavior. Victimization surveys find that more than half of all robberies are reported to the police (Rennison, 2001).

3. The *burglary rate* measures crimes in which private residences and commercial establishments are invaded, usually to commit a theft. This crime elicits fear that private space will be invaded by strangers and concern that valuable property will be stolen, and thus leads to the installation of costly security measures. Victimization surveys find that half of all household burglaries are reported to the police (Rennison, 2001). Even though the FBI expresses the burglary rate as the number of crimes per 100,000 people, it is actually residential dwellings and commercial buildings that are the targets, so burglary rates per number of dwellings and buildings might be a better indicator of how this crime has changed over time.

4. The *motor vehicle theft rate* is the number of recorded stolen vehicles per 100,000 people in the country. As with burglary, the target of this crime is a form of property rather than a person. Therefore, a rate of motor vehicle thefts per 100,000 people makes less sense than a rate of motor vehicle thefts per 100,000 vehicles. Unlike burglary, data are available on the number of such targets; therefore, changes in motor vehicle theft can be examined in terms of changes in the number of opportunities for that crime. Because the owners of stolen vehicles want to be reimbursed by insurance companies for their losses, avoid responsibility for accidents, and minimize the inconvenience of being without their means of transportation, most motor vehicle thefts (about four-fifths of them, according to victimization surveys) are reported to the police (Rennison, 2001).

Looking at trends in these four crime indicators avoids the trap of developing an explanation for declining crime rates that is specific to a single offense. This has been a problem with recent work that has focused narrowly on the decline in murder rates (Blumstein and Rosenfeld, 1998; Fagan, Zimring, and Kim, 1998; Karmen, 2000; Monkkonen, 2001).

Relative and Absolute Changes in Crime Rates

The FBI presents its UCR statistics at an annual press conference that highlights changes in crime rates since the previous year. These changes are expressed in percentage terms, as in the following headline: "Violent Crime Falls 7 Percent, to Lowest Level in Decades" (July 19, 1999: A10). This 7 percent figure is the result of subtracting the 1998 rate of violent crimes per 100,000 people from the 1997 rate, then dividing the difference by the 1997 rate. Expressing change as a percentage increase or decrease from an earlier time is useful for comparing different jurisdictions. For example, from 1992 to 1993, Chicago's murder rate decreased by 9 percent while Los Angeles's murder rate increased by 1 percent. Percentage changes in crime rates are also helpful when comparing different types of crime statistics; for instance, from 1994 to 1995 the FBI's UCR robbery rate dropped by 7 percent, while the Bureau of Justice Statistics's NCVS robbery rate dropped by 14 percent.

In comparing trends *within* a single jurisdiction, the use of percentage increases or decreases risks erroneous interpretation. For example, the murder rates per 100,000 people in the United States were 7.9 in 1970, 10.2 in 1980, and 7.9 in 1984. From 1970 to 1980, the murder rate increased by 29 percent (= [10.2 − 7.9]/7.9). However, when the murder rate dropped back to its 1970 level in 1984, the 1980–1984 decrease was only 23 percent (= [7.9 − 10.2]/10.2). Even though the absolute magnitude of the change in murder rates was exactly the same for the 1970–1980 and 1980–1984 periods (2.3 murders per 100,000 people), the percentage increase (29 percent) in the first period was greater than the percentage decrease (23 percent) in the second period. Percentage increases in crime rates can be, and often are, greater than percentage decreases because percentage decreases cannot exceed 100 percent but percentage increases can.

When looking at changes in crime rates within the same jurisdiction, this book sometimes employs an unconventional measure: the absolute increase or decrease in the number of crimes per 100,000 people. Thus, the previously mentioned changes in murder rates can be described as an increase of 2.3 murders per 100,000 people from 1970 to 1980, and a decrease of 2.3 murders per 100,000 people from 1980 to 1984. This conveys the return in 1984 to the murder rate that prevailed in 1970 better than a statement that the murder rate first increased by 29 percent then fell by a 23 percent, a description that erroneously implies a net increase in the murder rate.

Crime Trends, 1960–1999

This section examines changes in the four crime indicators from 1960 to 1999 and compares the magnitude of the 1990s decline to earlier changes in crime rates. The highly publicized drop in New York City's crime rates during the 1990s is compared to reductions in rates in the country as a whole and in other cities with more than one million people.

Changes in Murder Rates

Figure 2.1 shows how murder rates have fluctuated in the United States since 1960. In the 1990s, the rate fell from 9.8 in 1991 to 5.7 in 1999, a relative decline of 42 percent and an absolute reduction of 4.1 murders per 100,000 people. Only the 113 percent increase and absolute increase of 5.2 murders per 100,000 people from 1963 to 1974 dwarfed the 1991–1999 change. By 1999, the nation's murder rate had fallen back to its 1966 level.

Trends in murder rates for the 1990–1999 period are displayed in Figure 2.2 (p. 14). Over this time, New York City's murder rate fell from 30.7 to 9.0, a 71 percent decrease and an absolute decline of 21.7 murders per 100,000 people, relative and absolute declines that greatly exceeded those for the nation as a whole. Figure 2.2 shows that New York's higher murder rate in 1990 fell faster than the nation's, so that by the end of the decade the gap between the two rates had nearly vanished.

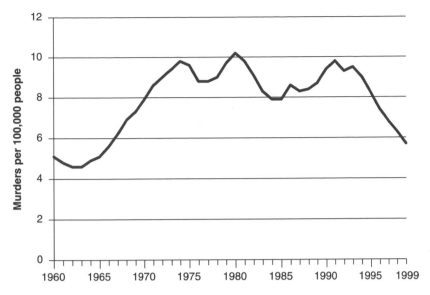

FIGURE 2.1   Murders in the United States, 1960–1999

Source: Based on UCR data in Kathleen Maguire and Ann L. Pastore, eds., *Sourcebook of Criminal Justice Statistics 2000*, Table 3.120, pp. 278–279. (Online: www.albany.edu/sourcebook [February 26, 2002])

Figure 2.2 contrasts changes in New York's murder rate with changes in the composite murder rate for all U.S. cities with populations over one million, exclusive of New York. This composite rate was calculated by subtracting New York's population from the total population of all cities over one million, subtracting the number of murders in New York from the number in all cities over one million, and then dividing the number of murders by the total population of those other large cities. Figure 2.2 reveals that New York's murder rate was lower than the combined rate for other large cities throughout the 1990s, and that the two trend lines more or less paralleled one another. Over the course of the decade, the murder rate in other large cities fell by 55 percent—not quite as much as New York's 71 percent decline. The other large cities had 17.8 fewer murders per 100,000 people by the end of the decade, compared to a decline of 21.7 murders per capita in New York. Murder rates in both New York and the other large cities fell faster and farther than the nation's murder rate.

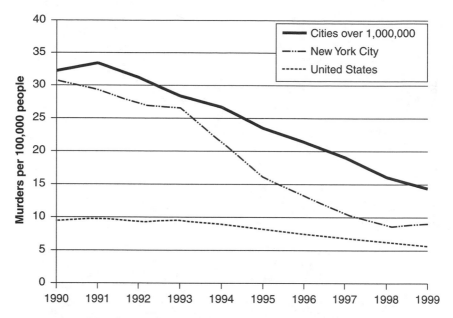

FIGURE 2.2 Murders in the United States, New York City, and Other Cities over 1,000,000, 1990–1999

Source: Based on data from Federal Bureau of Investigation, *Crime in the United States: Uniform Crime Reports, 1990–1999.* Washington, DC: U.S. Government Printing Office, 1991–2000.

Changes in Robbery Rates

Figure 2.3 shows that the nation's robbery rate dropped from 272.7 in 1991 to 150.2 in 1999, a 45 percent decline and a reduction of 122.5 robberies per 100,000 people. This reduction is comparable in magnitude to the absolute increase of 129.7 robberies per 100,000 people from 1961 to 1971. However, because the earlier increase was calculated using a lower starting base rate, the relative increase in that earlier period was much greater (222 percent). The decline in robbery rates during the 1990s left 1999's rate at roughly the 1969 level.

The Bureau of Justice Statistics's victimization survey provides additional evidence of a substantial decline in robbery rates in the 1990s. Figure 2.4 (p. 16) shows that the number of robbery victimizations per 1,000 people age 12 and over increased slightly from 1990 to 1994, then fell from 1994 to 1999, a decline that began three years later

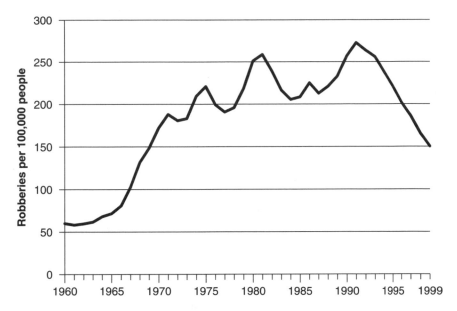

FIGURE 2.3   Robberies in the United States, 1960–1999

Source: Based on UCR data in Kathleen Maguire and Ann L. Pastore, eds., *Sourcebook of Criminal Justice Statistics 2000,* Table 3.120, pp. 278–279. (Online: www.albany.edu/sourcebook [February 26, 2002])

than the decline in the UCR rate. From 1994 to 1999, the NCVS robbery rate fell by 43 percent, similar to the 37 percent decline in the UCR robbery rate over that time.

During the 1990s, New York's robbery rate fell by 65 percent, resulting in 883.6 fewer robberies per 100,000 people and leaving the rate in 1999 close to 1967's rate. Both the relative and absolute declines in New York's robbery rate were greater than those for the country as a whole, even though the city's rate was still more than three times greater than the nation's rate in 1999. Figure 2.5 (p. 17) shows that New York's robbery rate was much higher than the nation's throughout the 1990s, although the two rates had begun to converge by the end of the decade as a result of the rapid decline in New York's rate. This figure also shows that New York's robbery rate was higher than the rate for other large cities in the first half of the 1990s, but that the decline in New York's rate resulted in virtually the same rates for 1995 through 1999.

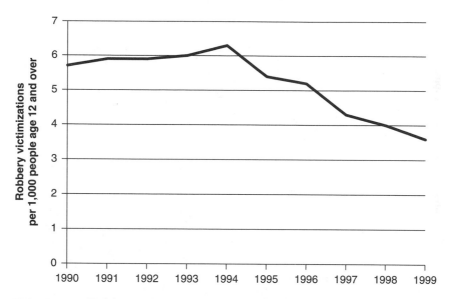

FIGURE 2.4   Robbery Victimizations, 1990–1999*

*1990–1992 rates may not be comparable to 1993–1999 rates because of a redesign of the victimization survey.

Sources: Based on Bureau of Justice Statistics, *Criminal Victimization,* reports for 1990–1999. Washington, DC: U.S. Department of Justice, 1992–2001.

Changes in Burglary Rates

The nation's burglary rate increased steadily from 1960 to a peak in 1980, then declined from 1980 to 1999 (see Figure 2.6, p. 18). The rate fell 38 percent from 1991 to 1999, a reduction of 482 burglaries per 100,000 people, leaving 1999's rate near the 1966 level.

The trend in burglary rates is distinct from those of the other three indicator crimes. Rates of murder, robbery, and motor vehicle theft began to drop after 1991, but the decline in burglary rates in the 1990s was part of a trend that began in 1980 and was only interrupted twice by short-lived upturns. In similar fashion, the burglary rate began to increase in the early 1960s, several years before rates of the other indicator crimes. The absolute increase of 1,023.5 burglaries per 100,000 people over the 1960–1975 period was somewhat greater than the absolute decrease of 914.1 burglaries per 100,000 people over the 1980–1999 period. In addition, the relative increase of 201 percent in the earlier period was greater than the relative decrease of 54 percent in the

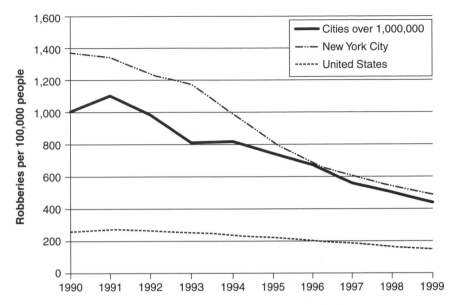

FIGURE 2.5   Robberies in the United States, New York City, and Other Cities over 1,000,000, 1990–1999

Source: Based on data from Federal Bureau of Investigation, *Crime in the United States: Uniform Crime Reports, 1990–1999.* Washington, DC: U.S. Government Printing Office, 1991–2000.

latter period because the earlier increase was calculated on 1960's low base rate.

NCVS data are limited to household burglaries and therefore are not directly comparable to UCR statistics, which include burglaries of both private residences and commercial establishments such as stores and office buildings. However, the results of victimization surveys can be used to determine if burglary rates fell in the 1990s. Figure 2.7 (p. 19) shows that the NCVS rate for household burglaries dropped by 41 percent from 1993 to 1999, comparable to the 30 percent decline in the UCR burglary rate over that period.

During the 1990s, New York's burglary rate declined by 67 percent and by 1,093.2 burglaries per 100,000 people. The city's 1999 rate was comparable to its 1963 rate. From 1990 to 1999, the nation's burglary rate declined less than New York's in both relative terms (38 percent vs. 67 percent) and absolute terms (465.9 vs. 1,093.2 burglaries per capita). Figure 2.8 (p. 20) shows the similarity of burglary rates for

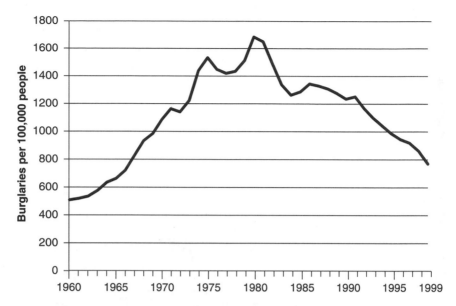

FIGURE 2.6   Burglaries in the United States, 1960–1999

Source: Based on UCR data in Kathleen Maguire and Ann L. Pastore, eds., *Sourcebook of Criminal Justice Statistics 2000,* Table 3.120, pp. 278–279. (Online: www.albany.edu/sourcebook [February 26, 2002])

New York and the nation during the 1990s. New York's rate started the decade higher than the national rate, but had fallen below the national rate by the end of the decade. New York's burglary rate was lower than the rate for other large cities throughout the 1990s, and fell by relatively more (67 percent vs. 48 percent) and absolutely more (1093.2 vs. 936.4 burglaries per 100,000 people) than the rate for other large cities.

Changes in Motor Vehicle Theft Rates

Figure 2.9 (p. 21) shows a big increase in the nation's motor vehicle theft rate from 1960 to 1971, a fairly steady rate from 1971 to 1983, another large increase from 1983 to 1991, then a dramatic decrease from 1991 to 1999. The rate dropped by 36 percent from 1991 to 1999, a reduction of 238.3 motor vehicle thefts per 100,000 people, leaving 1999's rate slightly below the rate for 1969. This decline, by far the largest during

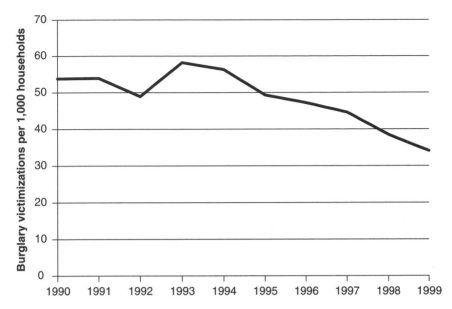

FIGURE 2.7   Burglary Victimizations, 1990–1999*

*1990–1992 rates may not be comparable to 1993–1999 rates because of a redesign of the victimization survey.

Sources: Based on Bureau of Justice Statistics, *Criminal Victimization,* reports for 1990–1999. Washington, DC: U.S. Department of Justice, 1992–2001.

the four decades, was comparable in relative and absolute magnitude to the 1983–1991 increase. The 1960–1971 increase was comparable in absolute terms to the decline in the 1990s; the larger relative change in the earlier period (a 151 percent increase) than in the latter period (a 36 percent decrease) is the result of the earlier increase being based on an initially low rate.

The FBI calculates its motor vehicle theft rate in crimes per 100,000 people, making it possible to compare it to rates of the other index crimes. The Bureau of Justice Statistics assumes that motor vehicles belong to households rather than individuals, and so calculates its motor vehicle theft rate in thefts per 1,000 households. Figure 2.10 (p. 22) shows that motor vehicle theft victimization rates started to fall after 1991, the same time that UCR rates began to drop. The 55 percent decline in the NCVS rate over the 1991–1999 period was greater than the 36 percent reduction in the UCR rate over the same time.

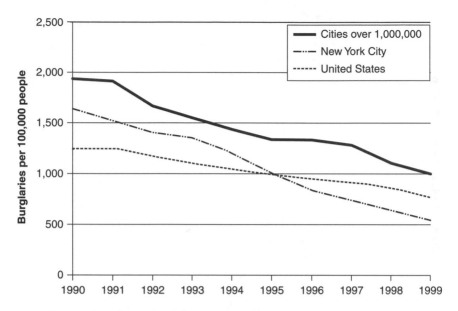

FIGURE 2.8   Burglaries in the United States, New York City, and Other Cities over 1,000,000, 1990–1999

Source: Based on data from Federal Bureau of Investigation, *Crime in the United States: Uniform Crime Reports, 1990–1999*. Washington, DC: U.S. Government Printing Office, 1991–2000.

A third way to measure motor vehicle theft rates is to calculate the number of thefts per 100,000 vehicles, a method that takes into account the fact that the number of vehicles in the country has grown faster than the population, so that today there are more targets for motor vehicle theft relative to the size of the population than there were in the past. Figure 2.11 (p. 23) shows that during the 1990s the number of recorded thefts per 100,000 registered motor vehicles fell by 336.1, a decline of 39 percent.

From 1990 to 1999, New York's motor vehicle theft rate dropped by 73 percent, a reduction of 1,474.9 thefts per 100,000 people, leaving the city's 1999 rate at about the same level as it was in 1966. The city's motor vehicle theft rate dropped by a greater relative amount and much greater absolute amount than the nation's rate. The city's rate had nearly converged with the nation's rate by the end of the decade (see Figure 2.12, p. 24). New York's rate was lower than the rate for other large cities throughout the 1990s and declined faster than the large-city rate over the course of the decade.

FIGURE 2.9   Motor Vehicle Thefts in the United States, 1960–1999

Source: Based on UCR data in Kathleen Maguire and Ann L. Pastore, eds., *Sourcebook of Criminal Justice Statistics 2000,* Table 3.120, pp. 278–279. (Online: www.albany.edu/ sourcebook [February 26, 2002])

New York City's Contribution to the Decline in National Crime Rates

When the *Times* reported that every major crime had declined in frequency in New York City from 1990 to 1991, the first time that had happened in thirty-six years, the paper pointed out that this ran counter to a national trend of smaller reductions, or even increases, in crime. By 1993, it was apparent that the city's decline in crime rates was part of a broader national trend that had begun just a bit earlier in New York. Five years later, the nation's crime rate was falling faster than New York's.

For several years in the mid-1990s, Mayor Giuliani claimed that New York's declining crime rates were the driving force behind the drop in the nation's rates: "Without us, there would have been much less than a 3 percent crime decline [in the nation's crime rate]" (cited in January 6, 1997: B3). Indeed, that 3 percent decline, which occurred

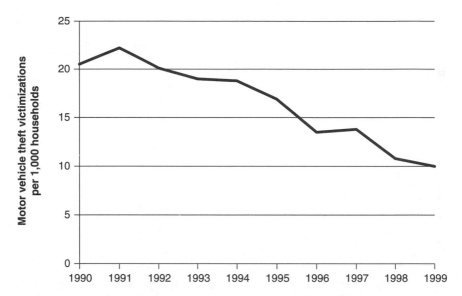

FIGURE 2.10   Motor Vehicle Theft Victimizations, 1990–1999*

*1990–1992 rates may not be comparable to 1993–1999 rates because of a redesign of the victimization survey.

Sources: Based on Bureau of Justice Statistics, *Criminal Victimization,* reports for 1990–1999. Washington, DC: U.S. Department of Justice, 1992–2001.

from 1993 to 1995, would have been only 2 percent if New York had been excluded (July 7, 1996, sec. 4: 2). Commissioner Bratton once asserted that the city accounted for one-third of the nation's recent reductions in murders and robberies and 70 percent of its reduction in motor vehicle thefts. Giuliani publicly stated on several occasions that both President Bill Clinton and U.S. Attorney General Janet Reno had told him that New York was largely responsible for the improvement in the nation's crime picture, a point reiterated in the *Times'*s observation that the city had given Clinton the opportunity to claim credit for the decline in the nation's crime rate during his 1996 reelection campaign.

New York's crime rates fell faster than the nation's in some years during the 1990s, but dropped more slowly in other years. The important question is the extent to which New York's decline in crime rates contributed to the reduction in the nation's rates over the course of the whole decade. One way to determine this is to look at the decreases in the nation's crime rates from 1990 to 1999, then calculate what those decreases would have been if New York's rates were excluded. This is

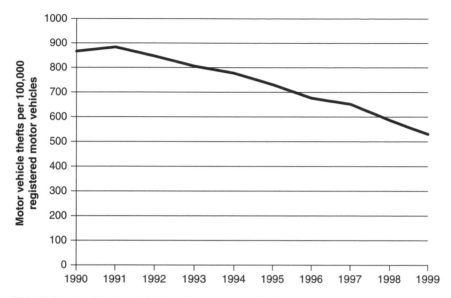

FIGURE 2.11   Motor Vehicle Thefts, 1990–1999

Sources: Based on data in Federal Bureau of Investigation, *Crime in the United States: Uniform Crime Reports, 1990–1999*. Washington, DC: U.S. Government Printing Office, 1991–2000; U.S. Department of Transportation, Federal Highway Administration. (Online: www.fhwa.dot.ohim [August 3, 2001])

done by subtracting the number of crimes in New York from the total number of crimes in the country and subtracting the population of New York from the nation's population, then calculating a "rest of the country" crime rate by dividing this number of crimes by the population of the country exclusive of New York. Similarly, the contribution of the falling crime rates in large cities to the decline in the nation's crime rates can be determined by subtracting the crimes and populations of all cities with more than one million people from national totals, and then calculating a crime rate for all of the country except its largest cities. Table 2.1 (p. 25) shows how much the nation's crime rates actually changed from 1990 to 1999, how the nation's rates would have changed if New York were excluded from national crime statistics, and how the rates would have changed if all cities with populations over one million were excluded from national crime statistics.

Though New York's reductions in crime rates did boost the national declines by a few percentage points, a comparison of the first two columns shows that even without the decline in New York's rates, the

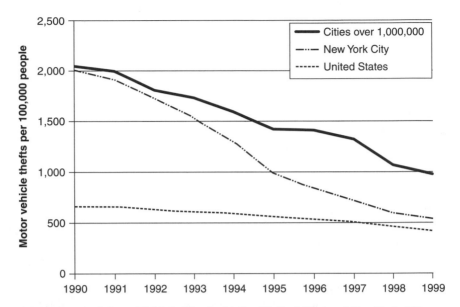

FIGURE 2.12 **Motor Vehicle Thefts in the United States, New York City, and Other Cities over 1,000,000, 1990–1999**

Source: Based on data from Federal Bureau of Investigation, *Crime in the United States: Uniform Crime Reports, 1990–1999.* Washington, DC: U.S. Government Printing Office, 1991–2000.

drop in the nation's rates would have been substantial. Contrary to the claims of Mayor Giuliani and Commissioner Bratton, these figures suggest that over the course of the decade New York was not, as Eli Silverman (1999: 6) asserts, "the major force driving down the nation's crime rate."

A comparison of the first and third columns shows that, as a group, cities with more than one million people (including New York) did contribute to the decline in nation's crime rates. Except for burglary, the nation's crime rates would have fallen by markedly less without the reduction in rates in the largest cities, though even without that contribution the nation's rates would have declined in impressive fashion.

The Failure to Report and Record Crime

Statistical evidence for the 1990s paints a picture of a substantial and sustained decline in the four crime indicators for the nation as a whole,

TABLE 2.1   **Change in Crime Rates, 1990–1999**

	U.S.	U.S. without New York City	U.S. without Largest Cities
Murder	–39%	–36%	–32%
Robbery	–42%	–37%	–32%
Burglary	–38%	–37%	–36%
Motor vehicle theft	–36%	–32%	–29%

for New York City, and for other large cities. However, early in the decade some criminologists, knowing that crime rates fluctuate over time, questioned whether the falling rates were really the harbinger of a long-term reduction.

Skeptical criminologists cited in the *New York Times* in the early 1990s suggested that the downturn might simply be due to a decline in the reporting of crimes to the police. H. Richard Uviller noted that because people fail to report many offenses to the police, it was difficult to know the true extent of crime, though he cited no evidence that reporting had declined in a way that would account for the drop in recorded crime (September 6, 1991: B3). George Kelling questioned the value of crime statistics for measuring the success of the police in fighting crime. A law-enforcement official supported Kelling, pointing out that the residents of one city might report thefts more often than the residents of another city, and that some people might even report crimes that had never occurred (August 16, 1992: 39). Hubert Williams, president of the Police Foundation, observed that new police rape units that encourage victims to report their victimization often generate rising rape rates (August 16, 1992: 39). Even though the *Times* reported views such as these, its position throughout the 1990s was that the changes in police statistics indicated that crime was actually declining, not that they merely reflected a growing unwillingness by citizens to report crimes. This conclusion was supported by experts' statements that crime reporting had not changed much (October 11, 1993: B2). The longer crime rates continued to fall, the less frequently underreporting was mentioned in the *Times* as a possible reason for the decline.

If the decline in crime rates was attributable to a growing unwillingness to report crimes, NCVS data should show that a decreasing percentage of all victimizations were reported to the police over the course of the decade. The percentage of robbery victimizations reported to the police fluctuated around 55 percent from 1990 to 1997, then climbed slightly in the last two years of the decade. The percentage of burglary victimizations reported to the police fluctuated around 50 percent throughout the decade. About 77 percent of motor vehicle theft victimizations were reported to the police during the 1990s, with slightly higher proportions for the last three years of the decade, when crime rates were at their lowest. For all three crimes, victimization survey data contradict the suggestion that a decreasing willingness to report crimes to the police caused crime rates to fall.

Police departments sometimes manipulate crime data, classifying serious crimes as minor ones to minimize the crime problem, or categorizing minor offenses as serious ones to exaggerate the crime problem and justify greater resources for the department. The failure of the police to record crimes surfaced as an issue several times during the 1990s. Five New York precinct commanders were caught downgrading felonies to misdemeanors in order to show lower rates of serious crimes; two were forced to resign for their falsification of data. Senior police officials said that such manipulation was the result of pressure on precinct commanders by headquarters and the mayor's office to reduce crime. Faced with evidence that some records were being falsified, the NYPD strengthened its auditing procedures and assigned precinct commanders more responsibility for the accuracy of crime reports. One NYPD official expressed his confidence in the overall accuracy of the department's crime statistics as follows: "The consequences of not bringing down crime can be embarrassing, but they are not as severe as being caught doctoring the numbers" (cited in October 26, 1996: 26).

A front-page story in the *Times* suggested that the problem of manipulating crime statistics might be nationwide: "Senior police officials around the nation are concerned that the sharp drop in crime in recent years has produced new pressure on police departments to show ever-decreasing crime statistics and might be behind incidents in several cities in which commanders have manipulated crime data" (August 3, 1998: A1). Because the news media and the public pay most attention to index crimes, the police can create the appearance of an improving crime picture by reclassifying serious crimes as minor ones. In Boca Raton, Florida, property crimes were systematically downgraded by reclassifying burglaries and robberies as vandalism, trespassing, or missing property, thereby reducing the city's felony rate. According to the local district attorney, the prevailing attitude in the police department was that crime reports "should be classified at the lowest possible level" (cited in August 3, 1998: A16). In Atlanta, the police reclassified or deleted some offenses in order to reduce the rate of serious crime for 1996, the year the Olympics were held there, so as to attract more visitors. In Philadelphia, systematic underreporting, downgrading, and sloppy recording practices produced an 8 percent undercount of serious crimes, forcing the FBI to exclude that city's crime statistics from its annual crime reports for 1996, 1997, and 1998.

Even though statistical manipulation might occasionally explain the drop in a city's or a precinct's crime rate, the *Times* and the criminologists it quoted agreed that the overall decline in rates in the 1990s was real, not the result of changes in police record-keeping practices. Murder and motor vehicle theft are the most accurately measured crimes, and rates of those offenses fell substantially and in parallel throughout the decade. In addition, both medical examiners' records for murder and victimization survey data for other serious crimes confirmed the downward trends revealed by police statistics.

Crime Cycles

Criminologists should be able to explain fluctuations in crime rates in terms of independent variables that influence those rates, but during the 1990s some experts quoted in the *Times* spoke as if crime cycles were natural occurrences not in need of further explanation. They implied that when rates rise they must inevitably come down, and that when rates fall they must rise again. For example, Richard Girgenti, New York State Commissioner of Criminal Justice Services, said that crime rates had peaked in the mid-1980s because of the crack epidemic, but that at some point they had to level off, saying, "Things do work in cycles" (cited in January 1, 1995: 37). After New York City's crime rate had fallen for several consecutive years, Michael Smith, director of the Vera Institute of Justice, commented, "It's possible the decreases in crime will accelerate. But the wheel of fortune turns against that possibility" (cited in January 1, 1995: 37). Howard Snyder of the National Center for Juvenile Justice made a similar observation after serious crime had declined from 1991 to 1994: "The figures wiggle from year to year, like the stock market. Crime has been up so high, you'd expect it to go back down" (cited in May 23, 1995: A14). In a similar vein, criminologist James Alan Fox stated, "Crime rates fluctuate much like the stock market. Good years are generally followed by bad years" (cited in November 8, 1994: A14). The following year, Fox questioned the U.S. Justice

Department's conclusion that juvenile arrests for violent crimes would double from 1995 to 2010, reasoning that because the juvenile arrest rate had increased by 100 percent from 1983 to 1992, "it would be hard to keep on going straight up" (cited in September 8, 1995: A16).

When New York City's crime rates fell more slowly in the last six months of 1995 than in the first six months of the year, police officials speculated that the decline in crime might be abating and that rates might not fall much more. The *Times* concurred, suggesting that there might be "a base as to how far crime can go down—and that base may not be far away" (December 17, 1995: 49). The following year, the paper reported that criminologists expected rates to continue to drop for a few more years, but perhaps at a slower pace (January 28, 1996, sec. 4: 5). Three years later, the *Times* questioned whether a recent upsurge in homicides in New York City—the first increase in a major crime category in eight years—indicated that the decade-long decline in rates was about to end. The paper noted that all of the city's seventy-six precincts had experienced a decline in crime from 1997 to 1998, but that four of them experienced an increase from 1998 to 1999. For the city as a whole, rape dropped by 16 percent, burglary by 13 percent, and motor vehicle theft by 10 percent from 1998 to 1999. Murder, however, increased moderately from 1998 to 1999. James Alan Fox interpreted this as follows: "I am leaning toward the conclusion that we have reached bottom. The years of double-digit declines may be over" (cited in December 19, 1999: 55). Jeffrey Fagan agreed: "If we are not at the bottom now, we are likely to hit the bottom very soon. You can't have unending crime increases or decreases, and the past is the best predictor of the future" (cited in December 19, 1999: 55). NYPD officials rejected the idea that the bottom had been reached, saying they had fought public and expert skepticism about falling crime rates throughout the decade, and proposing that the continued decline in the other crime categories suggested that the increase in murders was "an aberration, not a portent" (December 19, 1999: 55).

Fighting crime has sometimes been described as similar to battling an epidemic whose pattern of infection does not follow simple rules. According to sociologist John Laub, "Acts of violence lead to further acts of violence, creating a contagion effect and a sudden jump in crime rates that is hard to explain" (cited in January 19, 1997, sec. 4: 1). Such a "tipping point" in a crime trend can occur if one factor that affects crime triggers other factors that operate synergistically in the same direction to produce a more dramatic change in rates than any single factor could. According to Malcolm Gladwell, the substantial decline in New York City's crime rates in the 1990s was triggered by innovative policing methods that improved the city's quality of life by cracking down on minor offenses, such as fare-beating in the subways. He claimed that "tinkering with the smallest details of the immediate environment" reduced criminal behavior, which is responsive to even modest changes in the social environment (Gladwell, 2000: 146).

The rise and fall of crime rates could be linked to *issue-attention cycles*—fluctuations in policymakers' attention to the crime problem (Downs, 1972; Baumgartner and Jones, 1993). Variations in political attention to the crime issue are sometimes independent of actual changes in crime rates, but they can set in motion changes that influence those rates. Thus, increased attention to crime can generate control measures (such as more aggressive policing or more use of incarceration) that push rates down until they reach a "comfort zone" and attention to the problem diminishes. This reduction in attention can then set the stage for crime rates to rise once again.

Implicit in theories of tipping points and issue-attention cycles, as well as in wheel of fortune and stock market metaphors, is a tendency for unusually low rates to move over time toward higher, more average rates, and for unusually high rates to regress over time toward lower, more average rates. This kind of cycling often occurs with statistical measures, such as the crime rate, that result from the interaction of multiple variables. The variables and the interactions among them must be investigated to understand why crime rates rise and fall.

Conclusion

Crime rates fell significantly in the United States in the 1990s, and neither the underreporting of crime nor the manipulation of crime statistics can account for the decline. By 1999, rates had not fallen back to the low levels that prevailed in the early 1960s, but they had dropped well below the levels in 1971, the year that marked the end of an era of rapidly rising rates. The 1990–1999 reductions in the four crime indicators were the largest declines since 1960 and were comparable in absolute magnitude to the increases that occurred from 1963 to 1971.

The decline in crime rates in the 1990s encompassed all four indicator crimes and the nation as a whole; therefore, criminologists need to look for factors that had a broad impact on crime. Because rates fell more sharply in cities with more than one million people than they did in the nation as a whole, special attention must also be paid to changes that occurred in the country's largest cities.

Crime rates fluctuate in cyclical fashion, but cycles are descriptions rather than explanations of variations in rates. Perhaps criminologists will someday understand the dynamics of crime well enough to predict changes in crime rates, but today the most that can be hoped for is that theory and research can explain why rates changed as they did. That is the goal of this book.

CHAPTER

3

The Politics of
Falling Crime Rates
in New York City

When crime rates rise, as they did in the 1960s, politicians and law-enforcement officials rarely accept personal responsibility. Instead, they blame the upsurge on other politicians and law-enforcement officials, or on broad social changes such as rising divorce rates or diminishing respect for authority. When crime rates drop, however, politicians and law-enforcement officials are quick to claim credit, pointing to measures they have implemented to cut crime. Even though New York City's decline in crime in the 1990s was not unique, the city received an unusual amount of attention from both the local and national news media. Therefore, the claims made by its mayors and police commissioners about how they had reduced crime are well documented. Those claims may well have shaped public discourse on the reasons that crime fell elsewhere in the country.

For reasons that will become apparent, this chapter divides the 1990s into three periods: the administration of Mayor David N. Dinkins and Police Commissioners Lee P. Brown (January 22, 1990 to September 1, 1992) and Raymond W. Kelly (September 1, 1992 to January 9, 1994); the administration of Mayor Rudolph W. Giuliani and Police Commissioner William J. Bratton (January 10, 1994 to April 14, 1996); and the administration of Mayor Giuliani and Police Commissioner Howard Safir (April 15, 1996 until the end of the decade).

The Dinkins-Brown/Kelly Administration

When the *New York Times* reported in 1991 that crime in New York had fallen in every major crime category, Police Commissioner Lee P. Brown and other NYPD officials were unable to offer a convincing explanation for the decline. One police official noted that many factors influence crime rates; others suggested that a larger, more visible police presence might have deterred crime (April 23, 1991: A1). Criminologists, local merchants, and even offenders attributed the reduction in crime in midtown Manhattan to the increased number of foot patrol and narcotics officers in the area. An assistant police chief said that greater police activity had prevented crime rather than merely displaced criminals to nearby areas, but one street hustler disagreed: "Too many cops in sight—it's intimidating. They're tightening the bolts, and crime is definitely down . . . most people are going other places or sticking to small hustles. I wouldn't try to rob anyone. Well, I might if I saw they had a lot of money, but I'd follow them out of midtown to do it away from these cops" (cited in April 24, 1991: A16). The *Times* suggested another possible reason for the decline in crime: Perhaps fewer workers and shoppers were coming to midtown because of the city's economic slump, which could have reduced opportunities for crime. A city government official proposed that the closing of several action-movie theaters might have curbed crime by reducing the number of young people drawn to midtown. Other observers attributed the drop in crime to the private security guards hired by local organizations of property owners and businesses and to the greater deployment of transit and housing officers in the area.

A 1991 *Times* editorial concluded that the relationship between changes in policing and the decline in crime was "too compelling to be merely coincidental" (April 29, 1991: A16). The editorial credited Commissioner Brown with two important innovations: 1990's Operation Takeback, which added foot patrol officers supported by undercover narcotics officers and detectives to seven high-crime precincts, and a 1991 policy that required desk officers to patrol the streets one day per week. Crime fell in the seven precincts, even though it increased throughout the city as a whole. Crime had been increasing in those seven precincts before Operation Takeback. Other changes that the *Times* said had made the police more effective included increased manpower, a more coordinated and proactive response to crime, and greater community involvement. The paper did note that the waning crack epidemic, the economic slump, and the decline in crime in precincts that had not added patrol officers all raised questions about whether the reduction in crime in the seven high-crime precincts could be attributed solely to police measures.

By early 1992, Commissioner Brown and Mayor Dinkins were claiming that the police had reduced crime. Brown argued that the decline was the result of an increase in patrol officers and his community policing strategy, which put officers in contact with local residents in order to gather information and respond to specific neighborhood problems. He acknowledged that there was no one cause of crime and no single cure for it, and he agreed that a one-year decline did not make a trend. However, he asserted that his policies were making a difference. In 1997, after four years of declining crime under Mayor Giuliani, Brown remarked, "Anyone who's honest will tell you that crime is going down because of the foundation I laid. He's benefitting from the groundwork that David Dinkins and I laid there in New York" (cited in September 23, 1997: A1).

Mayor Dinkins believed that crime had fallen because of the Safe Streets, Safe City program he had initiated under a state law that allowed the city to raise property taxes and impose a surcharge on personal income taxes in order to pay for additional police officers. This program also provided high-risk youths with educational and social services. Another crime-fighting measure implemented by the Dinkins administration was a gun interdiction program. Despite these efforts, Dinkins's response to the decline in crime was understated. At one point, his spokesperson said that the mayor was "cautiously pleased, pleased that the numbers were down but cautious in knowing there was a lot more work to be done . . . to make sure the downward trend continues" (cited in March 25, 1992: B4).

The 1993 Mayoral Contest

During the 1993 mayoral race, candidates Rudolph Giuliani and Andrew Stein argued that the decline in crime during Mayor Dinkins's time in office looked impressive only because it came after years of very high rates. They also claimed that New Yorkers still felt unsafe on the streets (April 6, 1993: B3). Dinkins's response was that crime had fallen during his time in office and that New Yorkers had become less fearful. Noting that crime had declined for twenty-seven straight months, he commented, "If [the crime figures] were up in all seven major index categories, I'm sure it would be my fault" (cited in April 6, 1993: B3). Giuliani countered Dinkins, saying that the numbers were down only because discouraged New Yorkers were no long reporting crimes to the police. Giuliani offered no supporting evidence for this statement and he did not reiterate it once he became mayor and crime continued to drop. He also criticized Dinkins for his ineffectiveness in dealing with quality-of-life offenses and impulsive crimes, and for his unevenness in enforcing the law. This was an attempt to exploit racial tensions that had surfaced in a black boycott of a Korean grocer and a black–Jewish conflict in Crown Heights.

Dinkins's rivals for office claimed that the police were arresting fewer drug offenders. Indeed, narcotics arrests had fallen by 31 percent during the Dinkins administration, and arrests for other felonies had dropped by 17 percent. A police department spokesperson explained that mass arrests of drug offenders had declined because the number of officers devoted exclusively to narcotics crimes had been cut in order to put more uniformed officers on the street. Giuliani and Herman Badillo, another candidate for mayor, suggested that the decline in arrests during the Dinkins administration had actually reduced the number of recorded crimes because arrested suspects often confess to unreported crimes. Hubert Williams questioned this explanation, saying that both murders and motor vehicle thefts had fallen, and that because those offenses were almost always reported to and recorded by the police, statistics for those crimes would not be influenced much by changes in the number of arrests.

Commenting on the candidates' different positions, the *Times* concluded that the "uncertainties of crime statistics" made it difficult to determine whether Dinkins was responsible for the decline in crime. However, the newspaper noted that "for now the Mayor makes a plausible case" (April 10, 1993: 18). It alluded to the Safe Streets, Safe City program and community policing, observing that crime had fallen in all categories and in all precincts after those measures had been implemented, and concluded that "reported reductions seem to correspond more closely to the increased police presence on the streets than to any other factor" (April 10, 1993: 18). The following year, the *Times* attributed another modest decrease in crime to community policing, a view supported by a police official who said that the reduction in crime in twenty of twenty-two large cities in the first half of 1993 was partly the result of "a national trend in law enforcement toward community policing—taking officers out of patrol cars and putting them on city streets, where they can come to know a neighborhood and its problems, and the neighborhood can come to know them" (cited in November 8, 1994: A14). A Brooklyn resident agreed: "Things have drastically changed over the past few years. I attribute it to the community patrols. The officers are out there on the street. There is real problem-solving taking place" (cited in April 4, 1993: 42).

Thomas Reppetto, director of the city's Citizens' Crime Commission, acknowledged in 1992 that a meaningful downward trend in crime might be developing. He said that neither a decrease in the youthful population most prone to commit crime, a decline in crime reporting, changes in the drug culture, nor social and economic change could have produced such a marked reduction in crime over so short a time. He further stated, "the only explanation I can make is that the numbers are the result of the overall policing of the city" (cited in July 29, 1992: B3; see also March 25, 1992: A1, B4). He did question whether it was specifically community policing that had driven crime down, because that strategy had not yet been fully implemented.

Early in the 1990s, criminologists cited in the *Times* were skeptical about crediting the police for the reduction in crime, a decline that was still modest and of short duration. Marvin Wolfgang said that before reaching such a conclusion, he would want to know more about exactly how the police had reduced crime. David Bayley also questioned the impact of the police: "I doubt if the increment of added officers is that visible, and I'm not convinced that the quality of community policing has really improved that much in the past two years. I'd love to think that it's taking hold and these are the results, but I can't see the evidence" (cited in March 19, 1993: B4).

The Giuliani-Bratton Administration

After taking office in January 1994, Mayor Giuliani appointed William Bratton to head the New York Police Department. In his interview for the job, Bratton (1998: 194) promised to change the NYPD's policy of responding to crime after it happened to one of preventing crime before it occurred. He also said that he would cut crime by 40 percent in three years and public fear by a significant amount in four years. When crime fell more rapidly over the next twenty-seven months than it had in any comparable period in the city's history, both Bratton and Giuliani claimed personal credit, which sometimes caused conflict between them. For the most part, they ignored evidence that the drop in crime had started during the Dinkins administration and that it might be part of a national trend. Michael Smith commented that "Bratton and Giuliani may be the beneficiaries of a decrease in crime which is occurring in New York and elsewhere for a host of reasons, only some of which are related to police deployment" (cited in April 2, 1994: 24).

When Bratton announced that crime had dropped in 1993 for the third consecutive year, the *Times* noted that "the figures were released with a noteworthy absence of publicity" (April 2, 1994: 24). The apparent reason was that Bratton would have had to credit the reduction to the Dinkins administration, which Giuliani had criticized during the mayoral campaign as ineffective in fighting crime. When questioned about the most recent decline, Bratton attributed it to community policing and the expansion of the police force—policies initiated under Dinkins. Paradoxically, Bratton also asserted that the NYPD needed new strategies and that "for the first time in a generation, this organization is going to get serious about dealing with crime" (cited in April 2, 1994: 24). Rather than giving Dinkins credit for cutting crime, Mayor Giuliani minimized the importance of crime statistics, a position he abandoned when crime continued to fall during his administration: "I don't think a month or two months or even five months tells you the whole story. I have never been one who strongly relies on statistics as a way of measuring what we're doing. Obviously you prefer the trend in the direction of declining crime, but I don't want the department to be overly focused on statistics" (cited in June 2, 1994: B3).

In his book *Turnaround*, published two years after he had resigned as police commissioner, Bratton acknowledged that crime had indeed declined under Dinkins but said that the mayor had failed to use the crime issue to his political advantage. Rather than immediately hiring more police officers with Safe Streets, Safe City funds, which would have shown the public he was concerned with their safety, Dinkins spent two years' worth of that money on social-service programs. This could, at best, be seen as an indirect attack on crime. The additional officers for whom Dinkins secured funding did not actually start work until after the 1993 election, and Giuliani was then able to give the impression that he had been responsible for the additional officers. Bratton credited Dinkins and Police Commissioner Raymond Kelly with starting to improve the city's quality of life through their policy of arresting "squeegee people"—street denizens who greeted drivers entering the city by wiping their windshields with dirty rags and then soliciting money for their services. The threat of arrest and jail time cleared the streets of about thirty of the seventy-five squeegee people within a month. Actual arrests dissuaded the others from continuing their behavior. About half of those who were arrested had records of serious felonies, and about half had histories of drug offenses. Giuliani claimed that he had made the squeegee people an issue in the 1993 campaign, and he was widely perceived as the one who had eliminated this visible sign of urban disorder. However, Bratton (1998: 214) commented, "Only politics had kept Dinkins and Kelly from receiving their due."

The Quality-of-Life Initiative

In 1993, Bratton, then chief of the New York Transit Police, asserted that his "holistic" approach to policing had reduced subway crime. His strategy included daily meetings to review crime statistics; flexibility in shifting officers to the locations where they were most needed; an aggressive stance toward minor offenders, such as fare evaders, panhandlers, and graffiti artists, who often committed serious crimes such as robbery and assault; greater effort by the warrant squad to ensure that suspects who had been issued desk-appearance tickets showed up in court; and use of the media to publicize these measures. Bratton supported the harsh treatment of minor offenders with evidence that one in seven fare evaders had an outstanding warrant for another crime, and one in twenty-five carried a firearm (December 4, 1993: 23–24). He claimed that his strategy had cut subway felonies by 22 percent, subway robberies by 40 percent, and fare evasion by 50 percent.

On July 6, 1994, the *Times* reported on what Bratton (1998: 228) has called the "linchpin strategy" of the Giuliani-Bratton administration's crime-fighting program—the application of the approach he used in the subways to the city as a whole. This approach emphasized the NYPD's strict enforcement of laws against quality-of-life offenses such as subway turnstile jumping, aggressive panhandling, drinking and being drunk in public, truancy, selling alcohol to minors, scrawling graffiti, playing radios loudly in public, and soliciting prostitutes. This quality-of-life initiative also employed a Civil Enforcement Unit of lawyers to prosecute landlords and property owners whose buildings were being used for prostitution, drug dealing, pornography, and the sale of liquor to minors. The quality-of-life initiative was based on an influential 1982 article by James Q. Wilson and George Kelling entitled "Broken Windows," which proposed that

> just as a broken window left untended was a sign that nobody cares and leads to more and severe property damage, so disorderly conditions and behaviors left untended send a signal that nobody cares and results in citizen fear of crime, serious crime, and the "downward spiral of urban decay." The article also argued that whenever crime and communities verged on being out of control in the past, residents and authorities in neighborhoods moved to reassert controls over youth and over disorderly behavior.
>
> The implications of this point of view are that minor offenses have serious consequences for the life of neighborhoods and communities. (Kelling and Bratton, 1998: 1219)

The Giuliani-Bratton administration altered the norms of street behavior by increasing the probability of arrest for a minor offense. From 1993 to 1996, total arrests in the city increased from 261,329 to 345,041. Eighty-six percent of this increase was a growth in misdemeanor arrests, which rose from 133,446 to 205,277 (August 24, 1997: 1, 30). Before 1994, people arrested for minor offenses were usually released after being handed a desk-appearance ticket for a specified court date. These tickets were routinely ignored. Desk-appearance tickets were issued less frequently after 1994 because the police were more likely to jail suspects in minor crimes until their identities were verified by fingerprints and their records were checked to make sure they had no outstanding warrants. The most highly publicized success of this policy occurred in 1996 with the arrest of John Royster for the murder of one woman and assaults on three others. Royster was identified by a fingerprint taken when he had been apprehended for jumping a subway turnstile (September 12, 1997: B1).

Some observers believe that the crackdown on minor offenses contributed to the decline in serious crime, but critics point to the negative consequences of the quality-of-life initiative. The frisking of minor offenders for weapons, which seemed to discourage people from carrying unlicensed firearms and may thus have reduced handgun homicides, was criticized by civil liberties groups for increasing police misconduct and use of excessive force. Complaints of such police behaviors grew from 3,956 in 1993 to 5,596 in 1995. Critics also said that the aggressive treatment of minor offenders imposed punishment first and assessed guilt later. Being arrested, handcuffed, fingerprinted, and sometimes strip-searched were usually the only consequences of committing quality-of-life offenses, because judges rarely meted out additional penalties. One police sergeant described the quality-of-life initiative as follows: "[The police] were being told to go after things that they had been trained to ignore. It's like all bets were off, everything was fair game. You're talking about a greater level of intrusion in people's lives" (cited in August 24, 1997: 30). He said this strategy was effective when used with tolerance and common sense, but he believed that some officers used it disproportionately against minority youths. The *Times* suggested that many New Yorkers would consider it a good trade-off if more killers and rapists were apprehended, even if aggressive enforcement of laws against quality-of-life offenses occasionally led to abusive encounters between the police and the citizenry. However, former Mayor Dinkins dissented, pointing out that many New Yorkers actually felt less safe in recent years, despite the reduction in crime, because of the aggressive law-enforcement practices of the Giuliani-Bratton administration (September 12, 1997: B1).

The rising number of arrests for minor offenses increased police costs and taxed the courts and the correctional system. More overtime pay was required for the extra hours that arresting officers spent shepherding suspects through booking and arraignment. Most suspects charged with minor offenses were soon released because the limited jail space had to be reserved for more serious offenders. However, because some suspects were wanted for other, more serious crimes or for parole violations, the jail population grew. From 1991 to 1997, there was an 85 percent increase in misdemeanor cases in the courts, but little change in the number of judges handling these cases. Witnesses and defendants became disgruntled when they had to come back to court repeatedly to resolve charges, and many of those charges had to be dismissed when parties to the cases failed to appear. Patrick Joyce, a Legal Aid attorney, asked, "How can you make all these arrests and ignore the criminal justice system? Where do they expect the arrests to go?" (cited in September 26, 1994: B3).

Innovations in Police Management

An important component of Bratton's crime-fighting strategy was the introduction of corporation-style management techniques. He gave precinct commanders more autonomy in deciding how to reduce crime in their areas, and he had them meet regularly with their superiors and their peers to show how they had implemented departmental initiatives to cut crime and what the results of those efforts had been. Bratton called this management technique "a phenomenal accountability tool" (cited in August 15, 1994: B3).

Bratton deployed officers to crime "hot spots" that were detected through analysis of computerized statistics and pin maps. This method, called *Compstat*, had four components: accurate and timely intelligence, rapid deployment, effective tactics, and relentless follow-up and assessment. Weekly reports of crime statistics were systematically analyzed in meetings at police headquarters in which precinct commanders were held responsible for crime in their areas of command. Computer-generated maps with overlays were used to depict crime patterns. Tactics that proved effective in reducing crime were shared among precinct commanders, and those who had developed the measures were rewarded.

The Compstat model was used to fight motor vehicle theft in Brooklyn. The information that was compiled included daily reports of vehicle thefts, the places where stolen vehicles had been recovered, pictures of suspected vehicle thieves, and the location of "chop shops" that deal in stolen cars and parts. Increased vehicle-safety check-points, fingerprinting of recovered vehicles, and surveillance of chop shops were the methods of rapid deployment used. One effective tactic was the enforcement of licensing regulations for car repair shops, some of which were owned by members of organized crime. Relentless follow-up and assessment included following suspects arrested for motor vehicle theft through final disposition of the charges, keeping track of repeat vehicle thieves, visiting parolees with vehicle theft convictions, and sharing information with the parole and corrections departments. Public awareness, a fifth element added to the original Compstat model, was enhanced through crime-prevention lectures, press releases, and visits to local shopkeepers (Silverman, 1999: 161–163).

In 1996 and 1997, Giuliani and NYPD administrators attributed recent reductions in crime to Compstat, which had been used to shut down bodegas that trafficked illegal drugs and businesses that sold stolen jewelry. The police also closed five chop shops by mapping the locations where stripped stolen cars had been recovered, zeroing in on nearby repair shops, and tracing the license plate numbers of stolen cars brought to those shops. These steps were credited for a 40 percent decline in motor vehicle thefts over a one-year period.

Size of the Police Force

Mayor Giuliani occasionally acknowledged that Dinkins's Safe Streets, Safe City program had helped to reduce crime by raising the revenue with which to hire 6,000 additional police officers. However, after examining the relationship between the size of the police force and the city's crime rate from 1975 to 1994, the *Times,* in a rare allusion to the problem of simultaneity or reciprocal causation, concluded that it was unclear "whether the extra officers caused the reduction in crime or whether high crime produced pressure for more officers, who were hired and trained only after crime had begun to decline" (January 1, 1995: 37). A few months later, the paper reported that data from the nation's ten largest cities showed no clear-cut association between the size of a city's police force and its rates of murder, robbery, and motor vehicle theft (July 23, 1995, sec. 4: 1, 4).

Early in 1996, Giuliani announced that he would cut the number of police officers by 1,000 to help balance the budget, but that he would not reduce the number of officers on the street and in subways so as to maintain public safety (January 26, 1996: A1). He and Bratton noted that the 1995 merger of the city's police department, transit police, and housing police had freed more than 1,000 administrative officers, making an overall reduction in force possible without reducing the number of officers on the street. City council speaker Peter F. Vallone was critical of the proposed cut, saying, "It seems highly unlikely to us at this stage in the game, where we've finally established a safe city, that we're going to start diminishing the number of police officers you see in the streets" (cited in January 26, 1996: B3). Bratton argued that the management techniques, policing strategies, and computerized mapping he had introduced had increased police productivity and made it possible to maintain public safety with a smaller police force. He remarked, "The numbers [of officers] are very important, but maybe even more important is how we're using them. We're using them much more assertively, much more strategically" (cited in January 26, 1996: 1). In fact, Giuliani never made the proposed reduction in force, stating that it would have been wrong to do so.

Other Policing Measures

Bratton (1998) has stated that it is simplistic to attribute New York's decline in crime either to the quality-of-life initiative or to the increased size of the police force. Instead he proposed that attention should be focused on the multi-faceted nature of his strategy for changing police behavior, including measures aimed at arresting drug traffickers, taking firearms off the street, and reducing truancy.

To combat drug trafficking, Bratton gave all patrol officers the authority to deal with any crimes they uncovered, a change from Dinkins's policy of having patrol officers report drug offenses to teams that dealt only with drugs, a policy critics said had reduced narcotics arrests. Bratton also reallocated personnel after observing that work schedules left few narcotics officers on duty after 6 P.M. or on weekends, apparently leading drug traffickers to adjust their own schedules to minimize the risk of arrest. He used the police to close down open-air drug markets, which often displaced dealers to nearby communities or indoors to apartments and stores in the same community.

Bratton used several measures to get firearms off the street in one violence-ridden precinct in the East New York area of Brooklyn. An undercover unit scrutinized citizens for bulges or body language that could be caused by concealed weapons. Officers were told to apprehend as many accomplices in a given crime as possible, in contrast to the past policy of considering a case closed if a single suspect was arrested. Officers were also instructed to treat arrested suspects as sources of information about other offenders and their criminal activities, and to use that information to take aggressive action. Even suspects arrested for minor offenses were interviewed and searched for firearms, and any that were found were confiscated, matched to as many crimes as possible, and traced to their sellers if possible. Suspects were questioned about the location of other guns, and the police sought warrants to search people and homes. The overall strategy was based on "the view that a relatively small number of people commit most crimes, and that they are often loosely affiliated or come in contact with one another buying guns or drugs or selling stolen goods. With aggressive detective work, the theory goes, one arrest should lead to others" (January 1, 1995: 37). Compared to the same period a year before implementing these changes, this precinct experienced a 50 percent increase in confiscated firearms, a 20 percent decrease in shootings, nearly a 40 percent decrease in murders, and almost a 25 percent increase in total arrests for robbery, burglary, assault, and motor vehicle theft (July 25, 1994: B1, B4). Because no other precincts were compared to this one, and because many changes were introduced simultaneously in this precinct, it is impossible to say which, if any, of the measures were effective in cutting crime.

Bratton versus Academic Criminologists

In a *Times* op-ed piece, sociologist Richard Moran asserted, "As hard as it may be to believe, there is no direct relationship between the number of police officers and the rate of crime in a community" (February 27, 1995: A15). According to Moran, greater numbers of police officers are not associated with lower crime rates for the following reasons:

- The police are better at arresting criminals after crimes have been committed than at preventing crimes.
- More officers do not necessarily increase the number of offenders who end up behind bars, because prisons are already filled beyond capacity, and the incarceration of new offenders requires the release of old ones.

- Imprisoned offenders are often replaced by other criminals on the street without any overall reduction in crime.

Until recently, law-enforcement officials usually concurred with criminologists that there was little the police could do to affect the crime rate. They, too, assumed that the community, the family, the economy, and other institutions over which the police had no control were the underlying sources of crime, a position that exonerated the police when rates were high or rising. By the mid-1990s, however, the views of many police administrators and criminologists had changed, with the *Times* stating that crime experts had become more optimistic that crime could be reduced through "innovative and concerted police strategies on guns, teenagers and petty crimes" (January 19, 1997, sec. 4: 1). Police chiefs throughout the country seemed to believe that every change they had made had reduced crime, though a few of them remained cautious in claiming responsibility for the falling rates, perhaps realizing that doing so would expose them to criticism if rates began to climb. Andrew Karmen (2000: 84) has suggested that historically police chiefs "have pointed to forces beyond their control when the situation was deteriorating and have accepted full responsibility only when conditions were getting better."

In 1995, Bratton announced that his innovative methods had reduced New York City's crime rate to its lowest level in twenty-five years, bluntly stating that alternative explanations for the decline offered by academic criminologists were wrong. He disparaged criminologist James Alan Fox and the journalists who regularly quoted Fox's view that crime had fallen because of a decrease in the proportion of the population in the crime-prone years. Fox responded as follows: "Most of the decline that has occurred would have occurred anyway. The baby boom generation, which comprises almost a third of the population, is getting older. They are middle-aged, and they are not nearly as aggressive and violent as they were when they were younger" (cited in July 23, 1995, sec. 4: 4). Bratton rejected this explanation, noting that from 1990 to 1995 there had been a decrease of only 6 or 7 percent in the number of New York residents in the crime-prone age group from 15 to 29. No estimate was made of how much of a reduction in crime this change should have produced.

Bratton and academic criminologists exchanged views face-to-face at the November 1995 annual meeting of the American Society of Criminology in Boston. The commissioner asked criminologists to reconsider their views that New York City's drop in crime was simply part of a national trend or due to declining crack use, changed attitudes, or a demographic shift. He said, "I'm here to tell you that police make a difference, and we do take offense at some of your colleagues saying otherwise" (cited in November 19, 1995: 43). He dismissed the possibility that crime had fallen simply because there were more officers on the street, noting that in some years crime had dropped when the size of the force had declined. Instead, he attributed the 40 percent decline in homicides and 30 percent decline in robberies since 1993 to the NYPD's zero-tolerance policy toward quality-of-life offenses and to the change from reactive, random police patrols to proactive, carefully designed measures in high-crime areas. Again criticizing the argument that crime had fallen because of a decline in the number of people in the crime-prone age group, Bratton noted that public high school enrollments in the city had actually grown during the time that crime rates had fallen. He countered the argument that New York's experience was just part of a national trend by pointing out that the city itself accounted for a third or more of the national decline in murders, robberies, and motor vehicle thefts. Criminologists at the ASC meeting were impressed by the changes Bratton had made, but they called for more research to determine why crime rates were falling, proposing that social factors probably accounted for some of the decline. Criminologist Richard Frase remarked, "Bratton may want to take more credit than he's due, but we have to study it" (cited in November 19, 1995: 43).

Over time, the continued decline in New York City's crime rate convinced an increasing number of criminologists that the police can have an impact on crime. According to Mark H. Moore, "New York has enjoyed a significant drop in crime that can't be easily explained by sociological factors. Therefore, the claim that this might be the result of police activity looks pretty good" (cited in December 31, 1995: 32). Eli Silverman (1999: 5) was even more confident: "An effective NYPD presence on the streets is reducing crime." Other criminologists believed that the police had played some role in reducing crime, but that they had not been the sole reason for the decline. According to Jeffrey Fagan, "Cops deserve credit, but it would be a first in the history of social science for there to be a single reason for such a dramatic change in social behavior" (cited in July 23, 1995, sec. 4: 1). Agreeing that the police had contributed to the decline, Alfred Blumstein suggested that violent crime had also decreased because of an increase in the prison population and a "maturing" of the drug market (November 19, 1995: 43).

James Q. Wilson questioned the impact of the police on crime, pointing out that in Los Angeles, where homicides fell by 16 percent from 1995 to 1996, the police were doing less and making fewer arrests because they wanted to avoid getting into trouble. Characterizing the LAPD as a department with poor leadership, bad morale, and declining arrests, Wilson concluded, "I've asked several L.A. police officers why the murder rate is down in L.A., and they tell me, 'We haven't the faintest idea'" (cited in June 2, 1997: B10).

Bratton versus Giuliani

In July 1995, when it reported that the number of articles on crime in the city's newspapers had dropped by more than 50 percent from a year earlier, the *Times* asked whether the change was due to the decline in crime or due to manipulation of the news. The previous February, in what was widely interpreted as an effort to control the timing and source of announcements about new crime-fighting measures and thereby gain more personal credit for the decline in crime, Mayor Giuliani had reduced the staff of the NYPD's public information office from thirty-nine to seventeen, reassigned all current members, replaced them with people acceptable to City Hall, and forced Deputy Commissioner of Public Information John Miller to resign. After this reduction in staff, the NYPD supplied the press with less information about crime. The information it did supply was often delayed and lacking in detail, and police officers were less readily available for interviews. Pointing out that he had often found it useful to leak new police initiatives to the press to see how they would be received by the public, Bratton (1998) criticized this purge of the public information office for undermining his efforts because "the importance of the media cannot be overstated in reducing crime and disorder in New York."

Late in 1995, Bratton's aides became concerned about the mayor's reaction to the national and international attention being given to the commissioner, who had appeared on television in Brazil and Italy and been the subject of news stories in Australia, Japan, and Norway. In addition to cutting the department's press staff, Giuliani also turned down a proposed police parade on Bratton's birthday, pressured the commissioner to reduce his public profile, and controlled press ride-alongs with the police. Bratton repeatedly said that Giuliani deserved much of the credit for reducing crime, but the commissioner also routinely claimed personal credit for reducing crime. This claim was supported by criminologists such as Lawrence Sherman, who observed, "The message big-city police chiefs are getting from Bratton is that crime analysis works, and driving police operations in a military fashion based on clearly identified and mapped targets is the best way for police to reduce crime" (cited in December 14, 1995: B5). When Bratton's picture appeared on the cover of *Time* magazine with the caption, "Finally, We're WINNING the War Against Crime. Here's Why," implying that New York's decline in crime was due to the commissioner's efforts, Giuliani's press secretary commented that City Hall was pleased with the attention being given to the commissioner, but also claimed credit for the mayor: "It's a terrific story and it reflects the beautiful job this Commissioner and this Mayor are doing bringing crime down by record numbers" (January 8, 1996: 281).

On March 26, 1996, William Bratton announced his resignation after twenty-seven months as commissioner. He has said that he had planned to quit at the end of 1996, but that having his picture on the cover of *Time* had intensified his conflict with Giuliani. Aggravating the situation were City Hall's removal of some of the budgetary and personnel powers that the commissioner had traditionally held, and its insistence on reviewing a book contract that Bratton had before reappointing him as commissioner. At the time of Bratton's resignation, 60 percent of a sample of New Yorkers credited him with reducing crime, 18 percent credited Giuliani, and 10 percent believed that both shared the credit (April 21, 1996: 41).

During the press conference at which he announced his resignation, Bratton said there was enough credit to go around and that the reduction in crime could not have occurred without Mayor Giuliani's willingness to take the city "in the direction where the quality of life became a paramount concern" (cited in March 27, 1996: B5). Giuliani, in turn, respectfully noted Bratton's accomplishments. Even though they appeared mutually supportive and dismissive of any interpersonal rift, the *Times* observed, "The kind words, however, could not hide the two years of frustration that had preceded them" (March 27, 1996: B5). Two years later, Giuliani offered the following assessment: "Bratton was good at public relations and spending time at Elaine's [an upscale restaurant] and coming up with glossy presentations, but I had to supply the substance. Three-quarters of his ideas were ideas we gave him. The roles were reversed. I was the substantive person, and the Police Commissioner was the politician" (cited in August 16, 1998, sec. 6: 32). Bratton responded, "The Mayor doesn't know what he's talking about" (cited in August 16, 1998, sec. 6: 32).

The Giuliani-Safir Administration

In announcing that crime in the first half of 1996 had dropped from its level of a year before, newly appointed NYPD Commissioner Howard Safir said, "When I became Police Commissioner April 15 crime was going down a little more than 9 percent, and since I became Police Commissioner crime has gone down over 14 percent" (cited in July 3, 1996: A1). The *Times* suggested that this decline was due to an anti-drug initiative developed by Bratton and implemented just after he had resigned. Mayor Giuliani also claimed credit for the decline, contradicting the statement he made during the 1993 mayoral campaign that minimized the importance of crime statistics: "It's really remarkable. I don't think there's ever, in history, been a city with three consecutive years of double-digit drops in crime statistics. All the strategies that have been put in place are working better than anyone, including me, thought they would when we devised them" (cited in December 20, 1996: B4). Two district attorneys acknowledged the importance of the police, but they claimed that more prosecutions, especially of career criminals, and stiffer sentences had also helped to reduce crime (October 2, 1996: B3; July 1, 1997: B3).

The 1997 Mayoral Campaign

In his 1997 reelection campaign, Giuliani often spoke of the precipitous drop in crime during his first term in office: Homicides had fallen by 61 percent, robberies by 48 percent, and burglaries by 46 percent. Proudly observing that crime had fallen to its lowest level since 1967, he used crime statistics as evidence of the effectiveness of his approach to fighting crime, which included the quality-of-life initiative, the use of computers to map crime trends, and the concentration of police resources on drug trafficking (January 2, 1997: B3). The *Times* commented that although Giuliani could not be credited with all of the reduction in crime, he had translated dry crime statistics into a "tangible feeling of security" for many New Yorkers (October 27, 1997: A1). His timing was described as fortuitous, with the quality-of-life initiative beginning just as business improvement districts were having an impact on crime in the most visible commercial areas, years of renovating Times Square were coming to fruition, a national recession was ending, and greater civil order was emerging in many of the nation's cities.

Some of Giuliani's political rivals criticized his record on crime, claiming that rates had begun to increase in some precincts, that many

New Yorkers had yet to feel the effects of the reduction, and that fewer officers were visible on the street than during previous administrations (February 5, 1997: B4). However, most who had criticized the mayor in the past acknowledged that crime was down, tourism had increased, and residents were more satisfied with city life.

During the mayoral campaign, Giuliani introduced an idea apparently aimed at deflecting blame should crime increase prior to Election Day. If that happened, he suggested, it would be because five southern states had failed to curb the sale of firearms that were imported to New York for resale to criminals. According to Giuliani, 90 percent of the guns confiscated in the city that had been traced had come from sources outside the city, and 60 percent had originated in five states with lax gun laws: Florida, Georgia, Virginia, and North and South Carolina. Thomas Reppetto agreed with Giuliani: "We've pretty much done everything we could do here. We've taxed ourselves for more officers and used about every strategy in the book. If we got some help from people in other states on guns, we could cut our murder rate in half again. It would be nice if people in other states understood our problem, but they tend to be less inclined to firearm measures out there" (cited in March 7, 1997: B3).

Giuliani's effective use of the crime issue helped him win reelection in November 1997. When his new term of office began in January 1998, Howard Safir continued as police commissioner.

Crime and Safir's NYPD

In assessing Safir's performance as police commissioner, the *Times* described him as "a competent bureaucrat who implements the ideas of his larger-than-life predecessor. . . . Instead of the press, Safir cultivates the Mayor. Successfully, by all evidence" (August 16, 1998, sec. 6: 32). Trying to distance himself from Bratton, Safir said the former commissioner "didn't know what the hell was going on in this building [police headquarters]. I'm not here for press relations. I'm here to reduce crime" (cited in August 16, 1998, sec. 6: 32). Safir attributed his success in accelerating the pace at which crime was falling to the continued use of computerized crime maps; his rejection of community policing, which he described as "feel-good cops"; and the new Street Crimes Unit, which targeted illegal handguns (cited in December 24, 1998: A1).

During his first term in office, Giuliani sometimes attributed the reduction in crime to the expansion of the police force; more often, he claimed that the decline was due to the quality-of-life initiative and the systematic deployment of officers. In January 1999, he announced that he would add 1,500 officers to the NYPD in order to keep crime down, curb drug offenses, and reduce domestic violence. Even without the additional officers, the NYPD already had the most officers per capita of the ten largest cities in the United States. The *Times* suggested a political motivation behind the proposed buildup: Giuliani's reputation as mayor, and earlier as federal prosecutor, was based on crime fighting, and he had to keep the city's crime rate low, or better yet reduce it even more, in order to strengthen his expected campaign for the U.S. Senate. That plan was aborted in 2000 when he was diagnosed with prostate cancer and became involved in an acrimonious divorce.

Criminologist Eli Silverman supported the proposed addition of officers to the NYPD as follows: "If your expectations are to continue to drive down crime, you can't lose momentum. The truth is, I don't know when we'll hit diminishing returns until we hit it" (cited in January 29, 1999: B10). Even though it cited experts who concluded that cities' crime rates are not closely associated with the size of their police departments, a *Times* editorial also supported the buildup, saying, "With the Mayor's success rate, it makes sense to support a winning streak" (February 4, 1999: A26). The editorial urged that the increase be in officers who patrolled the streets and fought crime, rather than in officers who did office work, noting that the percentage of uniformed officers working as clerks, secretaries, custodians, and telephone operators in the NYPD was far higher than in other urban police departments.

When murders increased slightly in early 1999, in contrast to a continued decline in the total number of serious crimes, NYPD officials announced that murders arising from domestic disputes had grown especially rapidly. In response, Safir expanded the number of officers dealing with domestic violence in two precincts, having those officers work with social service agencies and visit homes with a history of violence. When reports of domestic violence dropped in those precincts, he proposed expanding the program to other areas of the city (March 11, 1999: B3).

The Diallo Shooting and Its Aftermath

Coming after several years of increasing complaints of police abuse, the February 1999 death of Amadou Diallo in a hail of forty-one bullets fired by four Street Crimes Unit officers aroused widespread concern that the police were exceeding acceptable limits in their war on crime. Civil rights lawyer Richard D. Emery worried that "once the crime rate drops to a certain point, police officers become like fishermen in fished-out waters, frequently catching not their prey, but hapless innocent victims" (February 19, 1999: A21). He pointed out that over the previous two years, the police had conducted 45,000 street searches that had yielded fewer than 10,000 arrests, but which had humiliated more than 35,000 innocent people in the hope of improving the city's quality of life. Emery believed that Bratton's 1994 reforms had been necessitated by a high crime rate, but that by 1999 crime had fallen to a low enough level that police aggressiveness could be curtailed. He suggested that Giuliani and Safir saw the apparent leveling off of crime as a failure and felt they had to implement new measures to cut crime even more.

In response to the Diallo shooting, *Times* reporter Bob Herbert wrote the following in an op-ed piece:

> Mayor Rudolph Giuliani insisted from the moment he took office that police officers adopt a much more aggressive approach to fighting crime and combatting the so-called quality-of-life offenses. What he didn't do was insist that this citywide crackdown be carried out by officers who were properly trained and closely supervised. And he never gave enough attention to the idea that law-abiding New Yorkers, including those who are black or Latino, should always be treated with respect by the police. (April 4, 1999, sec. 4: 11)

Herbert attributed the growing number of complaints of police abuse to the intense pressure on precinct commanders to reduce crime or be replaced. His statement that the "mayor and his police commissioners knew or should have known that their anti-crime strategies were dangerously flawed and likely to lead to tragedy" raises the question of why the *Times* had enthusiastically supported Giuliani's, Bratton's, and Safir's aggressive stance toward crime throughout the decade without warning of its supposedly predictable consequences (April 4, 1999, sec. 4: 11).

Another critic of the police in the aftermath of the Diallo shooting was U.S. Senator Charles E. Schumer of New York, who warned that hostility between the police and minority groups could hurt the continuing effort to reduce crime. Acknowledging that most officers behave honorably, he also pointed to the common practice of singling out blacks, most of them law-abiding, for searching and questioning. He recommended that the department get rid of its abusive officers and re-cruit more officers from minority groups.

Giuliani and Safir responded to these criticisms by citing FBI evidence that NYPD officers fired their weapons less often than officers in any other large city, and by pointing out that only a tiny percentage of all warrants led to raids on incorrect addresses. Safir observed that black New Yorkers had been the primary beneficiaries of falling crime rates, claimed that he did not tolerate racist officers, and pointed out that he had dismissed more officers than the two previous commissioners together.

Some NYPD officials used the Diallo shooting to explain the increase in homicides in early 1999, proposing that officers might have become less aggressive in stopping suspects because of the criticism and increased scrutiny they had faced after the Diallo shooting. Officials reasoned that if the police had become less aggressive, some New Yorkers might have been more likely to carry firearms because they were no longer concerned that the police would search them. Arrests for illegal possession of firearms did fall by 17 percent in early 1999 in comparison to the same period a year earlier (March 11, 1999: B3). A few weeks later, Safir announced that Street Crimes Unit arrests had fallen by 67 percent and that the unit was filing fewer stop-and-frisk reports, which Safir and Giuliani interpreted as evidence that SCU officers had been distracted by the Diallo shooting and its aftermath. Criminologist Andrew Karmen questioned this explanation of the short-term increase in homicides, observing that earlier the police had attributed the increase to a growth in domestic violence. He suggested that the police might be "seeing that crime is bottoming out, and they're preparing for criticism by developing this fingerpointing argument, that you the critics have ruined everything and caused crime to go back up" (cited in March 29, 1999: B3).

Highly publicized demonstrations at police headquarters protesting the Diallo shooting eventually led Safir to announce that fifty of the 380 SCU officers would be replaced with officers who were members of minority groups, that SCU officers would be more closely supervised, that some of them would be given promotions and raises (apparently to boost their morale), and that SCU officers would work in uniform rather than plainclothes to avoid confusion as to who they were. Critics said this last reform would hurt the unit's ability to fight crime by taking away the element of surprise. When gun seizures declined, perhaps as a result of a deliberate slowdown by the SCU, Safir allowed some officers to return to plainclothes. In October 1999, he broke the SCU into eight units that would report to regional commanders, saying this would increase supervision and accountability. However, this change was widely regarded as an effort to weaken the SCU.

In April 1999, Safir was the target of a no-confidence vote by the union representing police officers. They objected to pressure from headquarters to make arrests and issue summonses, and to the quality-of-life initiative, which they believed had made the public more hostile toward them. The union claimed that Safir should adjust his policing methods to the lower crime rate, something he was reluctant to do because of pressure from Giuliani to reduce crime even more. James Savage, president of the officers' union, said, "If we don't strike a balance between aggressive enforcement and common sense, it becomes a blueprint for a police state and tyranny. . . . I am advising our members to exercise the maximum degree of discretion in warning and admonishing citizens before issuing a summons or making arrests" (cited in April 14, 1999: A1). One officer remarked, "Crime has gone down, so now we're having to see how else can we find fault with the community. It's tough when you're going after people for riding bicycles on the sidewalk, pulling people over and giving them summonses" (cited in April 14, 1999: B6).

Asserting that the quality-of-life initiative was a major reason that crime had fallen, Safir called the union's no-confidence vote a political maneuver designed to enhance Savage's campaign for the union presidency. Safir acknowledged that the costs associated with reducing crime had to be considered, but concluded that the costs were justified by the advantages of less crime. He told the city council that in the twenty precincts where the SCU was active, the percentage of citizens stopped and frisked who were black (63 percent) was similar to the percentage of all offenders identified as black by crime victims (71 percent) and similar to the percentage of all arrested suspects who were black (68 percent). Rejecting Safir's contention that these statistics showed that the police were unbiased, Norman Siegel of the New York Civil Liberties Union said that race should never be used as a proxy for reasonable suspicion and that the great majority of police stops were not valid and had not led to convictions. New York State Attorney General Eliot L. Spitzer proposed that the problem might be even greater than suggested by police records because as many as several hundred thousand people might have been stopped and frisked without the police filing a report.

In 1999, Safir introduced the use of an integrated parolee database to make it easier for the police to learn whether someone stopped for a minor offense or with an outstanding warrant was also on parole. The police began to accompany parole officers on raids of the homes of parolees. Parolees were required to allow their parole officer to enter and search their home at any time, provide a urine sample at the officer's request, and answer questions about recent crimes. Because the police need warrants or emergency situations to do these things, the presence of parole officers allowed them more latitude in investigating parolees. Civil libertarians criticized this strategy as harassment and worried that it would make it harder for parolees to reintegrate into society. The police, however, said that the new approach helped them to solve crimes. In one case, they found firearms in the homes of two parolees, who then provided information that led to the solution of several murders (August 12, 1999: B8).

Despite the continued drop in New York City's crime rate, there were more arrests than ever in 1998. However, an increasing proportion of arrests were flawed, forcing district attorneys to reduce and dismiss more charges. One prosecutor remarked, "You have less crime and more junk." Another said, "It's a test of the evidence. The arrest that comes in is lacking in some way—the evidence is not sufficient to support the charge, or the search is a bad search and therefore would not withstand scrutiny" (cited in August 23, 1999: A1, B6). A study by the *Times* found that many of the cases that district attorneys refused to prosecute came from minority communities where there were increasing complaints of police harassment. NYPD officials responded that the department continued to encourage the arrest of suspects, that arrests were reviewed to make sure they would stand up in court, and that district attorneys had thrown out thousands of valid arrests they should have prosecuted.

Conclusion

The political response to the decline in New York City's crime rate focused narrowly on the impact of the police, with mayors and police commissioners repeatedly asserting that crime had been reduced by increasing the size of the police force, introducing community policing, implementing a quality-of-life initiative, holding precinct commanders accountable for reducing crime, and redeploying resources by using computerized statistics and maps.

Except for Bratton's attack on academic criminology, police administrators and mayors paid virtually no attention to forces outside their control that might have produced the decline in crime. Their interpretation of why crime had dropped might be the result of the limitations of local political power: Mayors and police commissioners affect the size of the police force and what the police do, but they are less able to influence the courts, the prisons, the economy, or the family. Usually, police commissioners defer to mayors and credit them with any reduction in crime. What was unusual in New York in the mid-1990s was that Commissioner Bratton effectively used the media to gain personal credit for the decline in crime. Mayor Giuliani had little he could offer to explain how he had reduced crime other than the policies implemented by Bratton, his appointee. The mayor seemed to be losing the competition for credit until he forced Bratton to resign in 1996. After replacing Bratton with Safir, a loyalist who did not compete with the mayor for credit, Giuliani was more successful in convincing New Yorkers that he was the one who had cut crime, even though he continued to focus almost exclusively on policing as the cause of that decline.

An alternative to ousting Bratton, but one not consistent with Giuliani's law-and-order approach, would have been for the mayor to have looked at crime reduction in terms broader than policing. He might have argued that attention to the crime problem had bolstered New York's economy by attracting new jobs and keeping employers from moving elsewhere, and then asserted that the booming economy had contributed to the decline in crime by offering potential offenders an alternative to breaking the law and by strengthening families and local communities. Giuliani paid little attention to such factors, and he did not acknowledge that the courts and the prisons might have played an important role in curbing crime, probably because he had no direct control over those institutions. By focusing on the police, the only visible crime-reducing institution over which he did have control, Giuliani put himself in direct competition with Bratton. Had Giuliani broadened the scope of his claims, he could have presented himself as a crime fighter who had done more than appoint a talented police commissioner.

Political discourse on the reasons that New York's crime rate fell suggests several testable hypotheses about how the police might have reduced crime, hypotheses that are evaluated with published research and available data in the following chapter. Alternative explanations for the decline in crime that were presented in the *Times* or offered by academic criminologists, but which were virtually ignored by New York's law-enforcement officials and politicians, are examined in subsequent chapters.

4 Did the Police Reduce Crime?

The police might reduce crime in either of two ways. The deterrence perspective suggests that offenders are rational individuals who can be dissuaded from committing crimes by increasing the risk of arrest and punishment. The incapacitation perspective proposes that more arrests will produce more convictions and prison sentences, and thus take more offenders off the street. Most researchers have not distinguished between deterrence and incapacitation in assessing the impact of policing on crime.

Critics such as David Bayley (1994: 1), who asserts that the fact that the "police do not prevent crime . . . is one of the best kept secrets of modern life," question whether the police actually reduce crime through deterrence and incapacitation, contending that they spend little time enforcing the law and that much of that time is devoted to minor offenses. Critics also doubt the rationality of offenders, claiming that many criminals, especially violent ones, do not give careful thought to the consequences of their actions and are therefore unlikely to be influenced by the threat of arrest. Those offenders who do think about the possibility of arrest might simply commit their crimes at different times, in different places, or in different ways in order to avoid the police. Crime is then displaced rather than prevented. Another problem is that any incapacitative effect of increased arrests might be offset by higher acquittal rates or reduced rates of incarceration. This could happen if a growth in arrests is not accompanied by an increase in court and prison resources (Marvell and Moody, 1996).

Law-enforcement officials and political leaders who asserted that the police reduced New York City's crime rate in the 1990s cited the following factors: (1) an increase in the size of the police force, (2) community policing, (3) more efficient deployment of resources, (4) aggressive action against specific targets, and (5) organizational reform. Mayor Dinkins attributed his administration's modest success in cutting crime to an increase in the number of police officers and the introduction of community policing. Mayor Giuliani stressed the use of computerized maps and statistics to redeploy resources and the implementation of measures that targeted firearms and drugs. Commissioner Bratton (1998: 198–199) cited the Compstat model, the quality-of-life initiative, the emphasis on arrest and interrogation, the assignment to all officers of the authority to arrest drug and firearm offenders, and the accountability required of precinct commanders.

The claim that the police "played an important, even central, role in getting people to stop committing crime in New York City" is made forcefully by Kelling and Bratton in a special issue of the *Journal of Criminal Law and Criminology* devoted to the question, "Why Is Crime Decreasing?" Asserting that "no evidence exists that the substantial drops in crime in New York City . . . were the result of economic change, changes in drug use patterns, or demographic changes," they state that their confidence in the impact of the police is based on the following:

1. We had a guiding "idea" about how to prevent crime; put another way, we had a theory of action;
2. We applied this idea in New York City's subway and, without anticipating it, the subway experience became the "pretest" for what was to happen later citywide;
3. Bratton, most importantly, but Kelling as well, had been struggling with issues of how to improve policing through police leadership, management, and administration for over two decades—principles developed in the context of organization and policy leadership and experience. (Kelling and Bratton, 1998: 1218)

Having a theory and applying it, and having experience, do not prove that a policy works. Determining the effectiveness of a policy instead requires a well thought out research design and the application of scientific methods. No such assessment has been done of the measures implemented by the NYPD in the 1990s. Despite Kelling and Bratton's claims, they offer no convincing evidence to refute the possibility that crime fell because of changes in factors other than policing that occurred during Bratton's administration but were unrelated to the measures he introduced.

Crime and the Number of Police Officers

Kelling et al. (1974: 2) once observed that "in the face of spiraling crime rates, the most common answer urged by public officials and citizens alike has been to increase patrol forces and get more police officers 'on the street.' " Bill Clinton used this reasoning in his 1992 presidential campaign, when he promised to support federal funding of 100,000 more officers for the nation's police forces. Five years later, he took credit for the drop in crime, saying, "At the beginning of my administration, we set out to change this country's approach to crime by putting more officers on the street through community policing, and taking guns out of the hands of criminals. We are making a difference" (cited in January 5, 1997: 10).

Research demonstrates that crime rates are affected by extreme variations in the number of officers on the street, such as a police strike or a police crackdown. However, such drastic changes probably alter the likelihood that crimes will be reported and recorded, making it difficult to assess the impact of large changes in the number of officers on the actual amount of crime that occurs. When the Nazis arrested the Copenhagen, Denmark, police force in 1944, robberies and larcenies increased tenfold, despite harsher penalties for offenders (Andenaes, 1974: 51). A 1969 police strike in Montreal led to a big increase in burglaries, bank robberies, and looting (Clark, 1969). There was a 50 percent increase in store robberies and a 42 percent increase in violence-related hospital admissions during a 1976 police strike in Finland (Makinen and Takala, 1980). Widespread looting has occurred in several U.S. cities that have experienced blackouts, which tax police resources (Sherman, 1992a). Contradicting this evidence that crime increases when the number of officers drops to a very low level, a study of eleven cities that had police strikes during the 1970s concluded that "strikes appear to have neither a significant nor a systematic impact on rates of reported crime" (Pfuhl, 1983: 498). At the other extreme, substantial increases in the number of officers on the street might also affect crime rates. Sherman (1990) found that fifteen of eighteen police crackdowns had a deterrent effect on crime, though the effect usually wore off after a brief time; five of the crackdowns continued to have deterrent effects even after they had ended.

More directly relevant to the question of whether the police contributed to the decline in crime in the 1990s is the effect of variations in police strength that are less extreme than strikes and crackdowns. Even if there is an overall association between crime rates and the size of a city's police force, that association might be spurious if certain characteristics of cities affect both the crime rate and the size of the police force. For instance, cities with high rates of poverty might be especially likely to have high crime rates (if deprivation leads to crime) and might have few police officers per capita because of limited tax revenue with which to pay for a larger force. It would be incorrect to assume that a low number of officers per capita causes a high crime rate, because the police–crime relationship might disappear when urban characteristics such as poverty are taken into account.

A few researchers have found that increases in police strength do lead to decreases in crime rates (Marvell and Moody, 1996; Levitt, 1997), but most have found that within the range of police officers per capita that exists in the United States, cities with larger police forces do not have lower crime rates than cities with smaller police forces (President's Commission on Law Enforcement and Administration of Justice, 1967; Loftin and McDowall, 1982; Greenberg, Kessler, and Loftin, 1983). Eck and Maguire's (2000) comprehensive examination of twenty-seven studies of the relationship between violent crime and police strength found that 49.4 percent of the estimates of this relationship showed no effect of police strength on crime rates, 30.3 percent showed that greater police strength was associated with higher crime rates, and only 20.2 percent supported the conclusion that greater police strength was associated with lower crime rates. They concluded that three decades of research had produced no "consistent body of evidence supporting the assertion that hiring more police is an effective method for reducing violent crime" (Eck and Maguire, 2000: 214). This view remained unchanged after they focused their attention on the results of the nine studies that had used the most rigorous research methods.

To illustrate the variation in crime rates among cities of similar size and with comparable police strength, I looked at all U.S. cities that had populations of 100,000 or more in both 1990 and 1999, had statistics for all four indicator crimes and for number of police officers published in both the 1990 and 1999 *Uniform Crime Reports,* and had not changed crime reporting practices or annexed population during the 1990s. I ranked these 157 cities by their 1999 rates of police officers per 100,000 people, which ranged from 97 to 672, then compared pairs of cities in which those rates were within 1.0 of each other and in which one city had a population no more than 5 percent greater than the other city. Table 4.1 shows the eight pairs of cities that met those criteria. What is striking, but not surprising in light of the many other ways that cities differ, are the often substantial differences in crime rates between the paired cities. If a substantial discrepancy in crime rates is defined as one of the paired cities having a crime rate more than 50 percent higher than the other city's, such discrepancies exist in six of the eight pairs for mur-

TABLE 4.1   **Police Officers and Indicator Crimes, Pairs of Cities, 1999**

City	Population	Police	Murder	Robbery	Burglary	Motor vehicle theft
			Rates per 100,000 people			
Buffalo, NY	301,069	318.2	10.6	489.3	1,470.8	993.1
Tampa, FL	292,941	317.8	10.6	792.3	2,056.4	1,959.4
Providence, RI	151,430	306.4	17.2	305.8	1,387.4	1,503.7
Fort Lauderdale, FL	155,740	306.3	14.1	457.8	1,935.3	1,148.7
Chattanooga, TN	149,230	300.9	14.7	397.4	1,790.5	993.8
Durham, NC	155,635	300.1	9.0	708.7	2,662.6	1,062.7
Topeka, KS	120,108	238.1	12.5	313.9	2,028.2	582.0
Alexandria, VA	119,721	237.2	1.7	132.0	464.4	586.4
Evansville, IN	123,689	225.6	4.0	82.5	1,004.9	348.5
Springfield, IL	117,905	225.6	8.5	205.2	1,520.7	316.4
Lubbock, TX	193,724	154.9	7.2	158.5	1,214.1	359.3
Spokane, WA	186,229	154.6	3.2	195.5	1,692.5	519.8
Eugene, OR	129,576	128.9	1.5	145.9	1,369.9	503.2
Sterling Heights, MI	124,928	128.9	0.0	30.4	244.9	239.3
Escondido, CA	122,344	116.1	2.5	125.1	503.5	802.7
Orange, CA	125,634	115.4	0.8	80.4	411.5	382.1

Source: Based on data in Federal Bureau of Investigation, *Crime in the United States: Uniform Crime Reports 1999*. Washington, DC: U.S. Government Printing Office, 2000, pp. 111–151, 300–367.

der and robbery and in three of the eight pairs for burglary and motor vehicle theft. Only two of the eight pairs—Providence-Fort Lauderdale and Lubbock-Spokane—had less than a 50 percent difference between all four crime rates. These comparisons are consistent with Eck and Maguire's conclusion that greater police strength is not consistently associated with lower crime rates.

Table 4.2 illustrates Eck and Maguire's (2000: 209) statement that they were "not aware of a single empirical study that supports the claim that increases in the number of police officers are responsible for recent

TABLE 4.2 Changes in Police and Crime per 100,000 People, 1990–1999

	Absolute changes in rates		
	New York City	*Los Angeles*	*Chicago*
Police	+ 195.9	+ 20.5	+ 41.0
Murder	− 21.6	− 16.6	− 7.8
Robbery	− 883.5	− 640.9	− 609.5
Burglary	− 1,093.2	− 887.5	− 728.7
Motor vehicle theft	− 1,474.9	− 1,149.1	− 629.3
	Relative changes in rates		
Police	+ 53.4%	+ 8.5%	+ 9.5%
Murder	− 70.3%	− 58.9%	− 25.5%
Robbery	− 64.5%	− 61.9%	− 45.7%
Burglary	− 66.7%	− 60.1%	− 40.4%
Motor vehicle theft	− 73.4%	− 63.0%	− 36.0%

Source: Based on data in Federal Bureau of Investigation, *Crime in the United States: Uniform Crime Reports 1999.* Washington, DC: U.S. Government Printing Office, 2000, pp. 111–151, 300–367.

decreases in violent crime" with data for the country's three largest cities—New York City, Los Angeles, and Chicago. The top part of the table shows that the absolute number of officers per capita increased in the 1990s by nearly ten times as much in New York as in Los Angeles, and by nearly five times as much in New York as in Chicago. New York did experience larger absolute declines in crime, but rates fell sharply in all three cities. The bottom part of Table 4.2 looks at this in terms of relative or percentage changes. New York City's rate of officers per capita rose by 53.4 percent during the 1990s, while its crime rates fell by 64.5 to 73.4 percent. Los Angeles had a much smaller 8.5 percent increase in officers per capita, but still recorded 58.9 to 63.0 percent reductions in crime rates. Chicago had a modest 9.5 percent increase in police strength, but saw its crime rates fall by 25.5 to 45.7 percent. Any claim that New York City's crime rates fell primarily because of an increase in the size of its police force is contradicted by the experiences of Los Angeles and Chicago, where crime rates plummeted without substantial increases in police strength. The somewhat larger reductions in

New York City's crime rates might be attributable in part to the much bigger increase in officers per capita, but published research does not support such a claim.

Focusing on changes in police strength and murder rates in New York City, Andrew Karmen (2000) found that the number of officers grew by 25 percent during the 1990s, leaving the city with twice the number of officers per capita as many other large cities by the end of the decade. He proposed that if this increased police presence deterred murder, there should have been a bigger decline in murders committed outdoors than in murders committed indoors, where the police are less visible. He discovered that in the mid-1990s murders on the street and in the parks did drop sharply as the police force grew, but that indoors murders fell by nearly as much, suggesting that factors other than changes in police strength had caused the decline.

Car and Foot Patrols

The ideal way to assess the relationship between police strength and crime rates is an experiment: Systematically change the number of officers in some areas, then compare changes in crime rates there with changes in rates in areas that have similar characteristics but where the size of the police force has not been changed. An experiment of this sort evaluated police effectiveness in reducing crime in Kansas City, Missouri, in 1972 and 1973 (Kelling et al., 1974).

The Kansas City Preventive Patrol Experiment was designed to assess the impact of police patrol cars on crime. Patrol cars increase the area the police can cover, enhancing the likelihood that officers will be at or near the scene when a crime occurs. However, patrol cars also isolate the police from the public, making it harder to maintain order, prevent crime, and arrest suspects. The police department provided officers in Kansas City with information about people in their patrol area who were wanted on warrants or for questioning, criminals thought to be operating in the area, and recent crimes committed in the area. Routine preventive patrol used this information for "observing from police cars, checking on premises and suspicious citizens, serving warrants, checking abandoned vehicles, and executing other self-initiated police activities" (Kelling et al., 1974: 7).

The Kansas City experiment doubled or tripled the number of cars in five "proactive" police beats, maintained the usual level of one car in five "control" beats, and took all cars off duty in five "reactive" beats (so-called because cars in nearby areas would respond to calls for help there). The reactive beats thus maintained police availability but reduced police visibility, though one critic contends that responses to calls in those areas made the police as visible as in the control beats (Larson, 1976). The fifteen police beats were matched by crime rates, numbers of calls to the police in the past, and population characteristics such as ethnicity, income, and length of residency.

Police crime reports and victimization surveys of households and businesses from before and after the experiment were used to measure the impact of patrol cars. After one year, the evidence showed that changes in patrol visibility were of "little value in preventing crime" (McNamara, 1974: iii). Police crime reports showed few differences across beats, and those that were found seemed to be random. Victimization surveys revealed no differences among beats in robberies, household or commercial burglaries, motor vehicle thefts, larcenies of car accessories, or vandalism (Kelling et al., 1974). The researchers warned that these results did not mean that police departments could be reduced in size without having an impact on crime, only that routine preventive patrol was ineffective in preventing crime. One critic was not surprised by the negative results, observing that crime is concentrated in certain "hot spots," whereas patrol cars are widely dispersed, making it unlikely that officers will encounter crime while on routine patrol (Sherman, 1992a).

If more patrol cars do not prevent crime, can increasing the number of officers on foot do so? The evidence is mixed, but offers little cause for optimism. A study in Flint, Michigan, found an 8.7 percent reduction in total crime in areas that had foot patrols, though the patrols had no impact on burglaries and larcenies (Trojanowicz, 1983). A study in Newark, New Jersey, found no changes in crime, as measured by police crime reports and victimization surveys, in areas in which foot patrols had been started, continued, or had ended (Kelling et al., 1981). Other researchers have also concluded that foot patrols do not reduce police reports of index offenses (Bowers and Hirsch, 1987; Esbensen, 1987). Overall, increased numbers of officers patrolling the streets on foot do not seem to have any consistent, substantial impact on crime.

The impact of car and foot patrols is difficult to determine because of displacement effects, which are altered crime patterns that result from changes that criminals make to avoid arrest. There is some evidence that police presence can displace crime from one area to another where there are fewer officers, or from a time when there are more officers around to a time when fewer are present (Reppetto,

1974), but neither the Kansas City experiment nor Sherman's (1990, 1995) study of police crackdowns found evidence of such crime displacement.

Directed Patrol and Compstat

Even if the size of a city's police force does not change, the number of officers in a given neighborhood can be increased or decreased through redeployment of existing resources. For many years, departments have strategically shifted officers from area to area on the basis of an analysis of crime statistics, an approach called directed patrol. The best-designed study supporting the effectiveness of this method was carried out in Minneapolis in 1988 and 1989 in 110 crime "hot spots" chosen on the basis of frequent calls to police. Fifty-five control hot spots continued to get the same attention from the police they had been receiving. Fifty-five experimental hot spots received two-and-a-half times as much patrolling as usual. The experimental areas showed a significantly greater decline in serious crime than the control areas (Sherman and Weisburd, 1995). What is unclear from this and other research on directed patrol is whether reductions in crime are "produced through general deterrence of all those who frequent hot spots, through specific deterrence of hot-spot offenders who come under closer scrutiny of the police, or through the incapacitation of repeat offenders following their arrest at these hot spots" (Eck and Maguire, 2000: 231).

Directed patrol became a high-profile strategy in the mid-1990s when the NYPD introduced the Compstat model. Because other measures were introduced at about the same time, assessing the impact of Compstat alone is difficult. Criminologists have tried to do this by closely examining the timing of the decline in New York City's crime rates. Compstat was announced in March 1994 and weekly sessions began in May 1994. Therefore, Karmen (2000) proposes that it could not have been implemented at the street level until mid-1994. He found that the number of murders declined significantly in January 1994 relative to January 1993, apparently because of unusually cold weather. Murders increased for a few months thereafter, then started to decline in May, a trend consistent with a Compstat effect. However, rapes and assaults were at least as common in the last half of 1994 as in the same period in 1993, and robberies, burglaries, larcenies, and motor vehicle thefts all began to decline months before Compstat was introduced. Karmen (2000: 99) concluded that "the findings of this inquiry into timing do not support the improved policing hypothesis across the board," though he acknowledges that Compstat could have accelerated the decline in crime.

In a similar analysis, Eck and Maguire (2000) found that homicides in New York City started to decrease four years before Compstat was introduced, but that the decline accelerated after it was implemented. However, the more rapid decline in homicides after 1994 than in the preceding years also characterized nearby states and the nation's ten largest cities, suggesting that New York City's decline was neither unique nor the result of Compstat, the quality-of-life initiative, or other measures introduced by Commissioner Bratton. Eck and Maguire (2000: 235) concluded that "the diffusion of the Compstat process to other cities throughout the United States came too late to have produced the national decline in homicides."

Crime and What the Police Do

Even though variations in police strength are not meaningfully associated with changes in crime rates, some police measures do reduce crime under certain conditions. This section considers what the police do rather than how many of them there are, assesses the effectiveness of different police measures, and then asks if the increased use of those measures contributed to the decline in crime rates in the 1990s. Measures specifically directed at drug and firearm offenses are examined in Chapters 6 and 7, respectively.

The Risk of Arrest

Law-enforcement officials, political leaders, and the public commonly assume that the police prevent crime through the threat of arrest, even though only one serious crime in five is solved. In fact, the rate at which the police solve or clear crimes overstates the chance that an offender will be arrested because many crimes are never reported to the police, some multiple-offender crimes are cleared with the arrest of a single suspect, and the police sometimes clear cases without making an arrest, such as when they believe that a crime was committed by someone who is currently incarcerated for a different offense or by someone who has since died.

Some research shows that the more crimes the police solve or the more arrests they make, the lower the crime rate (Block, 1972; Tittle and

Rowe, 1974; Logan, 1975; Wilson and Boland, 1976; Yu and Liska, 1993). Other studies, however, find no consistent evidence that higher clearance rates are associated with lower crime rates (Greenberg and Kessler, 1982). Higher clearance rates might not reduce crime rates because officers have to leave the street to do the paperwork associated with arrests, which decreases police visibility. In addition, the overburdening of the courts and prisons decreases the certainty of punishment by reducing the likelihood that defendants will be prosecuted and incarcerated (Sherman, 1995).

If an increased probability of arrest does prevent crime through deterrence or incapacitation, it would be reasonable to expect that clearance rates rose during the 1990s as crime rates fell. In addition to having a possible effect on crime rates, clearance rates can also be affected by changes in crime rates. If crime rates fall and the number of police per capita does not change, clearance rates might increase because the police have more time and resources to devote to investigating each crime. Clearance rates reported by the Federal Bureau of Investigation (1991, 2000) for the four indicator crimes for 1990 and 1999 are as follows:

	1990	1999
Murder	67.2%	69.1%
Robbery	24.9%	28.5%
Burglary	13.8%	13.7%
Motor vehicle theft	14.6%	14.9%

The robbery clearance rate increased modestly over this time, but there was little change in clearance rates for the other crimes. Because the per capita rates of all four crimes declined significantly during the 1990s, the absence of any meaningful change in the clearance rates for three of them suggests that crime rates fell for reasons other than growing police effectiveness at solving crimes.

Karmen (2000) has shown that the NYPD's clearance rate for murder increased steadily in the 1990s, to about 90 percent by the end of the decade, and that murders fell dramatically over that time. He suggested that the clearance rate might have increased somewhat because murders that involved the drug trade (which are especially difficult to solve) had decreased faster than other kinds of murders. Overall, he concluded that improvement in the clearance rate had not driven the murder rate down. Instead, the clearance rate had been artificially inflated because the NYPD had followed the FBI's instruction to count crimes committed in an earlier year but solved in a later year as cleared in the later year. As New York's murder rate declined, detectives reopened unsolved cases from earlier years and, having a smaller caseload, they were able to solve some of those older cases. When clearances of the older cases were added to clearances of new cases, the current clearance rate for murder was inflated. Karmen found that the proportion of new cases that were solved, about 55 percent, did not change much throughout the decade. He questioned the meaning of the association between changes in clearance rates and changes in crime rates by pointing out that the NYPD's clearance rate for motor vehicle theft changed little throughout the 1990s, ranging from 5 to 7 percent, but that motor vehicle thefts nevertheless decreased sharply during those years.

Evidence that an increase in the probability of arrest is ineffective in preventing crime comes from replications of the Minneapolis Domestic Violence Experiment (1981–1982). This experiment tested the impact of three different sanctions on men accused of domestic assaults that did not involve severe or life-threatening injuries. The sanctions, chosen randomly by police officers on the scene, were arrest, mediation or advice, and ordering the man to leave the home for eight hours. The results indicated that arrest deterred moderate domestic assault more effectively than the other two sanctions. Only 10 percent of the arrested men were involved in a new police report of domestic violence in the next six months, compared to 19 percent of those who had received mediation or advice and 24 percent of those who had been ordered from the home. Victim self-reports also showed that arrest was a more effective deterrent than mediation or being ordered from the home (Sherman and Berk, 1984; Berk and Newton, 1985). Because this conclusion was based on a single experiment, the National Institute of Justice funded six replications of the original study in other jurisdictions. Calling into question the generalizability of the Minneapolis experiment's findings, these replications concluded that arrest had no greater long-term deterrent effect on domestic violence than mediation or separation. Indeed, arrest actually increased the likelihood of repeat violence by unemployed suspects, while decreasing it among employed ones (Dunford, Huizinga, and Elliott, 1990; Sherman et al., 1991; Sherman, 1992b, 1992c; Hirschel and Hutchison, 1992). Sherman concluded that these "mixed results suggest that arrest is certainly no proven panacea and that mandatory arrest may not be justifiable on the grounds of crime control" (Sherman, 1992a: 206).

Aggressive Patrol

Scholars who study the police often distinguish order maintenance from law enforcement, the former describing efforts to maintain civility by dealing with interpersonal disputes and other disruptive behavior, and the latter referring to efforts to deal with serious crime through patrol, investigation, and arrest. Wilson and Kelling's (1982) broken windows theory proposes that disorder has a causal effect on serious crime. This theory was the basis of the NYPD's quality-of-life initiative, a zero-tolerance policy aimed at reducing serious crimes through strict enforcement of laws against minor infractions that disrupt the social order. According to one critic, this approach was based on the premise that "enforcing laws against public urination, graffiti, and inebriation will create an aura of regulation that helps prevent brutal crimes like rape and murder" (Parenti, 2000: 71–72). The quality-of-life initiative was an aggressive patrol strategy, which James Q. Wilson and Barbara Boland (1978: 370) define as one that "maximizes the number of interventions in and observations of the community." They claim that such a policy is not necessarily hostile or harsh, though the NYPD's quality-of-life initiative, which increased misdemeanor arrests by 73 percent from 1994 to 1997, was accompanied by a 62 percent increase in complaints of police abuse (Greene, 1999).

Some research completed before implementation of the quality-of-life initiative supported the impact of aggressive patrol on crime. The San Diego Field Interrogation Experiment compared an area where police questioning of citizens on the street was suspended for nine months, an area where officers who conducted field interrogations were specially trained to deal with citizens in a friendly fashion, and an area where interrogation methods were kept the same (Boydstun, 1975). Reported crime did not change in the two areas that continued to have field interrogations, but the total number of "suppressible" crimes (robbery, burglary, larceny, motor vehicle theft, assault, sex crimes, malicious mischief, and disturbances) increased from 75 to 104 per month in the area where field interrogations were suspended, then dropped back to 84 per month after they were resumed. "Street stops" apparently changed the perceived risk of apprehension, even though they did not actually lead to more arrests. Wilson and Boland's (1978) cross-sectional (one point in time) study of thirty-five cities found that robbery rates were lower where more moving traffic violation citations were issued, though that form of aggressive patrol was not associated with lower rates of burglary or motor vehicle theft. Their conclusion that aggressive patrol reduced robbery rates was challenged by researchers who analyzed longitudinal (over a period of time) data within cities (Jacob and Rich, 1981). A later cross-sectional analysis that controlled for various city characteristics associated with street crime supported Wilson and Boland's original conclusion, finding that more aggressive policing, as measured by traffic citations and disorderly conduct infractions, was associated with lower robbery rates but not with lower burglary rates (Sampson and Cohen, 1988).

Because Commissioner Bratton introduced many changes to the NYPD at about the same time as the quality-of-life initiative, but took no steps to evaluate systematically the impact of the measures, it is impossible to determine which, if any, of his policies reduced crime. Bratton's repeated assertion that aggressive action against minor offenders had made a major contribution to the decline in serious crime is called into question by evidence that other large cities experienced big reductions in crime without similar quality-of-life initiatives, as well as by evidence that crime began to drop in New York City several years before Bratton became commissioner. This suggests that he may simply have been fortunate enough to have taken over the department at a time when rates would have fallen anyway (Bouza, 1997). Some critics have proposed that the quality-of-life initiative might even increase serious crime in the long run by stigmatizing minor offenders, which would make it harder for them to find jobs and alienate them from conventional society (Sherman, 1993, 1997).

In assessing the impact of the NYPD's quality-of-life initiative, Karmen (2000) proposed that murders with firearms should have been affected more than other kinds of murders because aggressive patrol should have reduced the number of people carrying guns on the street. However, he found only a weak negative association between misdemeanor arrests and gun murders. The surge in misdemeanor arrests in the mid-1990s gave the erroneous impression that a record-setting number of New Yorkers were being apprehended for minor infractions, when in fact arrests and summonses had peaked in 1986 and 1987 without suppressing the rampant crack trade or the high rates of violence and theft that prevailed at the time. Karmen argues that most police stops of citizens after 1994 were occasioned not by the new zero-tolerance policy toward minor infractions, but rather by continuation of the traditional practice of stopping young minority males who had "the felon look" or were wearing "perp colors" but might not be breaking any law. As evidence that zero-tolerance policing does not necessarily reduce crime, Karmen presented the experience of the San Diego Police Department, which introduced community policing and reduced misdemeanor arrests in the mid-1990s but still saw the crime rate fall sharply. The limited body of research on zero-tolerance policing offers little support for the claim that the quality-of-life initiative reduced violent crime in New York City. There is also no reason to think that this measure was implemented widely enough to account for the decline in national crime rates (Eck and Maguire, 2000).

The quality-of-life initiative, and the broken windows theory on which it is based, assume that disorder and crime are distinguishable. However, the public often conceives of crime itself as a form of disorder, a kind of rule breaking or deviance that has much in common with graffiti and prostitution, both of which have been treated by scholars as disorder even though they violate the law. Some criminologists have defined disorder in ways that include behavior widely perceived as crime; for example, Wesley G. Skogan (1990) included gang activity and the use and sale of illegal drugs in his category "social disorder." Even if disorder and crime could be clearly distinguished, the causal link between them might not be one directional. The broken windows theory proposes that disorder affects crime but crime can also lead to disorder, as it does when fear of crime causes people to neglect or abandon a community.

Any reduction in crime that follows efforts to reduce disorder might be due to the deterrent effect that comes from having more police officers on the street, rather than due to the strengthening of the social order that supposedly results from greater police attention to disorder and quality-of-life offenses. Bernard E. Harcourt (2001) argues that the decline in crime in New York City from 1993 to 1996 paralleled the use of quality-of-life policing, but was not attributable to it. Harcourt cites evidence that over this time misdemeanor *arrests* increased by 54 percent, while misdemeanor *complaints* rose by less than 1 percent. He thus concludes that increasing police activity in making arrests could have reduced crime, but that the lack of any meaningful change in the number of citizen complaints of minor infractions indicates that there was no real change in the level of disorder in the city, which the broken windows theory specifically posits as the cause of the decline in crime.

Disorder and crime, which are separate variables in the broken windows theory, might both be influenced by other variables. In other words, any apparent association between disorder and crime might be spurious rather than causal. Skogan found that perceptions of neighborhood disorder were linked to rates of robbery victimization, and that this relationship held up when he controlled for neighborhood stability, poverty level, and racial composition. He cited this as support for "the proposition that disorder needs to be taken seriously in research on neighborhood crime, and that both directly and through crime it plays an important role in neighborhood decline. 'Broken windows' do need to be repaired quickly" (Skogan, 1990: 75). In reanalyzing these data, which he criticized for lumping together the results of five studies done over seven years and for having much missing information, Harcourt (2001) found that the association between disorder and robbery did persist after controlling for neighborhood stability, poverty, and racial composition. However, when he eliminated the data from five adjoining areas in Newark, New Jersey, the association between disorder and robbery vanished. Furthermore, the associations between disorder and four other crimes (rape, burglary, physical assault, and purse snatching) for which Skogan had data disappeared after controlling for neighborhood characteristics. Harcourt (2001: 78) concluded that "the data do not support the broken windows hypothesis" that order-maintenance policing reduces crime.

Sampson and Raudenbush's (2001: 1) study of Chicago neighborhoods reached a conclusion similar to Harcourt's. They uncovered moderate associations between five measures of predatory crime and disorder, which they measured by direct observation rather than with a survey of residents' perceptions, but only the association between robbery and disorder remained statistically significant after controlling for neighborhood characteristics (Sampson and Raudenbush, 1999). Although acknowledging that disorder might lead to robbery, they concluded that if curbing disorder cuts crime, it is probably because reducing disorder strengthens *collective efficacy,* defined as "cohesion among neighborhood residents combined with shared expectations for informal social control of public space" (Sampson and Raudenbush, 2001: 1). Collective efficacy, which they saw as a function of the level of structural poverty in a community, was directly associated with a community's crime rate. Their finding that there is "no direct link between disorder and most predatory crimes" suggested that "policies intended to reduce crime by eradicating disorder solely through tough law enforcement tactics are misdirected" (Sampson and Raudenbush, 2001: 5).

This conclusion is supported by an evaluation of a quality-of-life initiative in Arizona, which found that aggressive policing of social and physical disorder "had a far less substantial effect on serious crime than on disorder-related crimes and violations" (Katz, Webb, and Schaefer, 2001: 859).

In one of the few longitudinal studies of the relationship between disorder and crime, Ralph B. Taylor (2001) looked at the impact of changes in both physical and social incivilities on changes in homicide, rape, robbery, and assault rates in sixty-six Baltimore neighborhoods. Incivilities were measured by both researchers' assessments and surveys of residents' perceptions. Taylor found no impact of any incivilities on robbery rates, but concluded that

> [p]erceived social incivilities affect assault, perceived physical incivilities affect rape, and assessed incivilities affect homicide. The three incivilities indicators each predicted one crime change in the hypothesized direction. That the predicted impacts emerge is encouraging for the theory; that the impacts are not consistent across different and presumably comparable indicators is worrisome. (Taylor, 2001: 190)

These results suggest that curbing certain kinds of disorder might reduce some kinds of crime, but the inconsistency of his results led Taylor to conclude that "police planners and leaders should not automatically privilege a program that focuses on the reduction of incivilities" (Taylor, 2001: 371).

Community Policing

Since the early 1980s, many law-enforcement experts have advocated community policing, an approach that assumes that officers in patrol cars are too isolated from the community and that there must be more contact and cooperation between the police and local residents and businesspeople. In this way, neighborhood problems can be identified and solutions developed and implemented. This is accomplished by decentralizing the police department and assigning officers to the same areas for long periods of time. Rather than emphasizing arrest, community policing aims to reduce crime and fear, strengthen civil order, and solve local problems (Lab, 1997). Measures to achieve these goals include foot and bicycle patrols, concentration on crime hot spots, neighborhood police substations, crime newsletters, neighborhood watches, conflict resolution programs, recreational programs for

youths, truancy prevention, drug education, enforcement of municipal health and safety regulations, neighborhood cleanups, and building demolition (Skogan, 1990; Bratton and Kelling, 1993; Skogan and
Hartnett, 1997). In New York City, Bratton and Giuliani rejected community policing in favor of a traditional law-enforcement approach
that they applied to minor infractions that had previously been
treated as order-maintenance problems. Rather than asking someone
to turn down the volume of a boom-box or stop panhandling, a NYPD
officer in the mid-1990s would issue a citation and search and question the individual.

The federal Violent Crime Control and Law Enforcement Act of
1994, modeled on Mayor Dinkins's Safe Streets, Safe City program, established the COPS (Community Oriented Policing Services) program
to recruit, train, and pay for three years the salaries of 100,000 police officers in jurisdictions across the country. Due to turnover and redeployment, the peak net increase was about 84,600 officers in 2001. In
response to criticism that the new officers were spread too thinly across
all police departments, after 1998 COPS funds were directed to cities
that had high rates of crime and poverty (Roth and Ryan, 2000).

The extent to which community policing has actually been
implemented is uncertain. A survey of 1,606 city and county law-
enforcement agencies, in which community policing was defined as
measures "to increase interaction between police and citizens to improve public safety and quality of life in the community," found that
19 percent of the agencies had implemented such an approach and that
28 percent were in the process of doing so (Wycoff, 1995). However,
nearly half of the police chiefs and sheriffs who responded were unclear about what community policing meant in practical terms, raising
questions about the meaning of the survey's results. A more recent
study of all municipal police departments and sheriffs' offices in areas
with populations over 50,000 and with 100 or more officers found that
96 percent of responding municipal departments and 81 percent of responding sheriffs' offices had implemented community policing to
some extent (Cosgrove and Wycoff, 1999). This second survey does not
make clear exactly how the different departments defined community
policing or precisely what measures they had adopted. A third national survey found that the proportion of local police departments
with at least one full-time community policing officer increased from
34 percent in 1997 to 64 percent in 1999 (Hickman and Reaves, 2001).
What is unclear is whether this increase indicates a revamping of policing methods or whether it merely reflects a change in the way that old

practices are described, perhaps to secure funding from the COPS program. There is no evidence that the increase in community policing uncovered in the third survey had any effect on crime rates, which had started to fall several years earlier.

Most criminologists doubt that increases in community policing can explain the decline in crime rates in the 1990s. Writing before the decline, Skolnick and Bayley (1988: 29) concluded that the police could not provide data showing that community policing produced greater safety. More recently, Eck and Maguire (2000: 220–221) reached the following conclusion about the organizational changes associated with community policing:

> Although some police departments have undoubtedly changed their structures, cultures, and management styles, evidence suggests that overall, such shifts are occurring glacially. Changes in structure are just now starting to occur nationally. Evidence suggests that changes in culture, if they are occurring at all, are probably not widespread. There are no national data on changes in management style, though the limited research suggests that they are probably no more prevalent than changes in structure and culture.

Even if these organizational changes had occurred, according to Eck and Maguire (2000: 221), "there is little or no empirical evidence to support a claim that changing the management and organization of a police agency can lower crime. . . . Given that police agencies nationally have not experienced dramatic shifts in formal and informal organization, it is difficult to attribute recent declines in violent crime throughout the nation to such changes." Taylor, Fritsch, and Caeti (1998: 3) agree, noting that the key concepts of community policing "are only words that have found themselves in mission and value statements, but rarely in meaningful, structural and long-lasting changes reflected in police departments across the country."

Community policing is difficult to assess because there is disagreement over the precise meaning of the term, much of the material published on the topic is anecdotal, there are few good studies of its effectiveness, and the research that has been done is inconclusive (Taylor, Fritsch, and Caeti, 1998). In addition, police–community partnerships have frequently been introduced at the same time as other policing measures, attention has been focused on the process of implementing community policing more often than on its impact on crime, and researchers have studied the effect of community policing on fear of crime more often than its effect on crime itself. Overall, there is no "compelling evidence that police–community partnerships are either prevalent enough or effective enough to be responsible for recent national reductions in violent crime" (Eck and Maguire, 2000: 224).

Problem-Oriented Policing

Problem-oriented policing, which assumes that the police should deal with the underlying conditions that generate crime, shares with community policing an emphasis on cooperating with citizens to attack local crime problems. Crime statistics, officers' experiences, and information from people in the community are used to identify and analyze problems, develop and implement responses to them, and evaluate the effectiveness of those responses. The goal is to solve specific problems rather than merely establish good relations with the community (Eck and Maguire, 2000).

Problem-oriented policing was used to combat prostitution and robbery in Newport News, Virginia. Using crime statistics, the police estimated that about half of the robberies in a four-block area were associated with twenty-eight prostitutes. The police convinced judges to sentence convicted prostitutes to one year in jail, but suspend ten months of the sentence if they avoided the area. Law enforcement was stepped up for local bars and rooming houses associated with prostitution. As an apparent result of these measures, twenty-two of the prostitutes left the area, and robberies there declined by 43 percent (Eck and Spelman, 1987).

An evaluation of problem-oriented policing in Jersey City, New Jersey, compared the experiences of twelve matched pairs of places that had high rates of violent crime. Problem-solving policing was implemented in one of the areas in the pair, and policing methods were left unchanged in the other. Officers in the areas with problem-solving policing used their experience, crime reports, and information from local residents and businesspeople to learn of problems and devise measures to deal with them. The measures, which varied from place to place, were aimed at reducing social and physical disorder. They included cleaning up vacant lots, repeating foot and car patrols, dispersing loiterers, stopping and frisking suspicious people, issuing summonses for drinking in public, and disrupting drug dealing. These measures were not individually assessed for their impact; instead, the researchers focused on how crime in the areas with problem-oriented policing changed in comparison to crime in the areas that were policed in the usual manner. Comparison of the six-month periods before and after implementation of the measures concluded that problem-oriented policing had been "successful in reducing crime and disorder at violent places with little evidence of displacement" (Braga et al., 1999: 571).

A 1997 survey found that slightly more than half of large law-enforcement agencies at least encouraged their officers to engage in problem-oriented policing (Reaves and Goldberg, 1999). This approach was first used before crime rates started to fall in the early 1990s, and it might have been implemented in enough communities to account for some of the decline. However, Eck and Maguire (2000) conclude that the extent and rigor of problem-solving policing efforts are uncertain, and that too few evaluations of specific measures have been done to know whether the approach contributed significantly to the decline in crime rates.

Conclusion

Most criminologists have minimized the contribution of the police to the decline in crime rates in the 1990s. To Andrew Karmen (2000: 127), the experience of cities such as New Orleans, Washington, and Los Angeles indicates that "crime can go down even when police departments are in a reactive mode, in the throes of a severe morale crisis, embroiled in corruption scandals, and unsettled by changes in structure and leadership." As a result, he believes that factors other than policing, such as longer prison terms and improvements in the economy, better explain why crime rates fell. Ana Joanes's (2000: 267–268) study of crime trends in the seventeen largest U.S. cities led her to conclude that "further research is needed in order for any city to claim that its policies have produced, or even contributed to, the decrease in crime. . . . [T]he evidence that police strategies can deter crime is meager."

Police strength alone is not predictive of crime rates, but focused patrol methods might reduce some crimes under certain conditions. The decline in the nation's crime rate might be attributable, at least in part, to measures that were widely adopted prior to the early 1990s, especially directed patrol and problem-oriented policing. However, the extent to which such measures were implemented, and the effectiveness of those that were, is unclear. Eck and Maguire (2000: 249) suggest that innovative policing measures might have interacted with rising rates of incarceration, an aging population, or changing drug markets to drive crime rates down, but it is a myth that the "police [had] a substantial, broad, and *independent* impact on the nation's crime rate."

Did Increased Incarceration Reduce Crime?

Incarceration might reduce crime in several ways. Crime against the general public can be prevented through the incapacitation of offenders. As journalist Ben Wattenberg has remarked, "A thug in prison can't shoot your sister" (cited in Piehl and DiIulio, 1995: 23). Crime can also be stopped through specific deterrence: Imprisonment might cause offenders to weigh risks more heavily in considering the risks and rewards of crime, and thus make them less likely to break the law in the future. General deterrence is the idea that punishing offenders sends the message to the population at large that the rewards of crimes will be more than offset by their risks, thereby dissuading people from committing crimes. Another possibility is that prison treatment programs could reduce crime by rehabilitating inmates. Few, if any, observers suggested that the increased effectiveness of such programs contributed to the decline in crime rates in the 1990s. An additional justification for incarceration—retribution, or just deserts—proposes that offenders should be punished in proportion to the harmfulness of their crimes and their personal blameworthiness, but this approach does not purport to reduce crime, only to mete out justice. Since the mid-1970s, most research on the impact of incarceration on crime has focused on its incapacitative and general deterrent effects.

Many criminologists believe that the net effect of incarceration is to reduce crime, but the amount by which it cuts crime and its financial and social costs remain sources of contention. During the 1990s, researchers made substantial headway in determining the effects of incarceration, but deciding whether more or fewer offenders should be locked up still requires value judgments. For instance, Richard Rosenfeld (2000) estimates that averting a single homicide in the early 1990s required the incarceration of 670 additional prisoners at a cost of $13.4 million, figures that do not answer the critical question, "Is it worth spending $13.4 million to imprison 670 offenders in order to save the life of one homicide victim?" Related questions are whether that money could prevent more crime if spent in different ways, such as for the treatment of drug abusers, or whether it could be used to greater social advantage, such as for better medical care for the elderly.

Incarceration and Crime, 1960–1999

The relationship between incarceration and crime is complex and difficult to unravel, contrary to the widely held view that crime can be reduced simply by building more prisons, locking up more offenders, and lengthening sentences. Before turning to the research on this relationship, trends in incarceration and crime over the past four decades are examined, with emphasis on changes during 1990s.

Figure 5.1 shows the numbers of prisoners and indicator crimes per 100,000 people for 1960 to 1999. What is apparent is that although the crime rates fluctuate, ending up in 1999 at roughly the levels that prevailed in the late 1960s, the rate of imprisonment shows a dramatic, unbroken increase from 1972 to 1999. Between 1972 and 1980 the increase in the incarceration rate roughly paralleled the increases in robbery and burglary rates. After 1980, the rate of imprisonment continued to rise sharply although the crime indicators did not increase, and even dropped in some years in which incarceration grew. From 1990 to 1999, when all four crime indicators declined sharply, the incarceration rate continued its steep increase. The murder rate dropped by 39 percent, the robbery rate by 52 percent, the burglary rate by 38 percent, and the motor vehicle theft rate by 36 percent, but the number of prisoners per capita grew by 58 percent.

The growth in the prison population after 1980 was not the result of trends in crime rates or the number of arrests per crime. Instead, changes in punishment, particularly in the rate at which convicted offenders were sentenced to prison and in the amount of time they spent behind bars, explained most of the growth in the prison population. According to Blumstein and Beck (1999), from 1980 to 1996 the increased tendency to imprison arrested offenders explained 51.4 percent of the growth in the incarceration rate, and the increase in time actually served in prison explained another 36.6 percent of the growth. Only 11.5 percent of the growth in the incarceration rate was due to increased offending, and only .5 percent was due to increased police effectiveness in making arrests.

One reason for the dramatic upsurge in incarceration after 1972 was the increased skepticism about rehabilitation that developed after

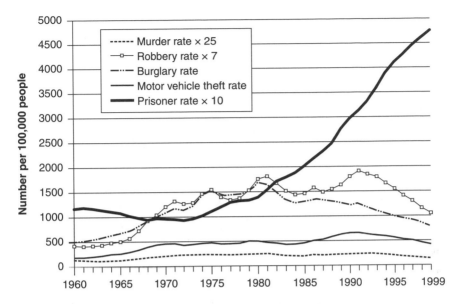

FIGURE 5.1   Indicator Crimes and Prisoners,* 1960–1999

*Rate of sentenced prisoners under jurisdiction of state and federal correctional authorities on December 31.

Sources: Based on data from Federal Bureau of Investigation, *Crime in the United States: Uniform Crime Reports, 1960 to 1999.* Washington, DC: U.S. Government Printing Office, 1961 to 2000; Kathleen Maguire and Ann L. Pastore, eds., *Sourcebook of Criminal Justice Statistics 2000,* Table 6.27. (Online: www.albany.edu/sourcebook/1995/pdf/t627.pdf [November 21, 2001])

publication of work by Robert Martinson and his colleagues (Martinson, 1974; Lipton, Martinson, and Wilks, 1975). Widely interpreted as showing that treatment does not rehabilitate offenders, their work led to more research on deterrence and incapacitation. Public punitiveness also grew: The percentage of Americans saying that the courts did not deal harshly enough with criminals rose from 65 percent in 1972 to 85 percent in 1978, remained at about that level until 1994, then began to drop. The proportion of people who believed that rehabilitation should be the main emphasis of prisons decreased from 73 percent in 1968 to 44 percent in 1982. There was a corresponding increase from 19 percent in 1968 to 51 percent in 1982 in the proportion who said that the primary emphasis of prisons should be punishment or the protection of society (Cullen, Fisher, and Applegate, 2000). Backed by this expanding public support for harsher sanctions, conservative politicians passed laws that reduced judicial discretion, established longer and often mandatory penalties, and restricted parole release (Blumstein, 1995a). Liberal critics contended that the increased funds being spent on incarceration would have a greater impact on crime if they were used to alleviate such underlying causes of crime as poverty and racial discrimination (Currie, 1998).

The juxtaposition of rising incarceration rates and falling crime rates in the 1990s elicited very different responses. The *New York Times* was puzzled by the divergent trends, as suggested by the following headlines:

- "Crime Keeps on Falling, but Prisons Keep on Filling" (September 28, 1997, sec. 4: 1)
- "Prison Population Growing although Crime Rate Drops" (August 9, 1998, sec. 1: 18)
- "Less Crime, More Criminals" (March 7, 1999, sec. 4: 1).

The accompanying articles implied that if crime rates were falling, there ought to be fewer criminals and fewer prisoners, rather than more. Other observers were less bewildered by the divergent trends, reasoning that if more criminals were being sent to prison there should be less crime because incapacitated prisoners could not commit crime, and because their imprisonment sent a message to potential offenders to avoid crime. What these contrasting interpretations highlight is the complexity of the relationship between crime and imprisonment, specifically the problem of simultaneity or reciprocal causation. In simplest form the problem is that more incarceration might reduce crime through incapacitation and deterrence, but less crime might reduce incarceration because there are fewer offenders or less public demand that offenders be imprisoned. Because the two cause-and-effect processes work in opposite directions, they can cancel out or mute one another. Before looking at research that has tried to unravel the relationship between crime and incarceration, the *Times*'s presentation of this issue is examined.

Crime and Incarceration in the *New York Times*

During the last half of the 1990s, the *Times* featured several in-depth discussions of the rising rate of incarceration and its relationship to falling crime rates. Rather than accept statements by law-enforcement officials, politicians, and a few criminologists that the increase in incarceration had driven crime rates down, the paper adopted a skeptical stance, pointing to the absence of any clear-cut association between trends in incarceration and trends in crime. For instance, in response to a claim by George W. Bush, then governor of Texas, that a 29 percent decline in crime during his administration was due to his support of tougher laws and longer sentences, the *Times* noted that crime rates had dropped as much or more in other states over the same time (August 18, 1999: A1, A22). The paper also pointed out that the nation's crime rates had fluctuated from 1975 to 1994, even though the incarceration rate had increased significantly over that time. Alfred Blumstein commented that the view of some politicians that more prisoners mean less crime "ignores the fact that throughout the 1980s crime rates were going up when the prison population was rising just as fast as it has in the 1990s" (cited in January 11, 1999: A10). Adopting a longer time perspective, Lawrence Friedman claimed that broad social, economic, and cultural trends have a greater effect on crime rates than changes in the criminal justice system and that crime rates were much lower in the 1940s and 1950s than in the 1990s, even though the earlier decades were characterized by much lower rates of incarceration (cited in May 6, 1996: A1, B8). Steven Levitt disagreed: "The underlying amount of crime would have grown faster had we not locked so many people up" (cited in January 20, 1997: A10). The problem with statements such as these is that it is possible to support practically any conclusion by selecting a time frame consistent with one's argument: Sometimes rates of incarceration and crime move in the same direction, sometimes they move in opposite directions, and other times they appear unrelated to one another.

On several occasions the *Times* quoted criminologists who not only questioned whether imprisonment had reduced crime, but also argued that incarceration had been harmful. Blumstein remarked that tougher sentences for juveniles probably had little impact on violent crime because most incarcerated offenders are simply replaced by other offenders, producing no net reduction in crime (August 9, 1996: A1, A25). He also proposed that high rates of incarceration could weaken the stigma of imprisonment and thereby undermine the deterrent effect of punishment, and might increase crime by disrupting families and strengthening ties between prison gangs and offenders on the street (September 28, 1997, sec. 4: 4). According to Lawrence Sherman, the imprisonment of large numbers of young African American males harms the social fabric of inner-city communities, and might thus generate more crime than it prevents (April 16, 1997: D23). Other criminologists observed that longer

sentences and the elimination of parole could backfire because most offenders would eventually be released, and they might then be more
prone to commit crime than they had been before incarceration if they
had grown hostile during their confinement, learned new criminal skills,
met potential accomplices, or acquired records that diminished their
chances of finding jobs that paid well and offered hope for advancement
(September 28, 1997, sec. 4: 4). The *Times* alluded to research that indicated that keeping offenders behind bars into their twenties or later had
less impact on crime rates than anticipated because older prisoners were
often past the peak age for committing crime (January 26, 1998: B6). The
paper also suggested that a "multiplier effect" could make the two million U.S. children with a parent or close relative behind bars more likely
to commit crime if they lacked socialization and supervision, grew con-
temptuous of a justice system they saw as abusing people close to them,
emulated their imprisoned relatives, or became accustomed to prison
when visiting those relatives (April 7, 1999: A1, A18).

Even those criminologists quoted in the *Times* who acknowledged
that incarceration could reduce crime expressed doubts about it as a
policy. University of Maryland criminologists said that locking up serious, repeat offenders did stop some crimes, but that existing research
was inadequate to the task of measuring how much crime was prevented by incarcerating more offenders. Sherman pointed out that imprisonment was the most expensive crime-prevention measure, but
that there had been little scientific evaluation of its effectiveness. He
concluded that "we may have reached the point of diminishing returns" because the most serious criminals are probably already in
prison, and any additional offenders who might be locked up will be increasingly minor ones (cited in April 16, 1997: D23).

Rather than turning to published research on the relationship between incarceration and crime, the *Times* focused on the factors that had
caused the long-term increase in the prison population, an emphasis
consistent with the paper's implicit assumption that falling crime rates
should have produced lower incarceration rates. The growth in incarceration was attributed partly to the War on Drugs initiated during the
Reagan administration (1981–1989) and continued by George H. W.
Bush (1989–1993). The *Times* astutely noted that because drug offenses
are not included in the FBI's crime index, increases in the overall incarceration rate will not necessarily be closely associated with changes in
rates of index crimes.

Another factor driving up the incarceration rate was the increasing tendency for convicted offenders to be sent to prison, and for longer

terms. From 1990 to 1996, the number of offenders sent to prison per 1,000 arrests rose from 460 to 613, a 33 percent increase (January 11, 1999: A10). Many states had introduced specific or mandatory sentences; for example, in early 1999 forty states had "truth-in-sentencing" laws that required offenders to serve a fixed proportion of the maximum sentence meted out by the court. That proportion was typically 85 percent, a figure mandated by a 1994 federal law that made access to federal funds for state prison construction contingent on passage of a truth-in-sentencing law for violent offenders. Time served behind bars also increased because some states had eliminated parole, restricted early release, or adopted get-tough measures that returned increasing numbers of parolees to prison. From 1990 to 1995, the percentage of prisoners eligible for parole who were actually released fell from 37 to 31 (September 28, 1997, sec. 4: 4).

Yet another reason for increased incarceration was the development of a self-perpetuating prison industry. The unionization of correctional officers and the potential for more jobs created pressure for the construction of new prisons (March 7, 1999, sec. 4: 16). The growth of the prison industry was most apparent in California, which built twenty-one new institutions between 1977 and 1997. From 1990 to 1997, the proportion of California's budget allocated to corrections rose from 4.5 to 9.4 percent, while the share for education dropped from 12.5 to 8 percent. Over that time, 10,000 additional prison guards were hired, and 10,000 university employees were laid off (September 28, 1997, sec. 4: 1, 4).

California's highly publicized "three strikes and you're out" law, which took effect in 1994, established a prison term of twenty-five years to life for offenders convicted of a felony after two previous convictions for serious offenses, a doubling of the statutory penalty for a second felony conviction, consecutive rather than concurrent sentences for multiple counts, and limitations on the amount of "good time" that could be credited toward early release. Despite these efforts to deal harshly with dangerous criminals, by 1996 twice as many offenders had been imprisoned under this law for marijuana possession as for murder, rape, and kidnapping combined. More than 85 percent of those who had received enhanced sentences had been convicted most recently of a nonviolent offense (March 8, 1996: A14). Nonetheless, then Governor Pete Wilson credited the three-strikes law for a 13 percent drop in the state's overall crime rate and a 14.7 percent drop in its homicide rate. James Austin, executive vice president of the National Council on Crime and Delinquency, greeted this claim with skepticism, pointing out that crime rates had also dropped elsewhere over the same period of time, and even more sharply in some states that did not have three-strikes laws. The *Times* cited research by the Justice Policy Institute indicating that three-strikes laws were ineffective, with both violent and overall crime rates declining more from 1994 to 1995 in the thirty-seven states without such laws than in the thirteen states that had them (March 7, 1997: A20). Even those states that have passed three-strikes laws rarely use them, and when they do the laws have little impact because most of those states previously had statutory provisions in place for enhancing sentences for habitual or repeat felons (September 10, 1996: A1).

The *Times* correctly identified factors other than crime trends that had produced the long-term increase in the nation's incarceration rate. Implicit in the paper's reporting was the idea that falling crime rates should have reduced that incarceration rate, but the body of research relevant to evaluating this assumption was never adequately addressed. The *Times* relied on criminologists who were skeptical of the ability of incarceration to reduce crime, but largely ignored work published from 1994 to 1999 by scholars such as Thomas Marvell, Carlisle Moody, and Steven Levitt, who used sophisticated statistical methods to figure out the complex relationship between crime and incarceration.

Research on the Crime–Incarceration Relationship

Some of the disagreement among criminologists about the impact of incarceration on crime is the result of using different research strategies. One strategy uses self-reports to estimate how many crimes offenders commit in a given year. Those *offense rates* are then used to calculate how much crime would be averted through more incarceration. A second strategy uses aggregate state and national data to separate out the effects on crime rates of variables other than incarceration. *Elasticities* are then calculated to estimate how much crime is prevented through incarceration of a certain number of additional offenders.

Selective Incapacitation and Offense Rates

Selective incapacitation, a policy that seeks to identify and imprison the most active offenders, has received support from studies that show that a small proportion of all people of a given age are responsible for a high proportion of all crimes committed by people of that age (Wolfgang, Figlio, and Sellin, 1972; Blumstein, Farrington, and Moitra, 1985; Tillman, 1987; Shannon, 1988; Tracy, Wolfgang, and Figlio, 1990; Loeber and Farrington, 1998). In developing a system of selective incapacitation, Peter Greenwood (1982, 1984) used interviews with imprisoned robbers and burglars to show that the following characteristics were associated with high rates of committing crime:

- An earlier conviction for the same offense
- Imprisonment for more than half of the two years prior to the current arrest
- A conviction before the age of 16
- Previous commitment to a juvenile institution
- Use of heroin or barbiturates during the previous two years
- Use of heroin or barbiturates as a juvenile
- Unemployment for half or more of the preceding two years

Robbers with at least four of these characteristics reported committing an average of thirty-one robberies per year while on the street, but those with one or none of the characteristics reported committing an average of only two. Greenwood claimed that a selective incapacitation policy that incarcerates those offenders who commit the most crime would allocate prison space more efficiently and reduce crime rates. He estimated that one such policy would increase the number of prisoners by 15 percent but could cut the robbery rate by 10 percent, and that a more selective policy could reduce the robbery rate by 20 percent with no increase in the prison population (Greenwood, 1983). Other researchers have found the crime-reduction potential of Greenwood's system to be less than he claimed, and have concluded that the number of prisoners would have to be increased dramatically to achieve even a modest reduction in crime (Visher, 1986; Bernard and Ritti, 1991).

Critics of selective incapacitation assert that many errors would be made if Greenwood's system was implemented, with "false positives" being locked up on the basis of predictions of crimes they might have committed, but in fact would not have committed, had they been released (Cohen, 1983a, 1983b; von Hirsch, 1984; Decker and Salert, 1986). Some argue that punishment should reflect the seriousness of the crime rather than the offender's prior record, and point out that

Greenwood's system does not take into account the amount of harm done by offenders (von Hirsch, 1984). Critics also complain that some systems of selective incapacitation use predictive criteria over which offenders have no control. Of Greenwood's criteria, only unemployment might be regarded as a factor over which offenders have little or no control. The validity of the prisoners' self-reports used by Greenwood to develop his predictive scheme has also been questioned, as has the implicit assumption that the additional offenders who would be incarcerated under a selective incapacitation system commit crimes at the same rate as the prisoners who participated in his study.

Research such as Greenwood's uses self-report surveys of prisoners, data on the operation of the criminal justice system, and probability models to estimate the impact of incarceration on crime. Essential to this approach is information on the following: the likelihood of arrest, conviction, and imprisonment; the amount of time that offenders actually serve behind bars; the length of criminal careers; and the proportion of those careers spent in prison (Spelman, 2000a). This method of analysis begins with the offense rate—the number of crimes that an active offender commits in a given year. Using self-reports to calculate the offense rate assumes that surveys can accurately measure the number of crimes that prisoners have committed. Most research has found that offenders' self-reports are consistent with their arrest records. When the reports are untruthful, offenders who report low levels of involvement in crime tend to underreport their crimes and offenders who report high levels of involvement in crime tend to exaggerate their criminal activity. Overall, the use of uncorrected prisoner self-report data seems to exaggerate the incapacitative effect of incarceration (Spelman, 1994).

Research that uses offense rates to estimate the incapacitative effect of incarceration typically assumes that prisoners are not replaced by other offenders during their terms of confinement. In other words, taking an offender off the street is thought to reduce crime by the number of offenses that individual would have committed had he or she remained free. Sometimes this is true: Imprisoning a man who commits a rape once a month will probably prevent a dozen rapes if he is incarcerated for a year. In other situations, however, incarceration does not produce a net reduction in crime. For instance, a gang of five robbers will probably continue to function in much the same way if one of them is imprisoned, either by recruiting a new member or by continuing their operations with only four members. The number of robberies the gang commits will probably not be affected much by the incarceration of one member.

Researchers have estimated the aggregate impact of incarceration on crime by multiplying the average offense rate for a sample of prisoners by the size of the sample. This approach assumes that offenders commit crimes at a uniform rate over time, contrary to evidence that criminal activity peaks at a certain age then declines as offenders get older. If a group of prisoners were incarcerated when they had reached their peak age of criminal activity, they would have committed fewer crimes during the year after their incarceration than they had in the year prior to incarceration. Using an offense rate based on what they did during the year before they were imprisoned thus overestimates the amount of crime prevented by incapacitating them for a year. Donohue and Siegelman (1998: 12) illustrate this point as follows:

> Consider a 20-year-old who committed 40 crimes in the year prior to receiving a 10-year sentence. Simply multiplying 40 crimes/year by 10 years suggests that imprisoning this person would forestall 400 crimes over the next 10 years. But if the prisoner's criminal career would in any case have ended at age 25, the true crime reduction is only 200, and 5 years of the 10-year sentence produce no incapacitative benefit.

A major error in estimating the impact of incapacitation is applying offense rates derived from samples of prisoners to offenders who are still active on the street, but who might be incarcerated if the inmate population were expanded. If the criminal justice system already selects those criminals who commit the largest number of crimes for incarceration, then the offense rate for criminals still on the street will be lower than the offense rate for offenders who are behind bars. For example, if imprisoned robbers committed an average of fifteen crimes during the year prior to their incarceration, robbers still on the street probably commit fewer than fifteen crimes per year. Therefore, the imprisonment of additional robbers will not prevent as much crime as is suggested by the offense rate of the imprisoned robbers. A similar problem arises in estimating the amount of crime that might be prevented by retaining for another year those offenders who are the most likely to be released if the inmate population were reduced. Using the average offense rate for a sample of prisoners will probably exaggerate the crime-reducing impact of such a policy because the prisoners most likely to be released probably have lower offense rates than the prisoners least likely to be released (Donohue and Siegelman, 1998).

Using adjusted self-report survey data and arrest records to calculate an offense rate for all index crimes other than murder and rape,

Marvell and Moody (1994) concluded that the annual reduction in offenses for each additional inmate was between sixteen and twenty-five. Other research indicates that a range of twelve to twenty-five crimes per prisoner per year is more accurate (DiIulio and Piehl, 1991; Piehl and DiIulio, 1995; Levitt, 1996).

There is no way to determine the exact offense rate of the additional offenders who were locked up as the prison population expanded from 1990 to 1999, but it is possible to estimate the reduction in crime that would have occurred for offense rates ranging from one to twenty-five. This range assumes that in the year prior to incarceration the additional inmates committed at least the one offense for which they were imprisoned, but did not commit more offenses than the criminals already in prison had committed in the year prior to their incarceration. Figure 5.2 shows for each offense rate the percentage of the actual reduction in index crimes, other than murder and rape, that could have been expected from the incarceration of 564,094 more inmates in 1999 than in 1990. If the offense rate for the additional inmates was one, the expansion in incarceration would account for only 7.3 percent of the reduction in crime from 1990 to 1999. If the offense rate for the additional inmates was six, the increase in incarceration would explain 43.6 percent of the reduction in crime. Any offense rate greater than thirteen would account for all of the reduction in crime from 1990 to 1999; indeed, it would suggest that the reduction should have been even greater than it was.

These estimates reveal relatively little, however, because the actual offense rate for the additional offenders incarcerated during the 1990s is unknown. The flawed nature of the research on offense rates, especially the absence of self-report surveys of criminals still active on the street, has so far provided no reliable way to use offense rates to estimate the impact of increasing incarceration on changes in crime rates. Fortunately, a different research strategy exists for addressing this problem.

Incarceration, Crime, and Elasticities

The direction of causality between incarceration and crime is not obvious: More incarceration could reduce crime through incapacitation or deterrence, but falling crimes rates could also lead to less incarceration. Any impact of incarceration on crime, or of crime on incarceration, can also involve time-lags. For example, the specific deterrent effect of incarceration would not affect crime rates until after inmates are released,

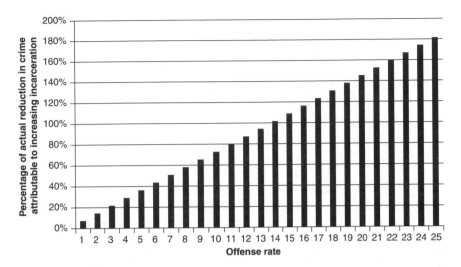

FIGURE 5.2   Percentage of Actual Reduction in Index Crimes* Attributable to Increasing Incarceration, 1990–1999†

*Index crimes other than murder and rape.

†The expected crime reduction is the product of the offense rate and the increase of 564,094 inmates in state and federal institutions from 739,980 in 1990 to 1,304,074 in 1999. The percentage of the actual reduction in crime attributable to increased incarceration is the expected crime reduction divided by the actual reduction in reported and unreported index offenses, exclusive of murder and rape. The actual reduction in these index offenses recorded by the FBI from 1990 to 1999 was 2,819,111 (= 14,349,620 − 11,530,509). National Crime Victimization Survey data were used to inflate the FBI figure to account for unreported crimes, using the 1999 NCVS estimate that 36.3 percent of victimizations were reported to the police. Not all of those victimizations were index crimes, but there is no other measure of the extent of underreporting. Thus, the actual increase in reported and unreported crimes from 1990 to 1999 was 7,766,146 (= 2,819,111 ÷ .363).

Sources: Federal Bureau of Investigation, *Crime in the United States: Uniform Crime Reports, 1990 and 1999*. Washington, DC: U.S. Government Printing Office, 1991 and 2000; Kathleen Maguire and Ann L. Pastore, eds., *Sourcebook of Criminal Justice Statistics 2000,* Table 6.26. (Online: www.albany.edu/sourcebook/1995/pdf/t626.pdf [November 19, 2001])

and the courts might not reduce the incarceration rate until crime rates have fallen for several years. Another possibility is that any association between incarceration and crime is the result of other variables that influence both the use of incarceration and the commission of crime. For instance, increasing poverty might generate crime because the poor turn to theft, and might also lead to more incarceration if indigent suspects are unable to afford effective defense counsel. Determining the impact of such factors on crime and incarceration has proved difficult because, with one exception, researchers have been unable to find variables that clearly affect crime or incarceration, but not both. The one exception was Steven Levitt's (1996) use of state litigation aimed at alleviating prison crowding as a variable that apparently influenced incarceration but not crime. By using this variable to account for simultaneity, he was able to separate the effect of incarceration on crime from the effect of crime on incarceration.

Regression analysis of aggregate state or national data is a commonly used method for sorting out the relative effects of independent variables (such as incarceration, age structure, and unemployment) on a dependent variable (such as crime). One study found that changes in murder rates from 1948 to 1985 were influenced by changes in incarceration and inflation, but not by changes in welfare assistance (Devine, Sheley, and Smith, 1988). Marvell and Moody (1994) showed that over the 1971–1989 period a state's incarceration rate influenced its crime rate for the following year, but that its crime rate did not significantly affect its incarceration rate in the short term. McGuire and Sheehan (1983) and Cappell and Sykes (1991) also found that incarceration rates affected subsequent crime rates, but, unlike Marvell and Moody, they found that crime rates influenced subsequent rates of incarceration as well. In a study that showed that changes in incarceration were associated with changes in rates of murder, robbery, and assault for the 1930–1994 period, Marvell and Moody (1997: 220) concluded that "prison expansion has been an effective crime-reduction strategy and presumably will continue to be so. It is probably the major reason why homicide declined after 1990."

Marvell and Moody (1994) used a form of regression analysis known as the Granger-causality test to calculate elasticities—the percentage reductions in crime that can be expected from a 1 percent increase in the prison population after controlling for the effects of other variables. If the effects on crime of variables other than incarceration are not fully accounted for, elasticities will incorrectly estimate the impact of incarceration. An elasticity of –.16 means that a 1 percent increase in the prison population will produce a .16 percent drop in crime. A doubling of the prison population (a 100 percent increase) would reduce crime by 16 percent. Using data for the 1976–1989 period, Marvell and Moody estimated that for every 1 percent increase in the prison population, there would be a .14 percent reduction in rapes, a .35 percent reduction in robberies, a .33 reduction in burglaries, a .16 reduction in larcenies, and a .28 percent reduction in motor vehicle thefts. Overall, twenty-one index offenses per year would be prevented for each additional inmate. Sixty-two percent of those offenses would be larcenies and 30 percent burglaries. Their estimate of twenty-one index crimes averted per year per additional prisoner falls within the twelve to twenty-five range of offense rates derived from research using prisoner self-report surveys and arrest data.

Levitt's (1996) analysis of data for the 1971–1993 period produced somewhat higher elasticities than Marvell and Moody: –.30 for property crime and –.40 for violent crime. He attributed these higher estimates to his success at separating out the impact of crime on incarceration, an effect that, if ignored, would have muted the reciprocal impact of incarceration on crime. Levitt's (1996: 324) elasticities "imply that each marginal prisoner released as a result of overcrowding litigation is associated with an increase of fifteen crimes per year, almost exactly the self-reported criminal activity of the median prisoner." Questioning whether Levitt's variable of state prison-crowding litigation is truly independent of crime rates, Donohue and Siegelman (1998) concluded that elasticities are probably in the –.15 to –.20 range, but might be in the –.10 to –.30 range.

Spelman's (2000b) assessment of published research found that most elasticities fall between –.16 and –.31, but he concluded that probably the low estimate was too low and the high estimate imprecise. He suggested that the best estimate of elasticity was between –.20 and –.40; thus, a 100 increase in the prison population would reduce crime by 20 to 40 percent. Despite the variation from one offense to another in elasticities that have been reported by researchers, Spelman (2000b: 484) concluded that "the most prudent course would be to assume the elasticity for each crime type is about the same, on average." He based this conclusion on his belief that criminological theories do not adequately distinguish among types of crimes, and his observation that researchers have not found statistically significant differences in elasticities among crimes.

To determine how crime rates would have been affected if state and federal governments had not increased their prison populations between 1973 and 1997, Spelman (2000a: 105) says

> all that is needed . . . are actual changes in prison and crime rates and an estimate of the elasticity. Briefly, one can apply the elasticity estimates to each year's prison expansion and calculate what the crime rate would have been, had that year's expansion not taken place. If one continues

these calculations, year after year, one eventually comes up with an estimate of what today's crime rate would have been, had *none* of the previous year's expansions taken place.

Using this method, Spelman concluded that expansion in the prison
population after 1973 resulted in a violent crime rate that by 1997 was
20 to 50 percent lower than it would have been without the growth in
incarceration. After accounting for an increase in elasticities over time,
which was the result of a growing prison population and a changing
age structure, Spelman concluded that the decline in the violent crime
rate over the 1973–1997 period would have been 27 percent less had the
prison population not expanded. He believes,

> with considerable conviction, that the prison buildup was an important
> contributing factor to the violent-crime drop of the past few years. Amer-
> ica would be a much more violent place had billions of dollars not been
> invested in prison beds over the past two decades; violent crime would
> not have dropped as fast and as far as it has. Nevertheless, violent crime
> *would* have dropped a lot, anyway. Most of the responsibility for the
> crime drop rests with improvements in the economy, changes in the age
> structure, or other social factors. (Spelman, 2000a: 125)

Spelman's method, described in the Appendix, can be applied to
changes in the four indicator crimes from the 1990 to 1999. Using low-
and high-end elasticities of –.2 and –.4 for each crime, the growth in imprisonment during the 1990s accounts for 31.7 to 53.5 percent of the
reduction in the murder rate, 32.4 to 52.8 percent of the reduction in the
robbery rate, 13.3 to 34.3 percent of the reduction in the burglary rate,
and 29.1 to 53.4 percent of the reduction in the motor vehicle theft rate.
With the exception of the burglary rate, which began to drop in the
early 1980s, growth in the incarceration rate accounts for approximately
one-third to one-half of the reduction in crime rates in the 1990s. This
estimate supports the claim that increased use of incarceration contributed in a major way to the decline in crime, but it is also consistent
with assertions that other factors played important roles in driving
rates down.

Working backward from the elasticity-based conclusion that 13 to
54 percent of the reduction in crime rates in the 1990s was due to growth
in the prison population, and using offense rates based on self-report
surveys and arrest data for prisoners (see Figure 5.2), it is possible to
determine an approximate offense rate for the additional inmates who
were locked up from 1990 to 1999, assuming the same elasticity for all

index crimes. Doing this reveals that the additional prisoners had an offense rate between two and eight, well below the range of twelve to twenty-five derived from studies of offenders already in prison, and consistent with the argument that criminals still active on the street have offense rates lower than inmates.

Conclusion

The growth of the prison population after 1980 was not due primarily to increased offending or increased police efficiency at making arrests; instead, it was mainly the result of an increase in the rate at which convicted offenders were sent to prison and a lengthening of the time they spent behind bars (Blumstein and Beck, 1999). Elasticities indicate that 13 to 54 percent of the decline in crime rates in the 1990s was due to growth of the prison population, a conclusion consistent with offense rates derived from prisoners' self-reports and arrest data.

How could increasing incarceration have reduced crime rates in the 1990s when it had not done so during some periods in the past? Perhaps expansion of the prison population in the past had kept crime rates lower than they would have been without such an expansion, but other factors drove crime rates up faster than expansion of the prison population could reduce those rates. Research on elasticities tries to tease out the effects of those other factors to determine the impact of incarceration on crime rates. Another explanation for the greater impact of incarceration in the 1990s is that elasticities might increase as the inmate population grows, and in the 1990s the size of the prison population was at an all-time high. Incarceration might also have had a greater impact on crime rates during that decade because the nation's population was relatively older then, and older people are apparently more affected than younger people by the threat of spending time behind bars (Spelman, 2000a). Another possibility is that growing confidence in the economy and a low unemployment rate might have made the threat of incarceration a stronger one in the 1990s than it had been in the past.

Despite evidence that much of the decline in crime was due to increased incarceration, the *New York Times* paid scant attention to the crime-reducing potential of incarceration. This might have been the result of the ideological preferences of the paper's reporters and editors and the views of the criminologists to whom they regularly turned for commentary. Those criminologists tended to minimize the crime-reducing role of prisons in favor of a multifactor approach that emphasized the effects of changes in the age structure, young people's attitudes, and the drug market. Marvell and Moody (1997: 221) suggest a disciplinary aversion to the idea that incarceration can reduce crime in the following comment from a paper in which they showed that expanding prison populations did curb crime rates:

> We have widely circulated these findings, along with the data used, to colleagues who specialize in quantitative analysis. The most frequent response is that they refuse to believe the results no matter how good the statistical analysis. Behind that contention is the notion, often discussed informally but seldom published, that social scientists can obtain any result desired by manipulating the procedures used. In fact, the wide variety of estimates concerning the impact of prison populations is taken as good evidence of the malleability of research. The implication, even among many who regularly publish quantitative studies, is that no matter how thorough the analysis, results are not credible unless they conform with prior expectations.
>
> A research discipline cannot succeed in such a framework.

This attitude toward incarceration is apparent in a National Policy White Paper issued in November 2000 by the American Society of Criminology. Unnamed criminologists are accused of presenting "essentially a two variable equation which claims that as incarceration increases crime rates decline" (Austin et al., 2001: 14). In reality, most researchers use multiple variables in their efforts to understand the relationship between incarceration and crime. In questioning "the utility of incarceration as an effective crime control policy," the White Paper cites research reviews by the National Academy of Sciences published in 1978 and 1986 (well before the steep decline in crime rates in the 1990s) and a 1998 review that concluded that incarceration could reduce crime, but which is dismissed because it found diminishing returns as more offenders were locked up. The authors of the White Paper ignore the published research on elasticities discussed in this chapter, research that provides strong evidence of a crime-reducing effect of imprisonment. Their ideological opposition to incarceration is revealed in the following statement: "In the United States, the use of incarceration may well have exceeded its potential benefits and needs to be reexamined and curtailed" (Austin et al., 2001: 14). Note that the conclusion that incarceration needs to be curtailed is reached even before its possible benefits are reexamined.

The *Times* might have slighted the impact of incarceration on crime because of the complexity of the relationship and the difficulty of understanding the statistical methods used to study it. The newspaper paid little attention to the timing of the growth in the inmate population and the drop in the crime rate, ignoring research that had found that growth in the prison population produces a subsequent decline in the crime rate (McGuire and Sheehan, 1983; Cappell and Sykes, 1991; Spelman, 1994; Marvell and Moody, 1994, 1996, 1997, 1998; Levitt, 1996). Implicit in the *Times's* treatment of the incarceration–crime relationship was an attitude expressed by criminologist Elliott Currie (1998: 55), who referred to research on the issue as "numbingly complex econometric studies that are difficult for ordinary mortals to follow."

It would be surprising if the increasing rate of incarceration during the 1990s, which resulted in 564,094 more prisoners in 1999 than there were in 1990, made no contribution to the decline in crime rates. The question is not whether there was such an effect, but rather what the magnitude of that effect was and what costs were associated with it. Application of the low-end estimates of the proportions of the reductions in crime rates explained by increased incarceration to the declines in the number of the indicator crimes detailed in the book's opening paragraph indicates that growth in prison population alone resulted in 10,800 fewer murders, 2,176,000 fewer robberies, 738,000 fewer burglaries, and 748,000 fewer motor vehicle thefts over the course of the decade. These benefits came at a cost: New prisons had to be constructed, new correctional officers hired, and more funds allocated for the care of inmates. The growing rate of incarceration, especially for drug offenses, fell especially harshly on young African American males from poverty-stricken urban areas, devastating families and social networks in those communities (Tonry, 1995). The toll of incarceration may not become apparent until minor offenders embittered at being locked up are released when their sentences expire.

Researchers have made different assumptions in assessing the costs and benefits of incarceration, and therefore they have disagreed in their conclusions. Using an average offense rate of 187 (a figure well outside the range that most criminologists agree on), an average annual cost of $25,000 per prisoner, and an estimated loss of $2,300 per crime (a figure Tonry [1995: 27–28] says is much too high), Edwin Zedlewski (1987) argued that imprisonment was cost-effective and should be used more. He estimated that incarcerating 1,000 more prisoners would cost $25,000,000 a year but save $430,000,000 in losses. Using a much lower offense rate of fifteen crimes per year, and acknowledging the tentativeness of his calculations, Levitt (1996: 319) remarked that "it appears that the social benefits associated with crime reduction equal or exceed the social costs of incarceration for the marginal prisoner." When they used $36,000 as the estimated cost of incarcerating an additional offender for one year, Donohue and Siegelman (1998: 2) concluded that "the effects on crime of further increases in the number of prisoners are likely to be modest." Because of their different assumptions, researchers have provided no clear guidelines as to how much incarceration should be increased or decreased, or exactly what the impact of such changes would be on crime. However, the evidence examined in this chapter suggests that expansion in the prison population did contribute in an important way to the reduction of crime rates in the 1990s.

6 Drugs and Falling Crime Rates

This chapter and the next one look at drugs and firearms, two facilitating factors that do not cause crime but do increase the chance that a situation will lead to violence or theft. Because of the association between these facilitating factors and the four indicator crimes, changes in policing and incarceration that affect drug and gun offenses can indirectly affect rates of murder, robbery, burglary, and motor vehicle theft.

The Drugs–Crime Relationship

The distribution and possession of illegal drugs are crimes themselves, but in this chapter the term "crime" is limited to the four indicator crimes. The connection between drug offenses and crime in this restricted sense is complex and varies over time, with the type of drug, and by place. Paul J. Goldstein (1985) suggests that drugs can generate criminal behavior in the following ways:

1. Drugs have *psychopharmacological* effects (e.g., paranoia, excitability, irrationality, and loss of self-control) that can lead to criminal actions, such as murders and assaults.
2. The *economic-compulsive need* to raise money to pay for drugs that are expensive because they are illegal, and thus in short supply, can lead to predatory crimes such as robberies and burglaries.
3. The *systemic* nature of the drug trade can lead to violence among those involved in the sale and use of drugs.

Drug-related crimes sometimes involve more than one of these factors. For example, all three would be present if a heroin addict used a stimulant for its courage-building effect prior to robbing a drug dealer to get the money to pay for his next fix.

Different drugs have different psychopharmacological effects, and some of those effects increase the likelihood of becoming an offender or a victim (see Box 6.1). Marijuana and heroin typically reduce aggression, though heroin can increase irritability and perhaps violence during withdrawal. Cocaine, even when smoked as crack, does not necessarily make users more violent, but it can do so in some circumstances. Smok-

---

BOX **6.1**

Alcohol Use and Crime

This chapter does not consider at length the possibility that changes in the use of alcohol, an intoxicant that is strongly associated with crime, account for the decline in crime rates in the 1990s. This suggestion was rarely part of the public discourse on why crime rates fell.

Because there is an well-established connection between alcohol use and crime (see Greenfeld, 1998), a reduction in alcohol consumption might have led to a lower crime rate. Parker and Cartmill (1998) have shown that from 1934 to 1995 declines in alcohol consumption preceded reductions in homicide rates by a year or two. Whether changes in alcohol consumption were also associated with reduced rates of robbery, burglary, and motor vehicle theft is unclear. The following figures for average gallons of alcohol (beer, wine, and distilled spirits) consumed per individual per year for five-year periods indicate that alcohol consumption did decline somewhat over the time that crime rates fell: 27.7 gallons in 1985–1989, 26.3 gallons in 1990–1994, and 25.2 gallons in 1995–1999 (U.S. Department of Agriculture, 2001) .

The reason for the association between alcohol consumption and crime rates is uncertain. Parker and Cartmill (1998) propose that homicide rates might be higher in areas with more outlets for alcohol (e.g., bars, clubs, restaurants, and liquor stores) because of the greater likelihood that people near such places will have consumed alcohol, and because alcohol's effects on judgment and information-processing increase the chance of arguments, fights, and murders. A second possibility is that outlets for alcohol attract people who are especially likely to engage in violence that leads to homicides. People seeking "action" or a good time might be more prone to violence, even if they do not consume alcohol. If alcohol outlets are associated with weakened social control, they might attract gangs, prostitutes, and drug dealers who are prone to violence. If this were true, homicide rates would be higher where there are more alcohol outlets, even if the homicides are not directly caused by alcohol consumption.

ing crack produces intense euphoric effects within five minutes of use, but dysphoria shortly after, leading to "missions" to get the money to pay for additional hits. Crack can produce paranoia and flawed judgment, leading to arguments and assaults. In addition, it often keeps users awake and active for days. Less frequently used drugs such as amphetamines and PCP have psychopharmacological effects that sometimes increase violent behavior. Boyum and Kleiman (1995: 297) have concluded that "sweeping assertions about intoxication and aggression do not withstand scrutiny; the relationship holds only for people with certain types of personalities, using certain substances, in certain situations." The strength of the relationship between drug use and criminal behavior also varies with stage of involvement in drug-related activities and with age (Menard, Mihalic, and Huizinga, 2001).

The economic-compulsive explanation of the drugs–crime connection assumes that people who use expensive drugs need more money than they can raise from legitimate sources. Users often earn money by selling small amounts of drugs, carrying drugs from one place to another for dealers, steering buyers to dealers, or performing other tasks associated with the distribution of drugs. Some users, especially those who heavily consume expensive drugs, rely on income-producing property crimes such as robbery. Overall, however, drug use is not strongly associated with the commission of property crimes because many more people use drugs than commit property offenses, and many thieves do not use drugs. Among adolescents, criminal behavior starts before drug use about as often as drug use precedes criminal behavior, raising doubts about the causal significance of drug use. Variations over time in drug use are not strongly associated with changes in criminal activity. Heavy and persistent users, who account for most of the overall association between drug use and crime, are an exception (Chaiken and Chaiken, 1990). The amount of property crime committed by heavy drug users declines sharply during periods of abstention and treatment, but their criminal activity increases if they relapse to daily use (Johnson et al., 1990).

Systemic factors are the basis of Jeff Grogger's (2000) explanation of the rise and fall of crack-related violence. Because crack was inexpensive to make and produced an intense, quick high at a low cost, it attracted many users and dealers soon after its introduction. Violence was instrumental in marketing the drug, because dealers lacked legal means to enforce their agreements, encountered intense competition from one another, and needed to impose discipline on lower-level dealers. Violence also occurred in robberies of drug dealers and in disputes with customers over the price and quality of crack. To gain an edge in the dangerous crack market, participants armed themselves with increasingly lethal firearms. When their violence was met with violence, the cost of dealing and using crack increased dramatically. According to Grogger, this evolution of the crack trade eventually imposed limits on drug-related violence because dealers and users quit or were killed and could not be replaced. Interviews with drug users and sellers in New York City in the late 1980s support the systemic explanation, showing that a high frequency of selling crack and interacting with other dealers was strongly associated with the commission of robberies and assaults (Johnson, Golub, and Fagan, 1995). A study of 122 large U.S. cities found that variations in drug market activity from 1984 to 1997 were positively associated with variations in homicide rates over that time, and that the association was stronger in cities with higher levels of social and economic disadvantage (Ousey and Lee, 2002).

To determine the relative importance of the systemic, psychopharmacological, and economic-compulsive explanations of the drugs–crime relationship, Goldstein et al. (1997) examined 414 homicides recorded in New York in 1988, the peak year for that city's crack trade. They found that 218 of the homicides were drug-related, and 118 of those were primarily crack-related. Of the 218 drug-related homicides, 14 percent were classified as psychopharmacological, 4 percent as economic-compulsive, 74 percent as systemic, and 8 percent as multidimensional (involving two or three factors). Of the 118 crack-related homicides, only five were psychopharmacological in origin, somewhat surprising in light of the reputed effects of the drug. Eight of the crack-related homicides were classified as economic-compulsive. This small number was probably due to the low cost of crack and the ability of many users to finance their habits by selling drugs rather than committing property crimes. One hundred of the 118 crack-related homicides were systemic in origin. The most common circumstance, accounting for forty-seven homicides, was a territorial dispute between competing dealers. Next most common were attempted robberies of dealers, which accounted for nineteen homicides. Other crack-related systemic homicides involved drug-related debts (twelve cases), punishment of workers by dealers (ten), disputes over drug thefts (nine), and the sale of bad drugs (six).

In addition to the three ways that Goldstein suggests drug use can generate crime, there are several ways that criminal behavior can lead to drug use. Offenders who plan to commit crimes sometimes use drugs to deal with the stress of violating the law, confronting a victim, and evading the police. Robbers, burglars, and other thieves commonly spend the proceeds of their crimes on illegal drugs (Shover, 1996). Thus, the drugs–crime relationship is characterized by simultaneity or reciprocal causation. The relationship could also be spurious, the result of a third factor (such as unemployment or low self-control) that can affect the likelihood of both drug use and crime. A recent study concluded that drug use and crime have mutually causal effects after accounting for the possibility of spuriousness (Menard, Mihalic, and Huizinga, 2001).

Drugs, Crime, and the Criminal Justice System

Law-enforcement officials assume that their efforts to curtail the distribution and use of drugs will reduce crime. However, interdiction and street sweeps aimed at reducing the drug supply have uncertain results. If these measures drive up prices they could diminish the number of users, but they might also increase the number of crimes that have to be committed by the remaining users in order to pay for the more costly drugs. Rising drug prices could also increase systemic violence by fostering competition among a growing number of dealers attracted to the more profitable drug trade. One indication that higher prices might have a net effect of reducing drug use is that increasing heroin and cocaine prices seem to be associated with decreasing drug-related deaths and emergencies and with decreasing proportions of arrestees testing positive for the drugs (DuPont and Greene, 1973; Boyum, 1992; Hyatt and Rhodes, 1992). Nevertheless, Boyum and Kleiman (1995: 312) reached the following conclusion from their research review: "Overall, we simply do not know whether, on balance, higher drug prices increase or decrease crime. . . . Furthermore, there is no reason to assume that there is a consistent relationship between drug prices and crime. More likely, the connection is context-specific, different for different drugs, time periods, and price levels." For instance, higher heroin prices might reduce crime when treatment programs are available to users, but increase crime when treatment programs are unavailable (DuPont and Greene, 1973).

In addition to any effect that they have on prices, police anti-drug measures could reduce systemic crime by arresting dealers and scaring off potential buyers. Some research indicates that the police can reduce robbery and burglary through crackdowns on outdoor drug markets, but other studies have found that such measures are ineffective or even counterproductive (Sherman, 1990, 1992a). One police crackdown reduced robberies and burglaries in Lynn, Massachusetts, for two years without any apparent displacement of crime to adjacent areas. However, a crackdown in Lawrence, Massachusetts, produced no apparent reduction in drug use and actually increased violent crime. Operation Pressure Point in Manhattan curbed robberies and homicides, but a crackdown in Harlem had no obvious effects on the drug trade or crime (Kleiman, 1988). Operation Clean Sweep in Washington, D.C., seemed to increase homicides by posing a threat to participants in the drug trade and by endangering nonparticipants living in the buildings into which dealers had retreated to avoid the police (Reuter et al., 1988). Police measures can increase crime by destabilizing established patterns of drug distribution, thereby encouraging new dealers to start selling in the area. This can lead to violence when old dealers try to hold on to or reclaim their turf (Brownstein, 1996).

The benefits of police crackdowns are usually short-lived. In addition, they sometimes displace the drug trade to other areas, rather than stopping it altogether (Sherman, 1990; Eck and Maguire, 2000). Nevertheless, Eck and Maguire suggest that the police might wear down users and dealers by making their daily routines more arduous and risky, and might deflate the market by forcing dealers off the street and into buildings where it is harder to sell drugs. Police measures of this sort were widespread enough and implemented early enough to explain some of the decline in crime rates in the 1990s, but Eck and Maguire (2000: 239) find little direct evidence that the police curbed violent crime through such measures, and thus conclude that "police drug enforcement may have had only a minor impact on the collapse of the crack cocaine market."

The demise of the crack trade was probably hastened by the increasing use of incarceration. Figure 6.1 shows that the percentage of all new inmates admitted to state prisons for drug offenses grew dramatically from 1983 to 1990, then leveled off after 1990. The growth was primarily the result of an increase in the number of arrests for drug offenses and an increase in the likelihood of a drug offender being sentenced to prison. There was no marked increase in the length of time that drug offenders actually served behind bars (Blumstein and Beck, 1999). This increase in the imprisonment of drug offenders immediately preceded the steep decline in crime rates in the 1990s, suggesting that the incapacitative and deterrent effects of incarceration might have

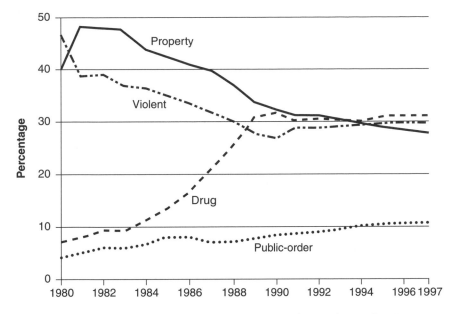

FIGURE 6.1   Percentage of New Court Commitments Admitted to State Prisons, by Offense Type, 1980–1997

Sources: Bureau of Justice Statistics, *Correctional Populations in the United States, 1995.* Washington, DC: U.S. Department of Justice, 1997, p. 16; Bureau of Justice Statistics, *Correctional Populations in the United States, 1997.* Washington, DC: U.S. Department of Justice, 2000, p. 12.

pushed rates down. Before assessing this possibility, the way that the *New York Times* presented the drugs–crime issue is examined.

Drug Use and Crime Rates in the *New York Times*

Brownstein (1996) and Reinarman and Levine (1997) claim that from 1984 to 1992 the news media, law-enforcement officials, and policymakers distorted crime data to create the impression of a crack epidemic and an associated growth in violence. These criminologists do not suggest that the subsequent drop in crime rates was the result of distorted interpretations of crime data, and their social constructionist approach offers little insight into why rates did fall. Their critique of the news media's role in shaping public perceptions of the crack–crime nexus is not consistent with the *New York Times*'s in-depth discussion of the drugs–crime relationship.

In examining the reasons for the decline in crime rates in New York City, the *Times* devoted more attention to the systemic nature of the crack market than to the psychopharmacological or economic-compulsive aspects of the drug. Relying on an explanation offered by Alfred Blumstein (1995b), the paper reported that when crack arrived in the city in the 1980s, it destroyed a relatively stable heroin distribution network and increased the number of drug dealers, creating more competition for turf and customers. To protect themselves, dealers armed themselves with semiautomatic handguns and other powerful weapons. Residents not involved in the crack trade responded by acquiring guns to protect themselves and their families from the armed dealers or to enhance their own standing on the street. This proliferation of firearms increased the number of shootings in neighborhoods where crack was sold.

According to the *Times*, crime rates fell in the 1990s as the number of drug-dealing operations decreased. Those still in existence became less violent and more like legitimate enterprises, and turf wars were settled (June 8, 1997, sec. 4: 1, 4). A 1997 National Institute of Justice report discussed in the *Times* claimed that the waning of the crack epidemic, rather than the innovative police measures touted by police commissioners and politicians, was the most important reason for the sharp decline in homicide rates from 1991 to 1996. This report showed that changes in homicide rates were closely associated with changes in cocaine use in five of the six cities studied (Detroit, Washington, Atlanta, New Orleans, Miami, and Indianapolis). Critics responded that the six-city sample was too small for drawing reliable conclusions, and that the omission of large cities such as New York made it hard to generalize from the study. Former NYPD Commissioner Lee Brown commented that it was difficult to isolate a single factor as the cause of the drop in homicide rates, saying, "I think it is a combination of factors, from crack going down to community policing to demographics" (cited in October 27, 1997: A12).

The October 1997 article presented the results of research that had established a link between crack and violent crime. Eric Baumer and Richard Rosenfeld's multi-city study concluded that the "early and pronounced decline in crime rates for New York City, widely attributed to enforcement measures, is also consistent with New York being among the first cities where crack appeared and, in turn, plateaued" (cited in October 27, 1997: A12). Andrew Golub and Bruce Johnson found that the rate of detected crack use among juveniles being admitted to jail dropped from 70 percent in 1988 to 22 percent in 1996 in Manhattan, from 30 percent in 1989 to 10 percent in 1996 in Washington, and from 45 percent in 1987 to 5 percent in 1996 in Detroit. Washington and Detroit were both well below Manhattan in the percentage of juveniles testing positive for crack in the late 1980s, suggesting that Manhattan was more likely than the other two cities to experience crime reduction from a decline in crack use.

The *Times* repeatedly cited evidence that police measures had curbed drug trafficking, which had, in turn, reduced the crime rate. A 1996 editorial noted that a police crackdown on drugs in ten Brooklyn North precincts was followed by nearly a 25 percent decline in felonies from a year earlier. The addition of 800 officers and the consolidation of all local narcotics, housing, and patrol officers under one commander were cited as the reasons the police had been able to close more than fifty drug organizations and padlock more than one hundred businesses and social clubs that sold drugs (September 2, 1996: 20). Two years later, the *Times* again attributed a reduction in crime to police measures aimed at drug trafficking, including aggressive action against quality-of-life offenders, increased arrests of dealers, and cooperation with state and federal agencies in attacking violent drug gangs. In Washington Heights, a community with extensive drug trafficking, the district attorney gained the permission of apartment building owners to let the police patrol indoors, leading to thousands of arrests that otherwise could not have been made (May 18, 1998: A1, B6).

In addition to suggesting that the crack trade had diminished because of more arrests, the *Times* raised the possibility that police pressure had displaced dealers and users from one area of the city to another, or even to other cities and states. Responding to a report that crime in New York City had dropped by 4.4 percent from 1990 to 1991, while crime had increased by 3.9 percent elsewhere in the state, Richard Girgenti, New York State Commissioner of Criminal Justice Services, noted that the number of new crack addicts had declined in New York City but increased in Buffalo, raising the possibility that some users had migrated because of intensified police patrols in New York City (April 10, 1992: B6). Five years later, the *Times* suggested that increased drug trafficking in nearby Rockland County might have been due to the increasingly aggressive police measures used against drug traffickers in New York City (February 27, 1997: B4).

Another explanation for the declines in crack use and crime that was given considerable attention by the *Times* was attitude changes in young people. This factor was also mentioned by criminologists, local youths, and the probation officers and social service professionals who worked with those youths (June 8, 1997, sec. 4: 1, 4). From his research on juvenile drug users in New York City, Bruce Johnson concluded that in the 1980s crack was considered "cool" because it offered an opportunity to make a lot of money quickly, easily, and without serious consequences. Attitudes turned more negative after young people had witnessed firsthand the way that crack had ravaged their families, friends, and neighborhoods through violence, incarceration, parental abuse, and AIDS. Richard Curtis's (1998: 1276; see also July 23, 1995, sec. 4: 4) ethnographic research in Brooklyn led him to conclude that youths responded

> to the multiple threats against their daily lives and futures by repudiating those elements which endangered them: unchecked street-level drug markets, out-of-control violence, and hard drugs. The palpable change which washed over the neighborhood beginning in 1993 was initiated and carried through by young residents who, though far from uniform in their responses to those dangers, shared a conviction that they would not succumb to the same fate that nearly erased the preceding generation.

Jeffrey Fagan's study of youths recently released from jail led him to a similar conclusion: "There has been some cultural adaptation to the slaughter" (cited in July 23, 1995, sec. 4: 4). Because of this shift in attitudes, fewer young people started using crack, depriving dealers of new recruits and reversing the epidemic.

Another expert who cited the role of attitude change in reducing drug use and crime was Geoffrey Canada, president of Harlem's Rheedlen Centers for Children and Families. He claimed that 1995's drop in juvenile crime, the first in a decade, reflected "a real sense among young people that this business about murder has gotten out of control. I think some of the glamour of being a thug, walking around with a gun, is being removed, because people 13, 14 and 15 years old have seen so many of their friends or relatives being killed or going to prison" (cited in August 9, 1996: A25). He acknowledged that the drug market still existed, but said that it had passed into the hands of older people who treated it like a business that required organization and stability. This differed from the market of a few years earlier, which he described as follows: "When you had 15-year-olds selling crack, they were wild cowboys who shot off their guns if somebody dissed them" (cited in January 19, 1997, sec. 4: 6). According to Canada, the "notion of the late 1980s and early 90s that crime was an option for young people, a way to get their sneakers or movie tickets or buy an apartment building, that whole way of thinking has changed dramatically" (cited in October 18, 1999: A19). He suggested that the change in attitudes was associated with the continuing prosperity in minority neighborhoods, observing that "people now see other people working and they get the message that work pays, crime doesn't" (cited in October 18, 1999: A19).

One 20-year-old New Yorker supported Canada's views as follows: "People are getting smarter. It's no more doing things on a whim. Before, people would say, I want to sell drugs, because it was the cool thing to do. Now people are thinking and planning, they are more educated about guns and drugs" (cited in June 8, 1997, sec. 4: 1). The turning point for this young man came when a close friend was shot and killed in front of him. Other youths cited in the article had also seen a shooting or had close friends and relatives in prison. According to a probation officer, "They saw what was happening and were witnesses to it. It was too unpleasant. They remember their mothers crying and their older brothers not coming home, for no reason, and they don't want to be a part of it" (cited in June 8, 1997, sec. 4: 1). A psychiatrist who had once belonged to a gang said that firearms and violent crime became less socially acceptable in the 1990s, and that more young people were aspiring to be drug addiction counselors or police officers.

Andrew Karmen (2000: 73) has interpreted the decline in crack use and crime among young people in terms of a change in behavior rather than attitudes, observing that "many of the socially disadvantaged teenage boys and young men who had gotten caught up in reckless illegal activities during the late 1980s adopted law-abiding life-styles— as did the next generation of teenage boys during the 1990s." This statement proposes that two things happened: Young people who had been involved in crime several years earlier had reformed, and those entering their teen years were engaging in crime at a lower rate. The second assumption is probably easier to defend than the first. The age group that had committed crime at a high rate in the late 1980s might have had a lower incidence of crime in the 1990s not so much because its members had changed their behavior, but rather because its most crime-prone members had died of overdoses, been murdered, or been sent to prison. Put another way, taking the most criminally active members out of an age group reduces the average number of crimes per individual for those remaining in the group. At this point, there are no data that persuasively demonstrate that the crack generation of the late 1980s experienced a change in behavior or attitudes that can account for the decline in crack use and crime in the 1990s.

Another factor briefly mentioned in the *Times* as contributing to the decline in drug-related violence was the development of community organizations aimed at ridding housing projects of drug dealers and neighborhood programs designed to counsel young people about alternatives to a life of crime. Richard Curtis believes that "churches, block associations and not-for-profit housing groups deserve more credit than they are given for reclaiming neighborhoods from the dealers. As abandoned buildings are redeveloped, families move in and crime-watch groups go into action. Dealers have fewer places to set up shop" (cited in September 2, 1996: 20).

Assessing the nation's War on Drugs at the end of the 1990s, the *Times* pointed out that crack use had never spread to the general population in the way that had been feared, the number of crack users had dropped soon after surveys had started to count them, and public and political response to crack had led to harsh new laws and a subsequent burgeoning of the prison population, a growing proportion of which were African Americans from poor inner-city neighborhoods. Barry R. McCaffrey, head of the National Drug Control Policy Office, warned that the War on Drugs was diverting resources from such important needs as education in order to lock up increasing numbers of drug offenders. James Q. Wilson claimed that this change had been beneficial: "Putting people in prison has been the single most important thing we've done to reduce crime" (cited in February 28, 1999: 20). Supporting this view was Bridget Brennan, Special Narcotics Prosecutor for New York, who said: "What plays havoc with a neighborhood are the low-level dealers. When they take over a street or a stoop, everyone else is terrified. When you put those people in jail, it gives the community a sense that order has been restored" (cited in February 28, 1999: 20).

The *Times* proposed that even though one-third of the nearly 900,000 drug arrests by the NYPD during the 1990s were for crack use and distribution, "it was not the incarceration of a generation, or the sixfold increase in the number of police officers assigned to narcotics, that turned the tide in New York, which the police called the crack capital of the world" (September 19, 1999: 1). Countering Commissioner

Safir's assertion that the decline in crack use was the result of constant pressure by the police, the *Times* observed that nearly every major city with a crack problem had seen use of the drug decline in the 1990s, even though police responses to the problem varied markedly from city to city. Bruce Johnson noted that the crack epidemic in Washington, D.C., had subsided despite a decrease in police officers on the street, a reduction in drug arrests, and the indictment of the mayor for crack use.

When the *Times* observed that the decline in drug use was long-term and predated any special attention by law enforcers, it missed an important point: The decline in crime was not long-term and did begin shortly after lawmakers, the police, the courts, and the correctional system began to focus on crack. The *Times* ignored evidence that even though crack use was never a major part of the nation's pattern of drug use, it was closely associated with the serious crimes, especially homicides and robberies, that plagued poverty-stricken urban neighborhoods. Those crimes contributed in an important way to the nation's overall crime problem.

Drugs and Crime in the 1990s

Drug use patterns vary over time. New drugs become popular for a while, then diminish in their attractiveness to new users. Older users continue to consume once-fashionable drugs. Drugs that have waned in popularity sometimes experience a resurgence and again attract new users. The result is that trends in the use of different drugs overlap at any given time. To further complicate matters, the timing of the trends varies from place to place, making it difficult to analyze trends at the national level.

Prior to the question of whether changes in drug use explain the decline in crime rates in the 1990s is the question of whether drug use actually decreased during that time. Michael Tonry (1995: 117) asserts that the War on Drugs of the late 1980s and early 1990s had no more than a "modest dampening effect on drug use and trafficking." He argues that the drop in cocaine prices during that time suggests that the drug actually increased in availability and that incarcerated cocaine dealers were replaced with new ones. Surveys indicate that drug use had started to fall prior to the War on Drugs, but because many of those surveys target high school seniors and college students, they reveal little about trends in drug use by the homeless, the incarcerated, and inner-city minority youths (many of whom leave high school before their senior year). Tonry's conclusion that drug use was stable or increasing in some segments of the population while it was decreasing in others is echoed by Reinarman and Levine (1997: 34), who question whether there ever was a crack epidemic in the nation as a whole, but do acknowledge that an "epidemic of crack *use* might be a description of what happened among a distinct minority of teenagers and young adults from impoverished urban neighborhoods in the mid to late 1980s."

Bruce Johnson and his colleagues (Lipton and Johnson, 1998; Johnson, Golub, and Dunlap, 2000) have examined shifting patterns of drug use in New York City. They argue that since the early 1960s, academic difficulties, the absence of job skills, high unemployment rates, and the growth of single-parent families have been conducive to the emergence of drug subcultures in certain neighborhoods. Using ethnographic accounts and arrest data, they identify a heroin injection era from 1960 to 1975, a cocaine/crack era during the 1980s, and a marijuana/blunt era beginning around 1990. The crack era incubated from 1980 to 1983, expanded from 1984 to 1986, plateaued from 1987 to 1989, and declined thereafter. As the trade stabilized, dealers moved indoors, and users moderated their drug consumption. Subcultural norms turned against crack use, the condemnation of "crackheads" grew, and the newest generation of drug users opted for drinking beer and smoking *blunts* (hollowed out cigars filled with marijuana). Each of the three eras was characterized by a drug that became popular for a while with the youngest users, as well as by the continued consumption of drugs that attracted diminishing numbers of new users as time passed.

Each drug subculture identified by Johnson and his colleagues has distinct conduct norms—the accepted standards of how users and sellers of the drug must behave in order to avoid sanctions from other members of the subculture. As drug subcultures and their conduct norms changed over time, so did involvement in crime. Johnson and his colleagues estimate that about one-fourth of the heroin generation of the 1960s and early 1970s resorted to robbery, usually with knives rather than firearms, to support their drug habits. Because heroin is a depressant, it did not generate much violence. When assaults were committed, they were usually against robbery victims by addicts who were not high at the time but were trying to get money for more heroin. In other words, their violence was economic-compulsive rather than psychopharmacological in origin. Systemic violence was at a minimum because New York City's heroin trade was highly organized and tightly controlled. Heroin use was also conducive to a low level of violence because it caused the dissolution of some juvenile gangs that did not want addicts as members. By the late 1990s, many who had injected heroin in the 1960s and 1970s had died, some from overdoses and AIDS. Others continued to inject the drug, though few of them were still committing robberies and assaults.

Beginning in the early 1980s, the NYPD and community organizations moved aggressively to "take back the streets" from heroin and cocaine dealers. However, they ended up replacing organized drug selling with disorganized selling by creating a vacuum into which sellers of new drugs could profitably move. Cocaine use patterns also changed: The snorting of powder was popular in the 1970s, *freebasing* (inhaling a heated mixture of powder cocaine and ether) developed in the late 1970s, and smoking crack (rocks of cocaine crystals) emerged in New York City around 1984 and elsewhere soon after. The growing popularity of crack was the result of several factors: Freebasing had demonstrated the demand for a smokable form of cocaine, an increase in the importation of cocaine from South America had led to an oversupply of the drug, crack was easy to make and provided an intense high, and cocaine in that form attracted youths and the poor because it was inexpensive to produce and buy (Brownstein, 1996).

The profitability of crack was so great that "by 1988 nearly the entire labor force of the illicit drug distribution industry [in New York City] was attracted to it" (Johnson, Golub, and Dunlap, 2000: 178). Because many sellers were competing for customers, they had to discount prices, undercutting profits but making crack even more accessible. Juveniles were hired to distribute crack because they were not subject to the same criminal penalties as adults, had not yet become consumers of large quantities of the drug, and would work for low wages or could be paid with crack. Perhaps because of their size or inexperience, these young dealers often carried firearms, increasing the risk of violence in the subculture. Most low-level dealers used their own product, often multiple times throughout the day, and few of them had much money left over from selling drugs after feeding their own habits. Those who were able to organize and manage crews efficiently and make "crazy money," at least for a short time, became role models who attracted other impoverished youths to the trade. Crack users were more likely than users of powder cocaine or marijuana to commit robberies, but they were no more likely than heroin users to do so (Lipton and Johnson, 1998). Because the crack trade and its violence drew the attention of the police, dealers and users were always on edge and sensitive to being "dissed," conditions exacerbated by the psychopharmacological effects of the drug.

By the end of the 1990s, many who had started smoking crack in the 1980s had given it up. Others were still using the drug, though often in a more controlled and surreptitious way. Many crack dealers who had been successful in the 1980s were dead, in prison, or unable to earn a living from selling drugs because they were regarded as untrustworthy due to their compulsive crack use. These changes set the stage for the emergence of the marijuana/blunt subculture in the early 1990s. National survey data show a steady increase in first-time users of marijuana from 1989 to 1997, and a drop in the number of first-time users of cocaine from 1989 to 1994, followed by an increase from 1994 to 1998. Thus, from 1989 to 1994 new drug users were decreasingly using cocaine and increasingly using marijuana (Office of National Drug Control Policy, 2001).

Johnson, Golub, and Dunlap (2000) propose that crime rates fell in the 1990s partly because of a shift from heroin injection and crack smoking to more widespread use of marijuana. Marijuana's high is less intense and of longer duration than the highs produced by heroin and crack. Furthermore, marijuana enhances sociability rather than producing paranoia (as crack does) or anxiety about staving off withdrawal (as heroin does). Homicides and assaults purportedly declined because of the mellowing psychopharmacological effects of marijuana and because the conduct norms of the marijuana/blunt subculture encouraged users to be laid back rather than hostile and aggressive. Property crimes might have declined because of the relatively low cost of marijuana, even when used on a daily basis. Burglary rates, however, had begun to fall a decade before the marijuana/blunt subculture emerged. Changes in law enforcement that made the possession of firearms riskier could have encouraged dealers and users to abandon the crack trade for the less violent marijuana/blunt subculture. According to Johnson, Golub, and Dunlap, the marijuana trade involved less systemic violence than the heroin and crack markets because marijuana was less profitable and therefore less likely to attract competing dealers, and because users bought quantities of marijuana that lasted longer and therefore were rarely desperate to replenish their supplies in the way that crack users often were.

In his study of changes in the drug market in the Williamsburg area of Brooklyn, Richard Curtis (1998) observed that gentrification had forced dealers to relocate to nearby communities, where dealing became concentrated in a few open marketplaces that were character- ized by competition among dealers and systemic violence. Leaders of drug-dealing organizations used violence to discipline low-level workers who had used the product entrusted to them or had kept the proceeds from their sales. Because the leaders often did not live in the community where they distributed drugs, and because they could eas- ily move their operations elsewhere, they were not committed to main- taining peace in the area. Over time, local youths who had not abandoned the drug world "for the relative safety of family, home, church, and other sheltering institutions" joined gangs, which "func- tioned as an alternative family which prescribed rules and justifica- tions for behavior, thereby bringing order and structure into potentially unmanageable social and emotional situations. The gangs imposed organization, government, and order on marginalized indi- viduals" (Curtis, 1998: 1263, 1265). Unlike earlier drug-dealing gangs that had been in conflict with local residents, these resurgent gangs be- came integrated into the community. They became part of a reconfig- ured drug market that was less violent, partly because it had moved indoors from parks and street corners in response to aggressive police enforcement of drug laws. Carrying on business indoors made dealers less vulnerable to robbers and decreased turf battles. Violence also de- clined because the gangs recruited members from established net- works of friends and acquaintances rather than relying on strangers (as they had at the height of the crack epidemic). These new members were older and more likely to be supporting families than earlier re- cruits, and therefore they were less prone to risk-taking and violence. Over time, crack dealing had shifted from a "freelance model" in which employee–employer relationships were loose and low-level dealers sold drugs purchased or taken on consignment from suppli- ers, to a "business model" characterized by hierarchical employee– employer relationships and tacit agreements among dealers about who controlled specific territories (Johnson, Hamid, and Sanabria, 1992). The earlier freelance phase was violent because of intense com- petition and lack of control over youthful dealers, but violence de- creased as dealers organized into confederations and drug distribution became more centralized and tightly controlled.

Research in New York City by Curtis and by Johnson and his col- leagues suggests that crime declined in the 1990s because of the reorga- nization of the drug trade and the waning popularity of crack. Did similar changes occur elsewhere in the country and, if they did, can they account for the decline in national crime rates? Analyzing cross-sectional data from twenty-four cities that participated in the federal Drug Use Forecasting (DUF) Program, later renamed the Arrestee Drug Abuse Monitoring (ADAM) Program, Eric Baumer (1994) controlled for variations among cities in racial and age composition, poverty, family instability, and home vacancy rates. He found that a city's level of cocaine use, which was measured by urinalysis of arrestees booked on serious charges, was strongly associated with its robbery rate, moderately associated with its homicide rate, and not at all associated with its burglary rate. Urinalysis cannot distinguish crack cocaine from powder cocaine, but self-reports indicate that most of the cocaine used by those arrested for serious crimes is in the form of crack.

In a later study of 142 cities, Baumer et al. (1998) found that robbery and burglary trends had been similar for decades, but began to diverge just as the crack trade peaked. From 1985 to 1992, robbery rates rose by 22.8 percent, while burglary rates fell by 16.7 percent. After controlling for differences among cities in population composition and socioeconomic factors, the researchers discovered that over this time cities with relatively more crack use had higher absolute rates of robbery as well as larger *increases* in robbery rates, and somewhat higher absolute rates of burglary but larger *decreases* in burglary rates. Cities with more crack use also had higher homicide rates than cities with less crack use. However, the rate at which homicide rates had changed over time did not vary much with a city's level of crack use, perhaps because overall homicide rates conceal trends in drug-related homicides.

Baumer et al. explain the divergent robbery and burglary trends in terms of the pattern of crack use. Crack's intense but brief high, which is followed by a crash and an intense desire for more crack, combined with the fact that the drug is typically used at night, makes burglary a crime ill-suited to a crack user's need for immediate cash. Most homes are occupied at night, and hence are risky targets for burglary. One offender remarks, "When you get high on crack, you want some more crack and you don't want to wait, so you got to do a robbery. Now a burglary, you might be high at three in the morning, now whose house can you go in at three in the morning and they ain't gonna be there?" (cited in Wright and Decker, 1994: 51). Commercial buildings are also unlikely targets because many crack users are young and lack the skills needed to break into buildings. Furthermore, burglaries usually net property rather than cash, and fences who buy stolen property are unavailable late at night. Baumer et al. suggest that the communities in which crack is most commonly used are already flooded with firearms, jewelry, and electronic goods (the items most likely to be stolen in burglaries), so the black-market value of such goods is low. This makes burglaries unprofitable and thus reduces the number of such crimes, whether by crack users or other thieves. In contrast to burglary, robbery produces cash quickly, and people walking on mostly deserted streets at night are vulnerable. Baumer et al. believe that most crack-related robbery is a result of the economic-compulsive need for resources with which to buy the drug, but they acknowledge that systemic violence, such as robberies of dealers who carry cash and drugs, accounts for some of the association between crack use and robbery. Because robberies involving participants in the crack trade are often not reported, police records probably underestimate the contribution of systemic factors to the association between crack use and robbery.

Changes in Crack Use and Crime

Measuring variations in drug use that lead to changes in crime rates is difficult. To explain changes in the four crime indicators, it is important to know the extent of the use of the drugs most commonly associated with those crimes (notably heroin and crack) by the segment of the population that commits indicator crimes at the highest rate (specifically young, minority-group males living in large cities). Unfortunately, there are no good longitudinal data on patterns of drug use by that demographic group. An imperfect approximation of drug use by those most involved in serious crimes is information gathered on arrestees by the DUF/ADAM Program. Golub and Johnson (1997) and other researchers have used the proportion of arrestees testing positive for a drug as an indication of the actual use of the drug. However, when the police emphasize drug arrests, a pool of suspects apprehended for serious crimes might yield a higher percentage testing positive for a drug than when the police place less emphasis on drug arrests. If crime rates later decline, the police might continue to focus on drug arrests because past policies are kept in place and squads devoted to drug enforcement are not immediately dismantled. In such circumstances, the proportion of arrestees testing positive for a drug might not decrease, even if drug use has actually diminished. Using arrests to measure drug use is problematic, but surveys of drug use are no better because they question high school and college students or the population at large. Such samples probably underrepresent the groups most likely to be heavy users of the drugs most closely associated with serious crimes.

Keeping in mind their limitations, DUF/ADAM data can be used to approximate changes in crack use. According to Golub and Johnson

(1997), an epidemic exists in a city if a substantial proportion of booked arrestees test positive for cocaine, and if those who test positive for cocaine constitute a large proportion of all arrestees who test positive for some drug. Looking at the twenty-four cities that had been in the DUF/ADAM program long enough to evaluate trends in drug use, Golub and Johnson found that by 1996 crack epidemics had abated in seventeen cities, had not abated in five cities (none of them on the East or West Coast), and had not occurred in two cities.

Table 6.1 compares changes from 1990 to 1999 in rates of the four indicator crimes with changes in the percentage of adult male arrestees who tested positive for cocaine in the fourteen DUF/ADAM Program cities that had participated in the program in both 1990 and 1999 and for which it was possible to calculate comparable crime rates in both years.* The table sorts cities into three groups based on the magnitude of change in the proportion of arrestees testing positive for cocaine: Seven cities had a substantial decrease in that proportion, five had little change, and two had a large increase. Because only two cities experienced increases and those increases were of quite different magnitudes, and because one of the cities (Denver) saw its crime rates drop while three of the four crime indicators increased in the other city (Omaha), average changes for those cities are not meaningful. Therefore, the comparison here is limited to the seven cities with substantial decreases in cocaine use and the five cities that had little change in cocaine use. The seven cities with substantial decreases in cocaine use averaged a 44 percent drop in murder rates and a 49 percent drop in robbery rates, greater than the averages of a 22 percent decline in murder rates and a 39 percent decline in robbery rates experienced by the five cities with little change in cocaine use. Reductions in burglary and motor vehicle theft rates, on the other hand, were much the same in cities that experienced either a substantial decline or relatively little change in cocaine use. These results suggest that declining crack use was associated with falling rates of murder and robbery, but not with changes in burglary and motor vehicle theft rates.

---

*Changes in UCR recording practices, or absent data, excluded the following DUF/ADAM cities from consideration: Cleveland, Houston, Indianapolis, New Orleans, Philadelphia, and San Jose. New York was excluded because 1990 DUF/ADAM data were for Manhattan only, but 1999 data were for the whole city. Miami was excluded because it collected no DUF/ADAM data in 1990. Because no data on female arrestees were collected in two of the remaining fourteen cities in 1990 and in one of those cities in 1999, and because there was substantial city-to-city variation in male/female ratios among tested arrestees, only the DUF/ADAM data for male arrestees were used.

TABLE 6.1   Change in Percentage Testing Positive for Cocaine and Change in Rates per 100,000 Population of Four Indicator Crimes, 14 DUF/ADAM Program Cities, 1990–1999

	Change in % Positive for Cocaine	Change in crime rate			
		Murder	*Robbery*	*Burglary*	*Motor vehicle theft*
Substantial decreases					
San Diego	− 62%	−62%	−62%	− 65%	−65%
Detroit	− 29%	−25%	−37%	− 26%	− 7%
Birmingham	− 26%	−35%	−45%	− 42%	−59%
Chicago	− 22%	−26%	−46%	− 40%	−36%
Dallas	− 21%	−61%	−44%	− 45%	−33%
Washington, D.C.	− 21%	−40%	−47%	− 51%	− 4%
Los Angeles	− 20%	−59%	−62%	− 60%	−63%
Average	− 29%	−44%	−49%	− 47%	−38%
Relatively little change					
Atlanta	− 14%	−41%	−36%	− 47%	−37%
San Antonio	− 12%	−62%	−52%	− 65%	−69%
Ft. Lauderdale	− 11%	−32%	−48%	− 54%	−29%
Portland, OR	+ 5%	− 9%	−52%	− 41%	−31%
Phoenix	+ 10%	+34%	− 9%	− 48%	−18%
Average	− 4%	−22%	39%	− 51%	−37%
Substantial increases					
Denver	+ 71%	−14%	−27%	− 47%	−23%
Omaha	+120%	+43%	−24%	+140%	+ 9%
Average	+ 96%	+15%	−26%	+ 47%	− 7%

Sources: Federal Bureau of Investigation, *Crime in the United States: Uniform Crime Reports, 1990 and 1999.* Washington, DC: U.S. Government Printing Office, 1991 and 2000; National Institute of Justice, *Drug Use Forecasting, Drugs and Crime 1990.* Washington, DC: National Institute of Justice, August 1991; National Institute of Justice, *ADAM 1999 Annual Report on Drug Abuse among Adult and Juvenile Arrestees: Adult Program Findings.* Washington, DC: National Institute of Justice, 2000. (Online: www.ncjrs.org/drgsuse.htm [March 19, 2001])

Conclusion

The absence of good data on the drug use patterns of those who commit the largest number of indicator crimes makes it difficult to determine the extent to which changes in those patterns explain the decline in crime rates in the 1990s. The reasons for any changes in drug use that did occur are also unclear. Richard Curtis and others claim that youths' attitudes changed in response to the toll taken by crack, but much of that toll was the result of criminal justice policies that led to more arrests and incarceration of drug offenders. However, those policies also increased systemic violence by disrupting established patterns of drug distribution. The net contribution of law enforcement to the decline in crime rates remains uncertain.

Changes in crack use during the decade explain some portion of the decline in murder and robbery rates, but probably had little or no effect on the reduction in rates of burglary and motor vehicle theft. The decrease in violent crime was largely attributable to systemic changes in the drug trade, as the shrinking crack subculture was supplanted by the marijuana/blunt subculture. Murders arising from competition for turf and the enforcement of discipline within drug organizations abated because of diminishing crack use and structural change in the organizations that continued to sell crack. Few murders or robberies were ever attributable to the psychopharmacological effects of crack, and the drug's low price and accessibility meant that few crack-related murders or robberies were economic-compulsive. The emergence of the marijuana/blunt subculture reduced the systemic violence associated with drug use, and little psychopharmacological or economic-compulsive crime was associated with marijuana use.

CHAPTER 7

Firearms and Changing Crime Rates

Firearms play an important role in two of the four indicator crimes: In 1999, 65 percent of murders and 40 percent of robberies were committed with guns. Guns do not cause murders and robberies, but they do facilitate them. Thus, the decline in the rates of these violent crimes in the 1990s might have been affected by a reduction in the availability or use of firearms.

Because burglars and motor vehicle thieves rarely confront their victims, there is little incentive for them to carry firearms. If they do use guns against their victims, their crimes become robberies, assaults, or murders. About one-eighth of the robberies reported by the FBI in 1999 occurred in residences, but there is no evidence of how many of them began as burglaries in which offenders carried guns but expected to find no one home or how many were planned as "home invasions" to rob residents at gunpoint. There are also no data on what proportion of motor vehicle thefts became robberies or "carjackings" when armed offenders confronted drivers. Some property offenders carry firearms for protection in case they unexpectedly confront a victim or a police officer, but guns play no role in most burglaries and motor vehicle thefts. Because rates of those property crimes dropped sharply in the 1990s, the factors other than changes in the availability and use of firearms that caused them to decline probably contributed to the reduction in murder and robbery rates as well.

Firearms and Crime in the *New York Times*

During the last half of the 1990s, the *New York Times* occasionally suggested that police tactics and gun-control laws might have contributed to the decline in crimes committed with firearms. In examining the decrease in murders in New York City from 1993 to 1996, the *Times* reported

121

that homicides by strangers had fallen by 74 percent, about twice as much as the 36 percent decline in homicides by acquaintances. There were also especially large reductions in murders that occurred in public places, resulted from spontaneous arguments or robberies, involved drugs, and were committed by teenagers (December 29, 1996: A28). Police officials said that a decrease in the number of guns on the street was a major reason for the decline in these types of homicide. Commissioner Safir asserted that the NYPD's quality-of-life initiative, roadblocks, and anti-drug measures, all of which involved searching suspects, had discouraged people from carrying guns. The quality-of-life initiative increased the interrogation of suspects, some of whom provided the police with information about the location of illegal weapons. Safir and Mayor Giuliani also claimed that tougher gun-control laws had made it harder for smugglers to purchase firearms in states that had permissive laws and resell them illegally in the city. Virginia, once a major source of guns for New Yorkers, had limited buyers to one gun purchase per month. Muting the impact of such laws was the relocation of some firearm traffickers to less restrictive states, particularly Florida and North and South Carolina. Cooperation between the NYPD and the federal Bureau of Alcohol, Tobacco, and Firearms was cited as effective in breaking up gun-trafficking rings and focusing attention on casual traffickers who brought guns into the city for resale.

Federal gun-control measures were mentioned by the *Times* as a reason for the decline in nation's crime rates. President Clinton was quoted as attributing the drop in crime to two programs he had supported, a 1994 ban on some semiautomatic assault weapons and the Brady Act's imposition of a waiting period for handgun purchases. He claimed that these measures had kept tens of thousands of felons, fugitives, and stalkers from buying weapons. He also announced that he wanted to expand a firearm-tracing program aimed at stopping illegal gun sales. In 1996, the first year of that Youth Crime Gun Interdiction Initiative, law-enforcement agencies had tracked 37,000 guns used in crimes back to their sources.

In a *Times* op-ed piece, former NYPD Commissioner William Bratton asserted that "easy access to guns is one of the biggest factors in violent crime" (June 20, 1998: A11). He urged the National Rifle Association to support law-enforcement agents in their efforts to get rid of cheap handguns, curtail multiple-gun purchases, and exercise discretion in granting concealed-weapon permits. Agreeing with Clinton, Bratton attributed the recent drop in homicides to the assault-weapon ban and the Brady Act. He pointed out that the cities that had been most successful in reducing firearm violence in the 1990s (notably New York, Los Angeles, and Boston) had been able to enact effective gun-control policies, whereas cities such as Philadelphia, Miami, and Houston still had high rates of firearm violence because their state legislatures had not allowed them to enact tough gun-control measures.

At the end of the decade, the *Times* reported that the 7 percent decline in the nation's homicide rate from 1996 to 1997 was entirely due to a drop in murders committed with firearms, and that a reduction in robberies committed with firearms contributed significantly to the 10 percent drop in the robbery rate over that time. To Alfred Blumstein these figures suggested that "efforts to control the availability of guns, especially in the hands of young people, are having some effect" (cited in October 18, 1999: A19). No mention was made in the article of the irrelevance of such efforts to the parallel declines in rates of burglary and motor vehicle theft.

The Firearms–Crime Relationship

The common assumption that more guns lead to more violence simplifies a complex relationship between firearms and crime. There would probably be fewer violent crimes if all guns in the United States were to disappear, but it is not clear that the crime rate is responsive to smaller variations in the number of firearms. Some observers have even suggested that a reduction in the number of guns could increase violence by taking firearms away from those who use them for self-protection, while leaving plenty of guns available for those who want them for criminal purposes (Kleck, 1997). A growth in the number of firearms could increase crime by making it easier for offenders to break the law, but more guns might also curb crime by deterring potential offenders who fear that victims are apt to be armed.

To complicate matters further, firearms and crime are probably reciprocally related. Not only does the number of firearms affect the crime rate, but the crime rate also influences gun ownership, with people buying more guns to protect themselves when crime rates rise, and perhaps giving up their guns when crime rates fall (Kleck and Patterson, 1993). The relationship between firearms and crime might also be spurious, with both influenced by variables that obscure the absence of any real relationship between them. For example, if communities with greater proportions of young men have both higher rates of firearm ownership and higher crime rates, comparing communities that have the same proportion of young men might erase what seems to be a cause–effect relationship between firearms and crime. In similar fashion, communities with thriving drug markets are likely to have both widespread ownership of guns and high crime rates, even though the guns cannot accurately be described as the cause of the high crime rates. Instead, the systemic nature of the drug market would explain both the extent of gun ownership and the high crime rate.

Do More Firearms Lead to More Crime?

The suggestion that crime rates fell in the 1990s because of a reduction in the possession, carrying, or use of firearms is based on the assumption that fewer guns lead to less crime. A better approach than simply assuming that the number of guns affects the amount of crime is to ask *how* guns contribute to crime. The role of firearms in assaults and murders that arise from interpersonal disputes is examined first, then their role in robberies and murders committed during robberies is explored.

Assaults and Murders.   Firearms could increase assaults and murders if the presence of guns somehow causes individuals who are otherwise unlikely to engage in violence to do so. Experimental research by Berkowitz and LePage (1967) supports this possibility, but Kleck's (1997) review of the evidence finds as much to contradict the idea of a "triggering" effect of guns as to support it. Most studies of this issue are laboratory experiments with college students, who are arguably so different from the criminals who commit offenses with firearms that the research might be irrelevant to understanding the real-world impact of guns on crime.

Another argument that guns increase crime is that assaults with firearms are more likely to result in death than assaults with other weapons or no weapon at all. Nearly fifty years ago, Marvin E. Wolfgang (1958) suggested that there might be no net reduction in homicides if killers substituted other weapons, presumably knives, for the firearms they used. He stated that what was important in producing a victim's death was the offender's lethal intent rather than the lethality of the weapon that was used. In other words, a person determined to take another's life would do so with a knife if a gun was not available, even though it might be easier to accomplish that goal with a gun. There is, however, little evidence that motivated attackers produce fatal results as often with knives as with guns.

In contrast to Wolfgang's claim that the significant factor in explaining lethal violence is the offender's intent rather than the kind of weapon that is used, Zimring and Hawkins (1997; Zimring, 1968) argue that the "instrumentality effect" is important: Assaults with guns are more likely to result in death than assaults with other weapons or no weapons, because bullets are especially injurious, guns have a longer range, and guns make it possible to attack victims multiple times. They present evidence that firearm assaults result in death about five times as often as knife assaults, implying that the substitution of knives for guns would reduce the number of attacks that result in death. They propose that many assailants are "ambiguously motivated," meaning they do not enter the crime situation intending to take a life even if they are willing to do so, and that a gun increases the chance that someone will be killed. Rather than providing any direct evidence of the intent of offenders, Zimring and Hawkins support their argument with questionable inferences from homicide data. Probably an attacker's intent and the lethality of the weapon he or she chooses are closely linked, with those who are determined to inflict serious injury being more likely to arm themselves with more lethal weapons. Because it is difficult to measure intent directly, it is not possible to specify to what extent the instrumentality effect accounts for the greater lethality of assaults with firearms.

Robberies and Robbery Murders.   Philip Cook (1983) asks whether the weapon or the offender's intent is more important. Does the tool determine the task; that is, does the availability of a firearm lead a potential offender to commit a crime? Or does the task determine the tool; that is, does a person first decide to commit a crime, then seek out a firearm? He suggests that robbers who plan to steal from well-protected, lucrative targets usually arm themselves with guns in advance, whereas opportunistic robbers who commit spur-of-the-moment thefts from vulnerable, less lucrative targets use guns only to the extent that they happen to have immediate access to them. He proposes that if this is true, a reduction in firearm availability should decrease the proportion of all robberies that are committed against commercial and other relatively invulnerable targets. The proportion of all robberies that were of commercial establishments, gas or service stations, convenience stores, and banks increased slightly from 21.8 percent in 1990 to 23.8 percent in 1999, contrary to what Cook suggests should have happened had firearms become less available over that time (Federal Bureau of Investigation, 1991, 2000).

Robbers armed with guns are more likely to kill their victims than robbers who are armed with knives or who are unarmed. In 1999, there were 4.5 robbery murders for every 1,000 firearm robberies, 3.0 robbery murders for every 1,000 robberies committed with knives or cutting instruments, and only 0.4 robbery murders for every 1,000 unarmed robberies (Federal Bureau of Investigation, 2000). As with assaults, it is unclear whether the higher proportion of gun robberies resulting in murders is the result of gun robbers' greater lethality of intent or the greater lethality of the firearms they use. Rather than being accidental, spontaneous, or aimed at overcoming victim resistance, many robbery murders are deliberate, though few are premeditated. Such excessive violence is most common among robbers who have committed violent crimes in the past, belong to robbery gangs that engage in recreational violence, or seek to enhance a reputation as a "hard man" (Cook, 1980, 1983; Katz, 1988).

Gun Availability and Crime Rates.   Evaluation of the firearms–crime relationship poses the problem of determining which of many possible measures of gun availability is most likely to be associated with the crime rate. Gun availability can be measured by the total number of firearms in the country, the proportion of households with a firearm, the proportion of households with a handgun (the firearm most often used to commit crime), the ownership of firearms or handguns by crime-prone demographic groups, the ownership of firearms or handguns by people with criminal records, or the extent to which crime-prone people carry handguns on a regular basis. The measures toward the end of this list are probably the ones most closely associated with crime rates, but unfortunately they are also the ones least available to researchers.

Surveys of gun ownership by U.S. households are conducted regularly. The Gallup Poll reveals that the proportion of households with a firearm fluctuated between 43 and 51 percent over the 1959–1993 period, with the exception of 1980. In the 1990s, the percentages of households reporting gun ownership in the years when the question was asked were 47 in 1990, 46 in 1991, 49.5 in 1993, 41 in 1996, 42 in 1997, and 35 in 1999 (Gallup Organization, 2001).* Because firearm ownership did not begin to decline until at least 1994, and perhaps as late as 1996, that decline cannot explain the change in crime rates, which began to fall after 1991. Indirect evidence of a decline in gun ownership also comes

*Results were averaged when two polls were done in the same year.

from data gathered by the Centers for Disease Control and Prevention (1999). From 1993 to 1997 there was not only a 27 percent drop in homicides and legal-intervention fatalities by firearms, but also a 36 percent drop in unintentional firearm deaths and an 8 percent drop in firearm suicides. These figures suggest that guns were used with declining frequency for both criminal and noncriminal purposes in the 1990s, though the downward trend began two years after the nation's homicide and robbery rates had started to fall (Centers for Disease Control and Prevention, 1997). The timing of these changes in the ownership and use of firearms raises the possibility that some people responded to the falling crime rates of the early 1990s by divesting themselves of their guns.

Even though it is relatively easy to get a firearm in the United States, there is no evidence that reducing the 250 million firearms in the country will keep potential offenders from acquiring guns. Kleck's (1997) review of twenty-five studies that examined the impact of aggregate gun levels on violent crime rates found that most were technically flawed, but that four of the five most methodologically sound studies uncovered no impact of gun ownership levels on violent crime rates.

Even though most firearms are never used to commit a crime, the likelihood that they will be increases when handguns are carried outside the home by young people, especially those involved in street gangs or the drug trade (Decker, Pennel, and Caldwell, 1997; see also Sheley and Wright, 1995). One survey found that 4 percent of elementary, middle, and senior high school students reported that they had brought a handgun to school in the previous year (LH Research, 1993). Research in Rochester, New York, found that 8 percent of a sample of students carried a gun regularly, and that 4 percent had used a gun in the previous year. This research also revealed that firearm crimes were least common among nongun-owning youths, more common among students who owned guns for sporting purposes, and most common among those who owned guns for self-protection (Lizotte et al., 1994; Bjerregard and Lizotte, 1995). Many juvenile gang members owned guns for protection prior to joining a gang, making them attractive recruits. After joining a gang, their delinquent activity increased, and they were more likely to be killed than juveniles who did not own guns and belong to gangs (Thornberry et al., 1993; Fagan and Wilkinson, 1998).

In looking at the reasons that adolescents acquire firearms, Fagan and Wilkinson (1998) propose that young inner-city males living in high-crime communities seek respect through displays of toughness when they lack other resources to achieve legitimate identities. They carry guns to ward off challenges to their reputations and threats to their lives. They learn street norms about what constitutes a dispute, how disputes should be resolved, the significance of displaying firearms, and when guns should be used. Social standing is achieved by being ready to use violence when street norms require it. Displaying or using firearms can prevent future attacks, but can also make one a target for others seeking to enhance their own reputations. The "ecology of danger" in inner-city communities creates the perception in adolescents, starting at about age 14, that others are likely to have guns and that they too must carry them for self-protection and be ready to use them at the slightest provocation. What is missing from this analysis is evidence of how this ecology of danger might have changed during the 1990s in a way that can explain the decline in crime rates.

Adult criminals also cite self-protection as a primary reason for owning firearms. Wright and Rossi (1986) found that 58 percent of their sample of incarcerated felons reported that they had acquired their most recent handgun for self-protection. Only 28 percent had acquired it for use in a crime. The felons interpreted *self-protection* quite differently from law-abiding citizens, including in their conception the use of guns against robbery victims who resist their efforts to steal and against police officers who try to arrest them. A high proportion of the felons carried guns most of the time, not just when they planned to commit a crime. Many of those who carried guns also carried other weapons (usually knives). The felons who carried guns most frequently were the ones most likely to have used guns in crimes. They also committed more crimes than felons who did not carry firearms. Carrying a gun was strongly associated with the carrying of guns by their friends and acquaintances, either because the felons had learned from their peers that carrying a gun was the thing to do or because they felt threatened by their gun-carrying peers. The strong association between peers' gun-carrying behavior and the felons' own gun-carrying behavior, and the more frequent commission of crimes by those who carried firearms, suggests that violent crime rates might have declined in the 1990s if the subcultural practice of carrying guns had abated. This might have happened in response to attitude change among young people, the emergence of the marijuana/blunt subculture, or the reorganization of the crack trade.

Do More Firearms Reduce Crime?

More guns in the hands of citizens could deter potential offenders from committing murders, robberies, assaults, and burglaries if they fear being shot or apprehended by their victims. Tom W. Smith's (1997) critical review of research on the extent to which people use firearms in response to being victimized concluded that the annual number of such defensive gun uses is between 256,500 and 1,210,000. Compared to victims who do not resist an offender's actions or who employ defensive measures other than guns, the victims of robberies, assaults, and possibly burglaries who use guns in their own defense apparently reduce the likelihood that they will be injured and the likelihood that the crime will be completed. They might also deter future crimes by increasing the risks perceived by offenders.

Offenders do consider the possibility that their victims will be armed. Wright and Rossi (1986) found that of the imprisoned felons in their survey

- Two-fifths had encountered an armed victim
- Two-fifths had avoided a potential victim whom they thought had a firearm
- Nearly two-thirds of those who had used a firearm said that the threat of confronting an armed victim had led them to carry a gun

Many offenders, however, are not deterred by the risk of encountering an armed victim. This was evident in the late 1980s when robberies of heavily armed crack dealers and drive-by shootings involving armed youth gangs were common.

Assuming that more guns in the hands of citizens will reduce crime, the majority of states have enacted laws that require law-enforcement agencies to issue permits to carry concealed handguns to qualified citizens. Anyone who does not have a criminal record or a history of mental illness usually qualifies for such a permit. These laws might increase offenders' perceptions that more people are carrying guns, and thus deter them from victimizing those they believe to be armed. On the other hand, by increasing perceptions that more people are carrying guns, these laws could increase the number of criminals who carry a gun without a permit for self-protection, or the number who use a gun preemptively against a victim they believe to be armed.

One reason to expect little impact on gun-carrying behavior from concealed-carry laws is that many of the people who applied for and received permits had carried their guns before getting permits. There is no way to know how many people started to carry guns only after acquiring permits, but it is less than the number of permits issued. In addition, many people who carried guns illegally before permits were required continued to carry them illegally after permits were required (Ludwig, 2000). Kleck (1997) suggests that the only people likely to have changed their behavior in response to new concealed-carry laws were those who did not carry guns illegally before permits were required, but who were willing and qualified to carry guns with permits after the laws were enacted. Overall, evidence suggests that "permissive concealed-carry laws may have only a modest effect on the overall prevalence of gun carrying" (Ludwig, 2000: 191).

Research on the effect of concealed-carry laws on crime rates is inconclusive. More than a simple comparison of states with and without such laws is needed, because states might enact such laws only when faced with high or rising crime rates. Because states with concealed-carry laws could differ in important ways from states without them, researchers must take into account state-by-state differences in crime trends, drug use, crime-reduction measures, urbanization, standard of living, and other variables. Lott and Mustard's (1997) analysis of counties with and without permissive concealed-carry laws controlled for some of these variables and concluded that concealed-carry laws reduced homicides, rapes, and aggravated assaults by 5 to 8 percent, but increased property crimes by 3 percent. They argued that violent crime had declined because criminals had grown more fearful that their victims would be armed, but they provided no direct evidence that this was true.

Kleck (1997) doubts that the decline in violent crime uncovered by Lott and Mustard was due to the deterrent effect of what was actually a small increase in the legal carrying of firearms. He believes it was more likely that the reductions in crime rates simply coincided with implementation of the concealed-carry laws, and that the lower crime rates were due to factors not controlled for by Lott and Mustard. Black and Nagin's (1998) evaluation of Lott and Mustard's research found that prior to enacting their concealed-carry laws, states had experienced significantly larger increases in crime rates than states that had not passed such laws. This suggests that the states that enacted the laws might have done so in response to rising crime rates, and that the subsequent decline in those rates could have resulted from changes in whatever factors had caused the rates to rise in the first place. One such factor might have been crack use. Controlling for variables ignored by Lott and Mustard, Black and Nagin found that the only meaningful impact of concealed-carry laws was an increase in assault rates. A similar study by Ludwig (1998) found a small but statistically insignificant tendency for concealed-carry laws to increase rates of adult homicide victimization. In summary, Ludwig (2000: 410) concluded that "concealed-carry laws are as likely to cause crime to increase as to decrease, though this evidence is far from definitive."

Firearms and Crime in the 1990s

Any change in the possession, carrying, or use of firearms by crime-prone people in the 1990s could only explain the decline in murder and robbery rates, because burglaries and motor vehicle thefts rarely involve guns.

Figure 7.1 (p. 132) shows that rates of robberies with firearms, other weapons, and no weapons rose slightly from 1990 to 1991, then fell more or less in parallel until the end of the decade. Because the other-weapon robbery rate fell by exactly as much as the firearm robbery rate (45 percent), and because the unarmed robbery rate also declined substantially (by 36 percent), these figures do not support the argument that changes in gun use caused the robbery rate to fall in the 1990s.

Murder is the other indicator crime that could be affected by changes in the possession, carrying, and use of firearms. Figure 7.2 (p. 133) shows that rates of homicides committed with firearms, other weapons, and no weapons all fell during the 1990s. From 1993 to 1999, the firearm homicide rate decreased by 44 percent, compared to a 34 percent drop in the other-weapon homicide rate and a 31 percent decline in the unarmed homicide rate. The larger decline in firearm homicides than in nongun homicides indicates that changes in gun use in the 1990s contributed to the overall decline in the homicide rate.

Using FBI Supplementary Homicide Reports for cities with more than 100,000 people, Blumstein (2000) found that from 1990 to 1997 the homicide rate for offenders between 25 and 45 years old declined steadily for homicides by handguns, homicides by firearms other than handguns, and homicides by means other than firearms. These changes were part of longer-term downward trends for this age group. For offenders under 25, there was a sharp decline after 1993 in handgun homicides, which was a

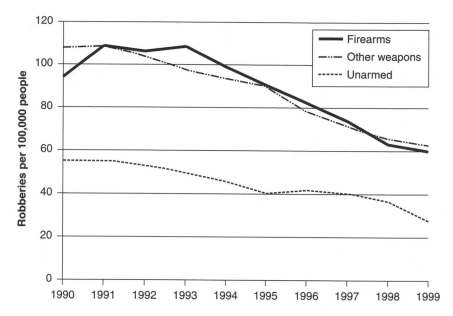

FIGURE 7.1   Robbery Rates, 1990–1999

Source: Based on data from Federal Bureau of Investigation, *Crime in the United States: Uniform Crime Reports, 1990–1999.* Washington, DC: U.S. Government Printing Office, 1991–2000.

dramatic reversal of a big increase in handgun homicides by this age group from the mid-1980s to 1993. For these younger offenders there was a slight drop in murders with firearms other than handguns, a reversal of a small, longer-term increase in such offenses. There was also a slight drop in murders with weapons other than guns, a continuation of a modest, longer-term decrease in such homicides. Blumstein concluded that most of the decline in homicide rates from 1990 to 1997 was due to the sharp reduction in handgun homicides by offenders under 25, a decline that was reinforced by a longer-term decrease in nongun homicides by these youthful offenders and a longer-term decrease in all types of homicides by offenders over 25.

Blumstein found that the sharp decline in handgun homicides in the 1990s was largely attributable to reductions in murders by black offenders between the ages of 18 and 24 and murders in cities with more than one million people. These findings suggest that the decline in handgun homicides might have been associated with the reorganiza-

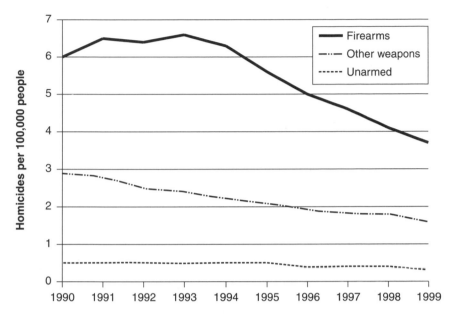

FIGURE 7.2   Homicide Rates, 1990–1999

Source: Based on data from Federal Bureau of Investigation, *Crime in the United States: Uniform Crime Reports, 1990–1999.* Washington, DC: U.S. Government Printing Office, 1991–2000.

tion of the crack trade and the waning popularity of crack. This would be consistent with Blumstein's (1995b, 2000) argument that the disorganized, intensely competitive nature of the crack trade in the 1980s caused dealers and users to arm themselves, and that guns diffused into surrounding communities as residents not involved in the drug trade bought guns for self-defense. According to Kleck (1997), the idea that guns diffused to these law-abiding residents is contradicted by survey data showing that between the start of the crack epidemic (1984–1987) and its end (1990–1993), there was no meaningful growth in the ownership of guns by males, blacks, black males, people aged 18 to 24, low-income people, or large-city residents. Most surveys indicate that gun ownership actually declined among those groups, when it should have increased if Blumstein's diffusion hypothesis was correct. Kleck suggests that the rise and fall of handgun homicide rates is more closely linked to changes in the drug trade and in street gangs than to the diffusion of guns into the hands of nonparticipants in the drug trade.

Changes in patterns of drug use probably contributed to the decline in handgun homicides (Johnson, Golub, and Dunlap, 2000). The shift from crack in the last half of the 1980s to marijuana in the early 1990s probably reduced the carrying and use of firearms because the new generation of marijuana users believed that nothing they were doing required them to have a gun. They needed relatively little money to support their drug consumption and, therefore, they infrequently turned to crime. The marijuana trade was also less violent than the crack trade because lower profit margins diminished the intensity of competition among dealers.

Firearms, Crime, and the Police

During the 1990s, many police departments introduced measures aimed at reducing firearm crimes. Evaluations of precisely how those measures affected crime rates are lacking, but there are some indications of what tactics might have worked.

In 1992 and 1993, the Kansas City, Missouri, Police Department created a patrol group to detect people who were illegally carrying firearms in an area that had a high rate of gun crimes (Sherman, Shaw, and Rogan, 1995; Sherman and Rogan, 1995). Officers looked for opportunities to conduct legal searches of cars and pedestrians, including curfew violations, traffic stops for driving a stolen car, illegal use of high-beam lights, and running stop signs. Guns were seized as a result of searching upon arrest, frisking for an officer's safety, and being in plain view. The twenty-nine-week patrol produced a 65 percent increase in gun seizures and a 49 percent decrease in gun crimes in the target area, in comparison to the six-month period prior to implementing the patrol. No comparable improvements occurred in a control area that had no such patrol; gun seizures there decreased by 15 percent, and gun crimes increased by 4 percent. The area with the gun patrol also experienced reductions in drive-by shootings and in all homicides, while the control area showed no meaningful change in either type of crime. There was no apparent displacement of gun crimes from the target area to other neighborhoods.

Sherman and Rogan suggest that gun patrols might reduce crime by increasing the probability that people who illegally carry firearms will be arrested and have their weapons confiscated, thereby encouraging potential offenders to leave their guns at home where they will be unavailable when disputes or robbery opportunities arise. A second possibility is that gun patrols lead to more incapacitation of firearm offenders; this implies that focusing police resources on any violent offenders, rather than just those who illegally carry guns, would reduce crime. A third possibility is that gun patrols deter crime in the same way that any visible patrol would. Sherman and Rogan conclude that the reduction in crime resulting from the Kansas City gun patrol was due to the deterrent impact of greater police visibility, rather than due to the confiscation of guns or the incapacitation of offenders.

Support for the effectiveness of directed patrols such as the one in Kansas City comes from a study done in Indianapolis. When suspects stopped for other infractions were given warnings rather than citations for carrying firearms, violent and property crimes increased. In the second phase of the study, when suspects carrying firearms were arrested rather than warned or issued citations, there was an 8 percent increase in seized firearms, a 40 percent decline in armed robberies and aggravated assaults, and a 29 percent decrease in all gun crimes. Homicides in the target area fell from eleven a year earlier to one during the experimental phase, even though homicides increased by 53 percent in the city as a whole over that time. The researchers concluded that gun patrols directed against suspicious activities and locations can reduce violent crime (McGarrell, Chermak, and Weiss, 1999; McGarrell et al., 2001).

From their examination of New York City's crime rates between 1985 and 1996, Fagan, Zimring, and Kim (1998) concluded that the long-term decline in nongun homicides and nongun robberies was "accretive" rather than a consequence of measures implemented by the police. However, they attributed the sharp decline in gun homicides and gun robberies after 1993 at least in part to policies introduced by Commissioner Bratton. They found it impossible to separate the impact of police tactics from the impact of other changes that might have reduced gun crimes. Even if the specific contribution of the police could be determined, they said it would not be clear which of the measures introduced by Bratton had reduced gun crimes. They did suggest that "the pattern in New York City is much more consistent with gun-oriented policing than with indiscriminate quality-of-life interventions as a cause of decline" (Fagan, Zimring, and Kim, 1998: 1322).

Bratton has made the following claim for the reforms he introduced in 1994: "People carrying illegal guns quickly realized that they risked gun charges after being arrested for minor crimes. After rising briefly in 1994, gun apprehensions then began to fall; the gunslingers were leaving their weapons at home. With far fewer guns on the street, far fewer people were shot and far fewer were killed" (Bratton and Andrews, 1999: 44). Karmen (2000) believes that gun seizures are an inadequate measure of the extent to which people are carrying guns. An increase in seizures can be the result of either greater police aggressiveness or an increase in the actual number of people carrying guns, and a decrease in seizures can mean less police aggressiveness or fewer people carrying guns. According to Karmen, better measures of the extent of gun carrying are changes in the number of gun crimes relative to the number of nongun crimes, as well as trends in shootings, bullet woundings, and firearm fatalities. Using this kind of evidence, he concludes that the anti-gun measures introduced by Bratton might have contributed to the downward trend in firearm crimes, but that the trend had started several years earlier and was more likely the result of changes in the crack trade.

Boston's Operation Ceasefire and Gun Project used a "pulling levers" approach that directly communicated to chronic gang offenders that violence would no longer be tolerated. A coordinated, multi-agency effort to attack illegal gun trafficking was implemented, in part through the interrogation of arrested gang members regarding who was selling firearms (Kennedy, 1998; Braga et al., 2001). This problem-oriented policing strategy was based on research that had found that firearm violence in Boston was overwhelmingly a youth gang problem, and that gun and knife homicides by youths were concentrated in three neighborhoods. Local and federal law-enforcement agents, probation and parole officers, federal and local prosecutors, youth corrections workers, and gang outreach workers joined together to disrupt drug dealing by gangs, stop and search gang members for quality-of-life offenses, serve outstanding warrants, enforce parole and probation conditions, and seek the harshest penalties in pending cases. Gang members were told that any gang-related violence would result in the fullest use of criminal justice resources against the whole gang, not just against the individual who had committed the crime. This strategy was credited for a 70 percent reduction in the number of young people murdered in the city. The degree to which the measures specifically directed at firearms were responsible for reducing homicides is uncertain because of the relatively small number of firearm homicides by Boston youths even before the project began, because other cities also experienced declines in youth homicides, and because Boston implemented several anti-violence measures at the same time (Eck and Maguire, 2000).

Homicide rates decreased in many cities in the 1990s, but there is no compelling evidence that the adoption of antigun measures by the police influenced the degree to which a city's homicide rate fell. A national evaluation of the Youth Firearms Violence Initiative concluded that arrest policies focused on gun crimes coincided with, but did not necessarily cause, reductions in gun crimes in some communities, but not in others (Dunworth, 2000). Eck and Maguire (2000) questioned whether gun patrols were a major reason for the decline in crime rates in the 1990s, because they did not know to what extent such patrols had actually been adopted, could not determine if cities that had implemented them had done so with the same rigor as Kansas City, were unsure if the patrols had been established early enough in the decade to account for the decline in crime rates, and did not fully understand how such patrols reduced crime. Overall, they concluded that "there is just enough evidence to suggest that gun-enforcement strategies contributed to the decline in homicides, but not enough evidence to be confident about such claims" (Eck and Maguire, 2000: 238).

Gun-Control Laws and Crime Rates

Research indicates that limiting the general availability of firearms will not reduce violent crime, but making guns less accessible to those most likely to commit crime and reducing the carrying of guns in situations that are especially likely to lead to violence might curb crime. Federal, state, and local gun-control laws have thus sought to restrict the acquisition of firearms by youths, convicted felons, domestic violence offenders, and the mentally ill. Firearm availability has also been curtailed through the regulation of gun dealers, the imposition of waiting periods before the acquisition of guns, and limitations on the number of guns that can be bought during a given period. If potential offenders do manage to acquire guns, the criminal use of those weapons might be minimized by requiring permits to carry guns, focusing police attention on people suspected of illegally carrying guns, screening people who enter public buildings such as schools and courthouses, and imposing add-on penalties for offenses committed with guns (Cook and Ludwig, 2000).

Kleck's (1997) evaluation of thirty-nine studies of the impact of gun laws on violent crime found that only four had directly measured gun availability, and only one had accounted for simultaneity. Sixteen of the studies provided mixed support for the conclusion that gun laws reduced violent crime, but twelve of them had evaluated the impact of just one law in a single area. In one of the best-designed studies,

Marvell and Moody (1995) concluded that state laws requiring minimum or add-on penalties for offenses committed with firearms did not consistently reduce rates of homicides or gun crimes. In another study, Kleck and Patterson (1993) found that only 3 of 102 tests showed unambiguously that gun laws affected violent crime rates: Prohibiting the mentally ill from possessing firearms reduced homicide rates, and banning handgun sales and licensing gun dealers reduced robbery rates. Fifteen additional tests provided ambiguous support for the impact of gun laws: Licensing gun owners might reduce homicide rates, and add-on penalties that were discretionary rather than mandatory might reduce rates of homicide and rape. Overall, Kleck and Patterson concluded that gun-control measures had little effect on the availability of guns to either the general population or the crime-prone segments of that population.

Implemented in 1994, the Brady Handgun Violence Prevention Act was designed to prevent felons from purchasing handguns from federally licensed dealers by mandating a five-day waiting period between initiation of a purchase and delivery of the weapon. From 1994 through 1999, 2.4 percent of the 22,254,000 applicants for firearm transfers had their applications rejected. Of those rejected in 1999, nearly three-fourths were turned down because of felony indictments or convictions, and one-eighth were turned down for domestic violence misdemeanor convictions or for restraining orders (Gifford et al., 2000). Gun-control advocates cited these figures as evidence that the Brady Act had prevented tens of thousands of potential offenders from acquiring guns, thereby contributing to the decline in crime.

When their applications to purchase guns from licensed dealers are rejected, some potential offenders probably do not seek guns from other sources, and some who do are probably unable to acquire guns. Though Wright and Rossi (1986) found that one-fifth of the felons in their sample who reported committing crimes without guns said that difficulty of access was one reason they had not used a gun, most potential offenders who want a gun are probably able to find one. Only one-sixth of Wright and Rossi's (1986) sample had acquired their last firearm from a legitimate source. Thirty-two percent had procured their firearm through theft, an additional 14 percent said that their gun had been stolen by someone else, and 24 percent thought it had probably been stolen. Wright and Rossi thus estimated that between 46 and 70 percent of the felons' most recently acquired guns had been stolen. In addition to stealing guns or buying stolen ones, people whose applications to buy firearms are rejected can get them by presenting false identification to dealers, by enlisting others to make "straw" purchases for them, or by buying from relatives, friends, fences, drug dealers, or unlicensed gun dealers (especially at flea markets and gun shows). Given the many ways that potential offenders can procure firearms, it is not surprising that three-fourths of the incarcerated felons in Wright and Rossi's sample said they could get a gun soon after their release with little or no trouble and at no great expense.

Despite the apparent ease with which potential offenders can acquire firearms, Garen Wintemute (2000) argues that screening potential handgun purchasers can reduce firearm crime. One study found that prospective handgun buyers who had prior felony arrests but no felony convictions, and who could therefore buy guns legitimately, were more likely to be charged with new violent crimes than convicted felons who had their applications to buy firearms rejected (Wright, Wintemute, and Rivara, 1999). If the prior arrests of the buyers who had not been convicted of felonies indicate their earlier involvement in crime, this finding implies that preventing offenders from buying guns from retail outlets can prevent crime. This conclusion is consistent with another study that found that people with at least one misdemeanor conviction who bought handguns were six times more likely than handgun purchasers without criminal records to be charged with new violent crimes (Wintemute et al., 1998). Wintemute et al. (1999) estimate that prohibiting offenders convicted of violent misdemeanors from buying handguns from legitimate outlets could reduce their risk of committing new violent or gun crimes by 20 to 30 percent.

Another approach to curbing firearm crime was an effort by the federal Bureau of Alcohol, Tobacco, and Firearms to trace guns used in crimes ("crime guns"). Fifty-thousand crime guns were traced in 1993, a number that had quadrupled by 1999. Starting in 1993, the ATF also began to look more carefully at firearm dealers who applied for new licenses or the renewal of old ones; this policy reduced the number of federally licensed dealers from 287,000 in 1993 to 86,180 in 1999. There is no evidence that either ATF measure reduced crime rates by keeping felons from getting firearms (Wintemute, 2000).

Many felons will procure guns from other sources if they cannot buy them legitimately from retail outlets. Potential offenders who cannot obtain guns from any source might give up the idea of committing a crime, but they also might commit a crime unarmed or with a different weapon. Because neither the Brady Act nor the ATF's measures were implemented until several years after homicide and robbery rates had begun to drop, they do not seem to explain the decline in violent crime, though they might have reinforced the downward trend once it had started.

Conclusion

Gun-control advocates claim that crime can be reduced by restricting access to firearms or by punishing firearm offenders more severely. In fact, the relationship between guns and crime is more complex than this argument suggests. Even the commonly accepted idea that more guns mean more crime is questionable: Crime rates are apparently insensitive to changes in gun ownership by the general population. Guns and crime seem to be reciprocally related: More ownership of firearms by crime-prone groups such as drug dealers and gang members leads to more violent crime, but more violent crime also increases gun ownership by these victimization-prone groups, as well as by the population at large. Guns in the hands of citizens deter some offenders from committing crimes, or at least divert them to unarmed victims, but research on the impact on crime rates of permissive concealed-carry laws is inconclusive.

Any change in the possession, carrying, or use of firearms in the 1990s that contributed to the decline in murders and robberies cannot account for the parallel decline in burglaries and motor vehicle thefts, because few offenders who commit those property crimes use guns. Murders and robberies committed with firearms declined in the 1990s, but so too did murders and robberies committed with other weapons or with no weapons at all. Firearm homicides did decrease more than nongun homicides, suggesting that changes in gun use contributed to the drop in the nation's homicide rate. The fact that handgun homicides fell most sharply in the 1990s among young black males and in large cities suggests that the decline might have been the result of systemic change in the crack trade and a shift from the use of crack to the use of marijuana.

Research in Kansas City, Indianapolis, New York City, and Boston indicates that police gun patrols can reduce crime, but it is not clear that such patrols were adopted widely enough to explain the decline in violent crime in the 1990s. Gun-control measures that target crime-prone groups, ban handgun sales, and license gun dealers can curb violent crime; measures that license gun owners and allow for add-on penalties for firearm crimes might have that effect. The problem with gun-control laws is that potential offenders who are denied the right to purchase guns from retail outlets often turn to other sources. The enormous number of guns in the country means they will have little trouble finding one. Some potential offenders who cannot buy guns legitimately are probably unable to get them from other sources; therefore, some violent crime is prevented by measures such as the Brady Act. That law was implemented after rates of violent crime had begun to fall, but it might have contributed to the decline.

CHAPTER

8   Age and Crime

When the *New York Times* turned to criminologists for an explanation of the decline in crime rates in the 1990s, they frequently pointed to demographic change. Demographic factors include sex, race, and marital status, but the population characteristic emphasized by the criminologists was age.

The strong relationship between age and crime is one of the most consistently documented findings in criminology, though there is disagreement over why criminal behavior varies over the life course. Noting that "the age/crime relationship is not backed by established theory," Marvell and Moody (1991: 239–240) propose that any of the following age-associated factors might affect criminal behavior:

> the physical ability to accomplish strenuous criminal acts, chemical factors such as testosterone levels that might predispose persons to crime, innate recklessness of juveniles, level of moral development, inability to balance immediate gains against long-term effects of crime, participation in peer groups consisting of frequent offenders, opportunities for gainful legitimate employment, extent of family ties, and greater legal penalties given adults and repeat offenders.

Measuring variations in criminal behavior among different age groups poses problems. Because many crimes are not reported to and recorded by the police, and because most recorded crimes do not lead to an arrest, there are no reliable statistics on the actual number of crimes committed by various age groups. As a result, research on the age–crime relationship has to rely on arrest data. The analysis in this chapter assumes that the likelihood that a crime will lead to arrest is the same for all age groups and does not vary over time—assumptions that could be incorrect. Arrest data are also flawed because crimes committed by youths are more likely to be carried out in groups than crimes committed by older offenders. Therefore, the age distribution of *arrestees* might differ from the age distribution of *offenses* (Marvell and

Moody, 1991). Despite their shortcomings, arrest data are used here as an indicator of criminal activity because no better data are available.

People between the ages of 15 and 24 are especially likely to be arrested for the four indicator crimes. The average proportion of the U.S. population in this age group from 1990 to 1999 was 14.0 percent. However, the average proportion of all arrestees in this age group was much higher: 53.4 percent for murder, 55.2 percent for robbery, 50.0 percent for burglary, and 59.6 percent for motor vehicle theft. Another way to describe the age–crime relationship is in terms of age-specific arrest rates, which are the number of arrests of people of a given age per 100,000 people of that age. Figure 8.1 presents age-specific robbery arrest rates for 1990 and 1999. The number of robbery arrests per capita in both years is highest for 15- to 19-year-olds and next highest for 20- to 24-year-olds. This pattern of high arrest rates for those in their mid-teens to mid-twenties, with a drop-off in rates for older groups, is also characteristic of the other indicator crimes. However, the peak age of arrest and the degree to which arrest rates decline after that age vary from crime to crime.

A Hypothetical Example

Because age groups differ in criminal activity, a society's overall crime rate can rise or fall with changes in its age structure, which is the distribution of its population among the various age groups. This is illustrated in Table 8.1, which shows the age structure of a hypothetical society at two different time periods. The total population during both time periods is 400,000, but during time 1 the proportion of the population under the age of 25 is 50 percent, while during time 2 the proportion under that age is only 25 percent. Correspondingly, the proportion over the age of 25 changes from 50 percent at time 1 to 75 percent at time 2. In other words, the population has become older from time 1 to time 2. At both times, however, the age-specific crime rate for each age group is the same: 10 per 100,000 people under 25, and 5 per 100,000 people over 25. The table shows that even if both the total population and the age-specific crime rates of two age groups remain the same over time, the society will experience a 16.7 percent reduction in its overall crime rate (from 7.5 to 6.25 crimes per 100,000 people) as a result of the demographic shift in the proportions of its population in the two age groups. This implies that crime rates might have fallen in the United States in the 1990s because of the aging of the population.

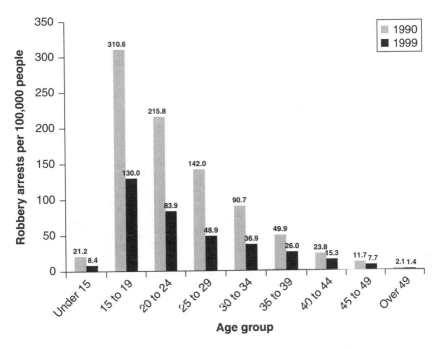

FIGURE 8.1   Age-Specific Robbery Arrest Rates, 1990 and 1999

Source: Based on data from Federal Bureau of Investigation, *Crime in the United States: Uniform Crime Reports, 1990 and 1999.* Washington, DC: U.S. Government Printing Office, 1991 and 2000.

TABLE 8.1   Changes in Age Structure and Crime Rates in a Hypothetical Society

Time Period	Age group	Population (% of total)	Total number of crimes	Crimes per 100,000 people
1	Under 25	200,000 (50%)	20	10
	Over 25	200,000 (50%)	10	5
	Total	400,000 (100%)	30	7.5
2	Under 25	100,000 (25%)	10	10
	Over 25	300,000 (75%)	15	5
	Total	400,000 (100%)	25	6.25

Age and Crime in the *New York Times*

In 1994, the *New York Times* attributed the recent reduction in the nation's crime rate to demographic change, specifically the low birth rates of the 1970s that left fewer people in the crime-prone age groups in the 1990s (November 13, 1994, sec. 4: 3). The following year, the paper cited sociologist Joan McCord's suggestion that the smaller number of people in the high-crime years might account for the decline in crime rates (January 1, 1995: 36). Rejecting a demographic explanation for the precipitous drop in crime in New York City, and touting instead the impact of his innovative law-enforcement policies, NYPD Commissioner William Bratton told criminologists at the 1995 American Society of Criminology meeting that enrollments in the city's public high schools had actually grown while crime rates had fallen.

Looking to the future, the *Times* made the following statement: "Criminologists are sure that in the next decade, crime will rise again to record levels because of the far different demographic trends of the 1980s" (November 13, 1994, sec. 4: 4). After the release of a report on the decline in crime from 1992 to 1993, Jack Levin boldly made this prediction, which soon proved to be wrong: "This may be the last good report that we see in a long time. This is the lull before the crime storm that we're going to have in this country in the next decade" (cited in May 2, 1994: A13). Levin based his prediction on an increase in murders by 14- and 15-year-olds and an imminent growth in the size of the high-murder-rate age group between 18 and 24. The next year, James Alan Fox warned that if changes in the age structure had contributed to the recent drop in crime rates, that decline would be short-lived because "by the year 2005 there will be 23 percent more teenagers between the ages of 15 and 19" (cited in January 1, 1995: 37). A U.S. Department of Justice report cited by the *Times* made a similar prediction, estimating that juvenile arrests for violent crime would double by 2010 as the result of a projected 20 percent increase in the number of teenagers (September 8, 1995: A16).

Implicit in the *Times*'s discussion of the demographic explanation of falling crime rates is the assumption that the decline was due to a reduction in the number of people in the crime-prone age group, rather than a reduction in the rate at which members of that group were committing crime. One of the few times the paper explicitly distinguished between the rate at which an age group commits crime and the number of people in that age group occurred in 1995: "The number of teenagers in the United States would increase by about one percent a year for the next 15 years. This means that *even if the juvenile crime rate held steady,* the total number of crimes committed by young people would rise" (August 9, 1996: A25; emphasis added). The *Times* and the criminologists it quoted typically drew attention to impending changes in the number of young people in the population, but ignored the possibility that the rate at which they committed crime might also change.

In a sidebar to a 1995 feature article, the *Times* questioned the demographic explanation, pointing out that crime rates had risen and fallen between 1975 and 1985 with little change in the proportion of the population in their crime-prone years (January 1, 1995: 37). Skepticism also surfaced in a 1997 letter to the editor from Kent Markus, Deputy Chief of Staff of the U.S. Attorney General's Office, who observed that even though experts had attributed the recent decline in crime rates to a drop in the number of people in their late teens and early twenties, in fact "the population of 15- to 24-year-olds has been relatively flat" since 1989 (October 18, 1997: A14).

In a 1999 article titled "The Coming Crime Wave Is Washed Up," the *Times* reported that the homicide rate of 14- to 17-year-olds, which had tripled from 1985 to 1993, had fallen by nearly half from 1993 to 1997. Criminologists were cited as having erroneously predicted that a growth in the youthful age group would produce a major increase in crime rates by the end of the millennium. These criminologists included James Alan Fox, James Q. Wilson, and John J. DiIulio, Jr., all of whom had pessimistically described the period of falling crime rates earlier in the decade as "the lull before the crime storm" and a "ticking time bomb" (cited in January 3, 1999, sec. 4: 4). Wilson admitted that the projected increase "clearly hasn't happened. This is a good indication of what little all of us know about criminology" (cited in January 3, 1999, sec. 4: 4). On the contrary, scholars who have published or examined research on the age–crime relationship knew all along that even increasing numbers of people in their crime-prone years would lead to higher crime rates only if the members of those age groups continued to commit crime at the same or higher rates. What happened in the 1990s was that young people, indeed people of all ages, became less likely to commit crime; that is, the age-specific crime rates of all groups declined (see Figure 8.1). Wilson acknowledged this point by commenting that he might have focused too much on population projections and too little on "the perception of young people about the costs and benefits of crime" (cited in January 3, 1999, sec. 4: 4). Fox continued to focus on age structure rather than age-specific crime rates, predicting that the number of young black males in the population would soon begin to increase faster than the number of young white males, and because young black males have relatively high rates of violent crime, the overall crime rate would increase. He did make this prediction more cautiously than his earlier ones: "We may indeed see a resurgence in youth violence. I say 'may.' I didn't say 'will' " (cited in January 3, 1999, sec. 4: 4).

One criminologist quoted by the *Times* who did make the distinction between age structure and age-specific crime rates was Alfred Blumstein, who explained the 1993–1994 decrease in murders, robberies, and assaults in twenty of the nation's twenty-two largest cities in terms of both a decline in the number of young people and a decline in the rate at which young people were committing crime. In a journal article, he and Richard Rosenfeld (1998: 1186) described recent homicide trends as follows:

> [A]ll of the increase in the level of homicide in the United States during the growth period of the late 1980s and early 1990s was due to the trends in the younger ages, because homicide rates for those 25 and older did not go up. However, some of the decrease during the decline period since 1993 is due to the drop in offending among young people, and some is attributable to the continuing decline in offending among older people.

According to Blumstein, nearly all of the decline in murders by young people in the 1990s was due to a reduction in firearm murders, apparently the result of changes in the drug market and police efforts to confiscate guns from young people. He attributed the longer-term decline in murders by people 25 and older to a reduction in spouse murders and barroom killings and an increase in the incarceration of adult offenders (November 8, 1994: A14; March 29, 1998: 16).

One reason that Levin, Fox, Wilson, and DiIulio erred in predicting the impact of demographic change on crime rates was that they focused on change in the size of the most crime-prone age group, but neglected change in the size of other age groups. In reaching a conclusion quite different from theirs, Steven D. Levitt (1999) looked not only at the 20 percent increase in the 15- to 24-year-old group that was projected to occur between 1995 and 2010, but also at projected changes in the size of other age groups, notably a 20 percent decrease in the 25- to 39-year-old group, which still commits much crime, and a 20 percent increase in people aged 65 and older, who commit very little crime. Taking all projected changes in the age distribution of the population into account, Levitt predicted that demographic change would actually reduce crime rates slightly by 2010.

Abortion and Crime Rates

The age structure of a population is a result of the processes of fertility, mortality, and migration. It is also influenced by historical events that deplete certain age groups; for example, the deaths of soldiers in a war or of drug users from overdoses can reduce the size of younger groups, while an influenza epidemic can have a big impact on the size of older groups. In a study discussed at length in the *Times,* economists John J. Donohue and Steven D. Levitt (2000) argued that another event reduced crime rates by depleting the age group that entered its crime-prone years in the early 1990s; this event was the legalization of abortion by the U.S. Supreme Court in its 1973 *Roe* v. *Wade* decision.

Because abortion purportedly increased in frequency with legalization, Donohue and Levitt argue that there were "missing" or unborn children in the 18-year-old age group from 1991 onward, a phenomenon they say might explain as much as half of the decline in the nation's crime rate from 1991 to 1997. They show that the first states to legalize abortion were the first ones to experience falling crime rates, and that the states that had the highest abortion rates experienced the biggest reductions in crime rates. In addition to its impact on crime rates through reduction of the crime-prone age group, legalized abortion might also reduce that group's age-specific crime rate in two ways. One is that the women most likely to have abortions might also be the ones most likely to have children who would later be especially prone to crime. Donohue and Levitt present evidence that abortions are most common among women who are in their teens, unmarried, economically disadvantaged, of low educational attainment, and black—all characteristics of mothers whose children are most likely to commit crime when they reach their teenage and early adult years. Donohue and Levitt also propose that age-specific crime rates might drop because of an improved-environment effect resulting from women's efforts to optimize the timing of their child bearing by recourse to abortion. If women are more likely to carry fetuses to term when they can provide them with a nurturing environment, their children might be less prone to crime. According to Donohue and Levitt, about one-fourth of the effect of legalized abortion on the decrease in crime rates was due to a reduction in the size of the crime-prone age group, and the other three-fourths was due to a reduction in that group's age-specific crime rate.

The *Times* devoted much space to criticism of Donohue and Levitt's research. Because there were no reliable data on the number of abortions performed prior to 1973, critics said that any study based on estimates of how much abortion had increased after legalization was suspect. They also argued that before 1973 the movement of women seeking abortions from states where they were illegal to states where they were legal made it impossible to do reliable state-by-state comparisons of abortion rates and their impact on crime rates. The harshest attack on the study focused on its policy implications—specifically, whether it could be interpreted as endorsing abortion as a crime-reduction measure. Some critics even contended that the authors' conclusions encouraged a genocidal policy toward poverty-stricken African Americans. Critics also questioned whether the legalization of abortion had affected crime rates as much as Donohue and Levitt claimed. Alfred Blumstein (cited in August 20, 1999: A14) commented, "These are very able guys, and I'm prepared to believe that they've discerned an effect. But I think they've gone too far in claiming that it can account for half of the decline, when there are a multitude of effects going on that are much more proximate to the situation." Levitt acknowledged that his research did not fully explain the decline in crime rates and thought it should have little impact on abortion policy.

Have Changes in the Age Structure Affected Crime Rates?

Before considering whether changes in the age structure of the population caused crime rates to fall in the 1990s, research on the impact of such changes on the increase in crime rates in the 1960s is examined. That earlier work developed a method for assessing the impact of the age structure on crime rates and strongly influenced criminologists' efforts to make sense of the decline in rates three decades later.

Age Structure and Crime Rates in the 1960s

The potential contribution of shifts in the age structure to changes in crime rates was highlighted by the President's Commission on Law Enforcement and Administration of Justice in 1967. The commission observed that the crime rate for people under 25 was much greater than the rate for those over 25, and that the post-World War II baby boom had increased the proportion of the population in the high-risk age group. Calculations based on 1960 arrest rates led the commission to conclude that "about 40 to 50 percent of the total increase in the arrests reported by UCR [from 1960 to 1965] could have been expected as the result of *increases in population and changes in the age composition of the population*" (President's Commission on Law Enforcement and Administration of Justice, 1967: 28; emphasis added). To reach this conclusion, the commission enlisted the FBI to prepare national estimates of arrest rates based on sex, age (under 14, 14–19, 20–24, 25–34, 35–44, over 45), race (white, nonwhite), and place of residence (central cities, outside central cities). Arrest rates for 1960 were then applied to the number of people in each category in 1965 to determine the expected number of arrests for 1965. The proportion of the increase in arrests that was accounted for by changes in population and age structure was determined using the following formula:

$$x = \frac{\text{predicted 1965 total arrests} - \text{actual 1960 total arrests}}{\text{actual 1965 total arrests} - \text{actual 1960 total arrests}}$$

Growth in the population alone accounted for 24 percent of the increase in arrests, and changes in population and age structure together accounted for 49 percent of the increase in arrests.

In a similar study, Theodore Ferdinand (1970) estimated the proportion of the increase in index crimes from 1950 to 1965 that was attributable to change in the age structure. He used two arrest rates, one for people aged 10 to 24 and one for all people under 10 and over 24. Growth in the proportion of the population between the ages of 10 and 24 accounted for 5.5 percent of the increase in murders, 13.4 percent of the increase in robberies, 12.3 percent of the increase in burglaries, and 13.8 percent of the increase in motor vehicle thefts.

To measure the extent to which the increase in crime rates from 1960 to 1970 was due to change in the age structure, I applied age-specific arrest rates for 1960 to the number of people in each age group in 1970 to determine how many arrests there would have been for each age group had 1960's age-specific arrest rates been the same in 1970. Census data for 1960 and 1970 made it possible to use seventeen age groups (under 15, single years from 15 to 24, five-year groups from 25 to 49, and over 49). The projected total of arrests for all age groups can then be used to calculate a projected total arrest rate per 100,000 people for 1970. The proportion of that projected 1970 arrest rate that was attributable to change in the age structure, exclusive of change in the size of the population, can then be calculated with a formula that uses per capita arrest rates rather than absolute numbers of arrests (see Box 8.1).

BOX **8.1**

Method for Measuring the Contribution of Changes in the Age Structure to the Increase in Crime Rates from 1960 to 1970

I made two adjustments to the number of arrests reported by the FBI. To account for the fact that UCR arrest data covered different proportions of the U.S. population in 1960 and 1970, I standardized arrest figures by calculating how many arrests there would have been in each year had UCR arrest data been reported for the entire nation. This adjustment assumes that the population not covered would have produced arrests at the same rate and with the same age distribution as the population actually covered by the UCR. The second adjustment modified the number of arrests reported in 1970 by applying 1960's clearance rate to 1970's arrest data. This was necessary because the police cleared different percentages of crimes in the two years.

The method I used to estimate the contribution of changes in the age structure to the increase in crime rates can be illustrated with data for murder. In 1960, fifty-three 15-year-olds were arrested for murder. That figure was for jurisdictions covering only 60 percent of the U.S. population, so I multiplied it by 100/60, producing an estimate of eighty-eight murder arrests of 15-year-olds for the nation as a whole. That number was divided by the number of 15-year-olds in the population in 1960 (2,802,230) to get an age-specific rate of 3.14 murder arrests per 100,000 15-year-olds. In 1970, 271 15-year-olds were arrested for murder. Arrest data for 1970 came from 75 percent of the population, so 271 was multiplied by 100/75 to get an estimated 361 arrests of 15-year-olds. That figure was multiplied by .923/.865 to account for the decline in the police clearance rate from 92.3 percent in 1960 to 86.5 percent in 1970. The resulting figure of 385 was then divided by the 4,029,034 15-year-olds in the population in 1970 to get an age-specific rate of 9.56 murder arrests per 100,000 15-year-olds. The next step was to subtract the 1960 population of 15-year-olds from the 1970 population of 15-year-olds to determine the increase in that age group (1,226,804). That figure was multiplied by the age-specific arrest rate of 15-year-olds in 1960 (3.14) to estimate the increase in murder arrests that would have occurred had there been no change in the age-specific arrest rate for 15-year-olds from 1960 to 1970. This produced a projected increase of 39 murder arrests based just on growth in the number of 15-year-olds in the population, assuming no change in that age group's murder arrest rate.

This method was then applied to murder arrests for the other sixteen age groups. The projected increase in murder arrests for the population as a whole was the sum of the expected increases in arrests for all age groups.

BOX **8.1** Continued

That projected total increase of 1,782 murder arrests was added to the number of murder arrests in 1960 to get a projected total of 10,931 murder arrests in 1970. That figure was then divided by 1970's total population (203,211,918) to get an overall projected rate of 5.38 murder arrests per 100,000 people. The percentage of the actual increase in the nation's murder arrest rate that was attributable to change in the age structure alone was then calculated as follows:

$$y = \frac{\text{projected 1970 arrest rate} - \text{actual 1960 arrest rate}}{\text{actual 1970 arrest rate} - \text{actual 1960 arrest rate}} = \frac{5.38 - 5.10}{8.99 - 5.10} = \frac{.28}{3.89} = 7.2\%$$

In other words, 7.2 percent of the increase in the nation's murder arrest rate from 1960 to 1970 was attributable to change in the age structure alone. This method was also applied to arrest data for the other three indicator crimes.

The proportions of the increases in arrest rates from 1960 to 1970 that are attributable only to changes in the age structure are 7.2 percent for murder, 9.8 percent for robbery, 10.1 percent for burglary, and 14.6 percent for motor vehicle theft.

Research demonstrates that the impact of age structure on crime rates is not the same everywhere. Using homicide data from 1901 to 1970, Gartner and Parker (1990: 363) found that "age structure exerts a significant positive effect on homicide rates in (1) England and Wales, but only for the full time period, and (2) Italy and the United States, but only in the post–World War II period." In neither Japan nor Scotland did the proportion of young males in the population influence the homicide rate. Gartner and Parker (1990: 366) concluded that the age–crime relationship is influenced by social context.

> Specifically, we propose that where violent conflicts between males or unrelated adults are more common, where firearms are more readily available and facilitate violent property crimes, and where cultural prohibitions of violence are weaker, changes in the proportion of young males in the population will most likely produce changes in the homicide rate. It follows that where family homicides and the killing of women and children constitute a larger proportion of the total homicide rate, where firearms are more strictly regulated and less available for use in the commission of other crimes, and where formal and informal control systems

more strictly limit interpersonal violence, changes in the proportion of young males will have weaker effects on the homicide rate.

They propose that from 1946 to 1970 the first set of conditions characterized the United States and Italy, and the second set of conditions described Japan, Scotland, and England/Wales.

Age Structure and Crime Rates in the 1980s and 1990s

Just as an increasingly youthful population contributed in a modest way to the rise in crime rates in the 1960s, so too might an aging population drive crime rates down, as illustrated by the hypothetical example in Table 8.1. From 1990 to 1999, the median age of the U.S. population rose from 32.8 to 35.5, while the proportion of those aged 15–24 (the crime-prone years) fell from 14.8 to 13.9 percent. These figures suggest that the decline in crime rates during the decade might have been affected by demographic change.

Looking at the impact of changes in the age structure on rates of murder and motor vehicle theft, Cohen and Land (1987) concluded that shrinkage of the youthful age group explained approximately as much of the decrease in crime rates in the early 1980s as the expansion in the size of that group had explained of the increase in crime rates in the 1960s and 1970s. In contrast, Steffensmeier and Harer (1987) found that change in the age structure had not affected rates of violent crime much from 1980 to 1984, but had caused rates of property crime, especially motor vehicle theft and larceny, to fall over that time: Change in the age structure accounted for 43 percent of the decline in the FBI's property crime rate, and 36 percent of the decline in the National Crime Victimization Survey's property crime rate.

In a later study, Steffensmeier and Harer (1991) found that adjusting for changes in the age structure from 1980 to 1988 significantly reduced the magnitude of the apparent decline in crime rates. An unadjusted crime rate based on NCVS data fell by 17 percent from 1980 to 1988, but after taking into account change in the age structure, that rate was down by only 7 percent. The FBI's unadjusted crime index rate dropped by 4 percent over the same time, but with adjustment for change in the age structure, it actually rose by 7 percent. Overall, change in the age structure over this time explained all of the decline in the FBI's crime index rate and about three-fifths of the decline in the NCVS crime rate. For the 1992–1996 period, however, the substantial reductions in rates of homicide, robbery, burglary, and motor vehicle theft were much the same with or without an adjustment for changes in the age structure, indicating that such changes had little impact on crime rates over that time (Steffensmeier and Harer, 1999).

I used the method explained in Box 8.1 to determine the extent to which change in the age structure accounted for the drop in crime rates from 1990 to 1999. Because 1999 was not a census year, data were available for only nine age groups (under 15, five-year groups from 15 to 49, and over 49), rather than the seventeen used in the 1960–1970 analysis. The proportions of the decreases in arrest rates explained by change in the age structure during the 1990s are 19.9 percent for murder, 16.6 percent for robbery, 11.9 percent for burglary, and 7.9 percent for motor vehicle theft. As with the 1960–1970 analysis, shifts in the distribution of the population among the various age groups explained modest proportions of the change in arrest rates (in no case more than one-fifth of the reduction).

Conclusion

Predicting crime trends from demographic data is risky. Marvell and Moody (1991) conclude from their research review that studies comparing jurisdictions at the same point in time have rarely uncovered a strong association between age structure and crime rates, but that nearly half of all time-series studies have found a strong impact of age structure on crime rates. Nevertheless, they are skeptical of the ability of criminologists to forecast crime trends from data on the age structure: "In all, the common practice of using demographic trends to forecast crime trends is not justified, either because the age/crime relationship is smaller than generally supposed, because the impact of age is too insubstantial to overcome other factors, or because the wrong age/crime curve has been used" (Marvell and Moody, 1991: 257). Allan Abrahamse (1997: 11) reaches a similar conclusion from his effort to determine whether a projected increase in the number of young people in California would substantially increase the state's homicide rate: "Demography will not prove to be destiny. It is the *behavior* of the next generation that will largely shape the future."

Change in the age structure of the population had a modest effect on the decline in crime rates in the 1990s, accounting for 7.9 to 19.9 percent of the decrease in the four crime indicators. These figures suggest that Donohue and Levitt's estimate that half of the decline in the crime rate was due to the legalization of abortion is exaggerated, because the effects of increased abortion are incorporated in the data for the age structure of the population. Changes in factors that reduced the age-specific crime rates of the different age groups were more important than change in the age structure in driving crime rates down, and changes in those factors are harder to predict than demographic shifts.

Changing Institutions and Falling Crime Rates

Sociological theories of crime focus on institutions such as the family, the school, the economy, and religion. Because these theories rarely specify how institutional change causes crime rates to rise and fall, the news media make little mention of them in their efforts to explain why crime rates are changing. None of the following factors central to sociological theories of criminal behavior was mentioned in the *New York Times* in the 1990s: the absence of self-control usually learned within families (Gottfredson and Hirschi, 1990), the strain that results from a disjunction between the goal of material success and access to the legitimate means to reach that goal (Merton, 1968; Agnew et al., 1996), and the lack of close attachments of students to their teachers and schools (Hirschi, 1969).

Generally overlooked by such institutional theories of crime is the problem of reciprocal causation or simultaneity. Families that do a poor job of socializing and disciplining their children contribute to high crime rates. However, high crime rates also weaken the ability of parents to protect their children, and rising crime rates that lead to the incarceration of more adults undermine family socialization and discipline. Another example of reciprocal causation involves the economic system. The strain and deprivation associated with unemployment can lead to crime, but increasing crime rates that result in more incarceration pull out of the economy people with demographic characteristics commonly associated with high unemployment rates, thereby reducing the overall unemployment rate below what it would have been without the high rate of incarceration. Simultaneity also occurs if political alienation generates crime, but rising crime rates further undermine political trust. The effects of crime on institutions is probably not as great as the effects of institutions on crime, but few researchers have assessed this process of reciprocal causation.

One of the few institutional theories that includes a time dimension, though it does not explicitly attend to the problem of reciprocal causation, is Gary LaFree's (1998a) explanation of the long-term, post–World War II increase in crime rates in terms of a decline in the legitimacy of the family, the economic system, and the political system. LaFree's (1998b) application of his theory to the falling crime rates of the 1990s is less convincing than his explanation of why rates rose in the postwar years, but he does offer a useful framework for looking at the way that institutional change might account for that decline. In addition to the three institutions central to LaFree's theory, this chapter considers religion, which was not proposed as a cause of the drop in crime rates by LaFree, the *New York Times,* or any criminologist quoted in the newspaper.

LaFree's Theory of Institutional Legitimacy

After demonstrating that the increase in crime rates following World War II was historically patterned and consistent across various types of crime, LaFree seeks to explain how changes in institutional legitimacy caused those rates to rise. He defines institutions as

> the patterned, mutually shared ways that people develop for living together. These patterns include the norms, values, statuses, roles, and organizations that define and regulate human conduct. Institutions encompass proper, legitimate, and expected modes of behavior. They are guides to how we should live and conduct our affairs, daily reminders of the conduct that we hold to be either acceptable or unacceptable. (LaFree, 1998a: 71)

Legitimacy, in LaFree's conception, is the ease or difficulty with which institutions such as the family, the economy, and the political system are able to get people to abide by norms that define and regulate human conduct. He argues that the preestablished "grooves" into which institutions channel behavior widened in the 1960s and 1970s, but narrowed in the 1990s, in ways that explain the rise and fall of crime rates. These changes especially influenced young black males, who disproportionately accounted for both the increase in crime rates in the 1960s and the decrease in rates in the 1990s. According to LaFree (1998a: 9), "African Americans experienced greater distrust in political institutions, greater economic-related stress, and greater changes in the structure and functioning of families during the postwar years."

Defining and measuring institutional legitimacy are difficult. LaFree uses indicators of the actual functioning of institutions, such as the divorce rate to measure family legitimacy and inflation to measure economic legitimacy. Legitimacy can also be defined in attitudinal terms, or the way that people perceive the appropriateness of an institution as it currently exists. LaFree uses an attitudinal measure for political legitimacy but not for the legitimacy of other institutions, instead inferring legitimacy from statistics on how well those institutions are working.

LaFree proposes that institutions produce law-abiding behavior when people perceive them as legitimate, and contribute to high crime rates when they do not instill the motivation to conform to the law, are unable to control criminal behavior, and fail to protect people from offenders. The motivation to break the law is reduced when parents and teachers foster in children a sense of right and wrong, and when people learn to regard the economic and political systems as fair and just. According to LaFree, the family declined in legitimacy after World War II because of rejection of the traditional two-parent, male-dominated family. This was reflected in rising rates of divorce and illegitimacy and the changing role of women in the economy. The economic system lost legitimacy because of growing income inequality, inflation, and the movement of industrial jobs to other nations. The legitimacy of the political system also declined, the result of growing distrust resulting from the black civil rights and other rights based movements, Vietnam War protests, and political scandals such as Watergate. LaFree argues that the attrition in institutional legitimacy set in motion countervailing responses that might account for the reduction in crime rates in the 1990s: Educational change resulted from the decreasing legitimacy of the family, welfare programs developed in reaction to the falling legitimacy of the economic system, and the criminal justice system expanded because of declining political legitimacy.

Crime and the Family

Families curb criminal behavior in several ways. Socialization instills values that reduce the chance that children will later break the law. Discipline produces self-control that minimizes the likelihood of committing crimes when opportunities arise. Parental supervision directly controls the behavior of children and adolescents. Families also protect their members against victimization. Even though a substantial body of research demonstrates that these family social processes play a crucial role in preventing or producing criminal behavior, changes in the family were virtually ignored by the *New York Times* in its consideration of why crime rates fell in the 1990s. In one of the few such references, the paper suggested that increased parental supervision might have contributed to the overall decline in school violence during the decade, a trend that contrasted sharply with several highly publicized mass murders by students (October 20, 1999: A1, A22).

LaFree claims that crime rates rose in the postwar era because of a decline in the traditional nuclear family—a household that has two biological parents, a male breadwinner and a female household manager. According to LaFree (1998a: 144), "although 84 percent of children born during the first half of the 1950s were, by the age of fourteen, living with both biological parents, only one-third of all children born in the early 1980s were still living with both biological parents when they reached the same age." The demise of the "Norman Rockwell family" was due to an increase in the number of widowed people living alone, a rise in average age at first marriage, and higher rates of divorce, illegitimacy, and remarriage. Change in the traditional nuclear family was also associated with a shift of men's jobs from agriculture to the industrial and service sectors, increases in income inequality and inflation that pressured women to move from unpaid work in the home to paid jobs in the labor force, and the feminist movement's challenge to patriarchy. The consequence of these changes was that fewer children and adolescents lived in households with two biological parents who played traditional gender roles. Therefore, according to LaFree, fewer children were positively influenced by the processes of socialization, social control, and guardianship that historically had been provided by nuclear families.

LaFree (1998a, 1998b) suggests that the declining crime rates of the 1990s were the result of increasing family legitimacy. He points out that the rate of growth in the proportion of all births that were to unmarried women abated, female labor force participation and the proportion of all households that were not families remained steady, and divorce rates stabilized and even fell somewhat. Even though the family showed few signs of returning to its traditional form, LaFree claims that in the 1990s it had begun to stabilize around a variety of more widely accepted alternative structures, enhancing its ability to prevent crime.

After World War II, not only did the percentage of all 6- to 17-year-olds who were in school increase, but the proportions of those under 6 and over 17 who attended school also grew, suggesting to LaFree that schools were increasingly relied on to supervise, control, and protect young people in the absence of families that could do so. He regards increased school enrollments as a measure of declining family legitimacy, and hence a factor associated with rising crime rates. He also treats growing school enrollments as the educational institution's response to the increase in crime rates. He proposes that the growth in the proportion of 3- and 4-year-olds who were enrolled in school from 44 percent in 1990 to 49 percent in 1995 is evidence of the educational institution's response to low family legitimacy, and proposes that this response might have contributed to the decline in crime rates.

LaFree does not elaborate on the social processes by which families and schools affect criminal behavior, looking instead at overall relationships between crime rates and measures of the health of those institutions. For example, he does not show precisely how higher rates of divorce and illegitimacy might cause children to become more criminal, or how early enrollment in school might make them less criminal. He does not consider in depth the problem of time-lags, which are important to understanding how changes in the family and the school affect crime rates. A divorce or enrollment in a preschool program will not immediately affect a 3-year old's propensity to commit crime, but it might have an impact some years later. Thus, LaFree's comparison of the divorce rate and the crime rate for the same year is questionable: A high divorce rate in a given year might indicate low family legitimacy, but it is unclear how that low legitimacy translates into a high crime rate for the same year. The supervision and protection functions of the family and the school could have short-term effects on adolescents' criminal behavior, but the socialization function of those institutions is more likely to have a long-term impact on crime.

LaFree's theory that crime rates are affected by low family legitimacy and the educational response to it yields to the following propositions about changes that should have occurred in the 1990s if family legitimacy contributed to the decline in crime rates:

1. The proportion of all births that were to unmarried women should have decreased.
2. The per capita rate of unmarried-couple households with children should have decreased.

3. The proportion of married women who had young children and were in the labor force should have decreased.
4. Divorce rates should have decreased.
5. The proportion of children living with both parents should have increased.
6. If family legitimacy increased, the proportion of young children enrolled in school should have decreased. On the other hand, if the educational institution's response to low family legitimacy increased, the proportion of young children enrolled in school should have increased.

Figures 9.1 to 9.6 show trends in measures of family legitimacy bearing on these propositions. Because data were unavailable for some years, the figures cover different time periods.

Figure 9.1 shows that the proportion of all births that were to unmarried women climbed steadily from 1960 to 1994, then leveled off from 1994 to 1999. There is no evidence here of any return to the traditional nuclear family. In fact, during the early part of the decade, when

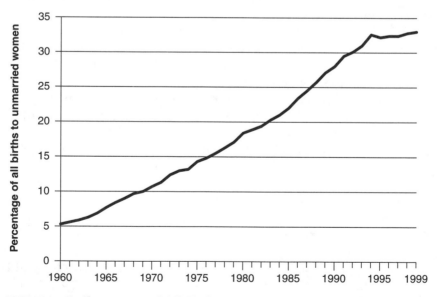

FIGURE 9.1   Percentage of All Births to Unmarried Women, 1960–1999

Source: National Center for Health Statistics, *National Vital Statistics Reports* 48 (October 18, 2000), 17 (Table 1).

crime rates were falling, the rate of illegitimacy was increasing as fast as it had since 1960. Figure 9.2 demonstrates that the per capita rate of unmarried-couple households with children under the age of 15 grew steadily from 1977 to 1998, then dipped a bit in 1999, well after crime rates had started to fall. Nontraditional families continued to become more common even after crime rates had started to fall, contradicting the theory that increases in family legitimacy accounted for the decline in crime rates.

Once women marry and have children, they are much more likely to be employed in the paid labor force than they were in the past. Figure 9.3 (p. 164) shows a steady increase from 1965 to 1995 in the proportion of married women with a husband present who had children under the age of 6 and were in the paid labor force. That trend levels off from 1995 to 1999, four years after crime rates had started to fall. Again, there is no evidence that a resurgence of the traditional nuclear family can explain the decline in crime rates.

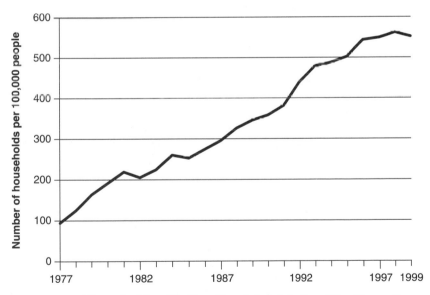

FIGURE 9.2   Households with Two Unrelated Adults of the Opposite Sex with Children under 15 Years Old, 1977–1999

Source: U.S. Census Bureau (Online: www.census.gov/population/socdemo/ms-la/tabad-2.txt [May 14, 2001]; www.census.gov/population/socdemo/hh-fam/p20–537/1999/tabH3.pdf [October 17, 2001])

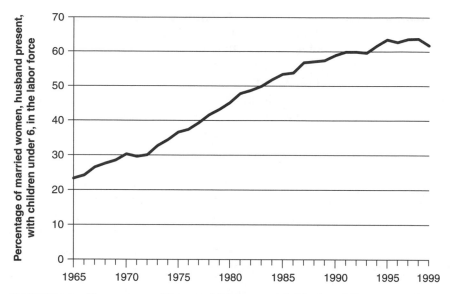

FIGURE 9.3   Percentage of Married Women with Husband Present and Children under 6 Years Old, in the Labor Force, 1965–1999

Source: U.S. Census Bureau, *Statistical Abstract of the United States 1965–2000.* Washington, DC: U.S. Government Printing Office, 1966–2001.

Figure 9.4 shows that the rate at which marriages ended in divorce rose sharply from 1967 to 1979, then dropped somewhat, though by the end of the millennium the rate was still well above the levels of the 1960s. In the 1990s, the divorce rate continued to decline, a change that could reflect an increase in the legitimacy of the family. Perhaps more importantly, the downturn in the divorce rate beginning in 1981 might have subjected fewer children to crime-generating influences, which could have depressed crime rates when they entered their crime-prone years in the 1990s. However, Figure 9.5 shows that the proportion of all children under 18 who lived with both parents fell slowly but steadily from 1968 to 1996, apparently because the effects of rising rates of illegitimacy and cohabitation outweighed the effect of declining divorce rates, leaving more children in nontraditional households in 1999 than in 1990.

The proportion of 3- and 4-year-olds enrolled in school increased gradually from 1972 to 1993 (if the anomalous year of 1990 is ignored), then rose sharply from 1993 to 1999 (see Figure 9.6, p. 166). This post-1993 trend is contrary to the decline in early school enrollments that

FIGURE 9.4   Divorces*, 1960–1999

*Includes annulments.

Source: Centers for Disease Control and Prevention, U.S. Department of Health and Human Services (Online: www.cdc.gov/nchs/search/search.htm [October 18, 2001]; www.cdc.gov/nchs/fastats/divorce.htm [October 18, 2001]); U.S. Census Bureau, *Statistical Abstract of the United States 1991–2000*. Washington, DC: U.S. Government Printing Office, 1992–2001.

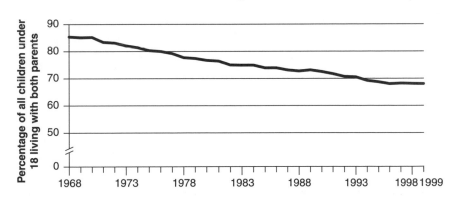

FIGURE 9.5   Percentage of All Children under 18 Living with Both Parents, 1968–1999

Source: U.S. Census Bureau (Online: www.census.gov/population/socdemo/hh-fam/p20-537/1999/tabC2.pdf [March 26, 2002])

would be expected if an increase in family legitimacy were the cause of the decrease in crime rates in the 1990s. The trend is consistent with LaFree's argument that the educational institution gained legitimacy as the family lost it, with the school replacing the family as the institution charged with socializing, controlling, and protecting the young.

Because most of the data point to a long-term, largely uninterrupted decline in the strength of the traditional nuclear family, there is little reason to think that family legitimacy increased as crime rates fell in the 1990s. Most of the evidence also fails to support the idea of a time-lagged effect of improved family functioning on crime rates. The exception is the decline in divorce rates, which might be associated with lower age-specific crime rates for people born after 1981. LaFree provides no evidence to support his contention that by the 1990s people in the United States had grown more accepting of such alternatives to the traditional nuclear family as out-of-wedlock births, single-parent families, or cohabitation.

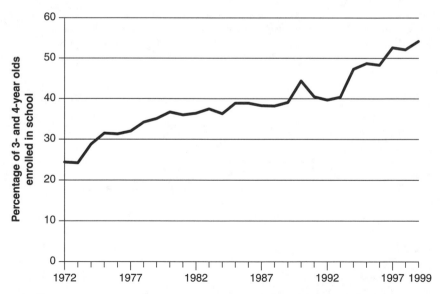

FIGURE 9.6   Percentage of 3- and 4-Year-Olds Enrolled in School, 1972–1999

Source: U.S. Census Bureau, *Statistical Abstract of the United States 1961–2000.* Washington, DC: U.S. Government Printing Office, 1962–2001; U.S. Census Bureau (Online: www.census.gov/population/socdemo/school/p20-533/tab01.pdf [October 18, 2001])

Indicators of family structure such as those used in Figures 9.1 to 9.6 might not fully or accurately reflect the family social processes that keep young people from committing crime. Socialization, social control, and protection might have improved even as the proportion of the population living in nontraditional households grew. For example, parental discipline might have improved in the late 1970s, instilling more self-control in children who committed crime at a lower rate when they entered their teenage years in the 1990s. There are, however, no available data on how family social processes have changed over time that can be used to test this hypothesis, or to test hypotheses that more effective teaching of values or closer supervision of adolescents contributed to the decline in crime rates.

Crime and the Economic System

Improving economic conditions were occasionally mentioned in the *New York Times* as a reason for the declining crime rates of the 1990s. One article suggested that increased employment opportunities and greater prosperity had made it possible for the residents of one Brooklyn precinct to buy and renovate buildings, purportedly increasing the residents' incentive to improve the neighborhood in other ways, such as joining together to fight crime (April 4, 1993: 35, 42). Another article suggested that a 17 percent drop in robberies in Brooklyn might have been partly the result of an increase in construction jobs there, though the paper did point out that robberies had also declined elsewhere in the city (January 1, 1995: 37).

Much of the attention paid by the *Times* to the role of economic improvement in reducing crime rates was not in news articles, but rather in brief letters to the editor. In one letter, Joydeep Mitra suggested that it was important to recognize that "a robust economy makes significant contributions to keeping crime rates low," rather than assume that low rates were due to police measures (August 22, 1997: A22). Milton Schwebel, professor emeritus of psychology at Rutgers University, wrote that it was odd that a *Times* article on the decline in property crimes had failed to mention the dramatic reduction in unemployment, because "[r]esearch has shown a clear relationship between unemployment and crime" (October 14, 1997: A26). He proposed that recognizing the importance of employment could lead to increased investment in the creation of new jobs rather than the building of more prisons. In a third letter, Jared Bernstein of the Economic Policy Institute argued that it was improvements in the low-wage labor market, rather than in the economy as a whole, that had reduced crime by creating "viable economic opportunities for those who want to play by the rules" (December 29, 1998: A18).

In a front-page story titled "Booming Job Market Draws Young Black Men into Fold," the *Times* considered the role of economic expansion in reducing crime (May 23, 1999: 1). The article cited a study by Richard B. Freeman and William M. Rodgers that found that black men between the ages of 16 and 24 who had a high school education or less were more likely to be employed, earned more money, and committed fewer crimes later in the 1990s than earlier in the decade. Even though the economic situation of young black men had improved faster than that of older black men or young men of all racial groups, by the end of the decade young black men still had unemployment rates more than twice those of their white peers. The *Times* attributed the improved economic condition of young black men to sustained economic prosperity and low unemployment, conditions that forced companies to hire workers they would not have employed a few years earlier. By the late 1990s, entry-level jobs had become better paid because the increased demand for labor required employers to provide more incentives to draw people into the workforce and take the jobs they were offering. Prolonged periods of low unemployment give young workers the chance to develop contacts, job experience, skills, and confidence, all of which are useful if the economy later weakens. Freeman concluded that the experience of the 1990s "shows how critical it is not to give up on these guys. If you give these kids a break, they come back" (cited in May 23, 1999: 24). Political scientist Jennifer L. Hochschild agreed: "Poor blacks never lost faith in work, education, and individual effort. What's different now is that they can do something about it" (cited in May 23, 1999: A1).

LaFree's Theory of Economic Legitimacy

LaFree proposes that a long-term decline in the legitimacy of the economic system was one reason that crime rates increased in the decades after World War II. His analysis of the reasons that rates fell in the 1990s also emphasizes changes in economic legitimacy and the social welfare system's response to the earlier decline in that legitimacy. Gallup Poll data show that the percentage of people expressing "a great deal" or "quite a lot" of confidence in big business moved generally lower in the decade prior to 1995, then increased sharply until 1998. Confidence in organized labor changed little after 1981, but did increase from 1997 to 1999 (Gallup Organization, 2001). Neither trend indicates that economic legitimacy increased soon enough to have produced the initial decline in crime rates, though the growth in economic legitimacy later in the decade might have reinforced the downward trend.

According to LaFree, measures of how people are faring in comparison to a fixed economic standard are less strongly associated with crime rates than measures of how they are doing relative to other people. Absolute measures fail to capture the sense of deprivation people feel when they compare their own economic standing to that of others and can obscure changes at the lowest income levels, which are critical to understanding the motivation to break the law. Measures of relative well-being include income inequality and inflation. Rising prices are important because they have greater impact on low- and fixed-income earners than on people with high incomes. LaFree argues that growing income inequality and inflation raise crime rates by undermining the legitimacy of the economic system, which reduces the effectiveness of social control by the family and the community and encourages people to break the law. He proposes that the decline in crime rates in the 1990s was associated with improvements in both absolute and relative economic well-being, basing his conclusion on the following evidence:

- Inflation and unemployment were low throughout much of the decade.
- Income inequality declined in 1995 and 1996.
- The federal spending deficit was lower in 1996 than at any time since 1979.
- In 1994 the poverty rate dropped for the first time in five years.

Social welfare, an institutional response to declining economic legitimacy, might reduce crime rates by convincing the disadvantaged that the economic system is fair and just, thereby weakening their motivation to commit crime. Researchers have shown that greater expenditures on welfare assistance are associated with lower rates of robbery, burglary, rape, and perhaps murder (DeFronzo, 1983; Fiala and LaFree, 1988; Devine, Sheley, and Smith, 1988). However, there is no direct evidence that changes in welfare spending contributed to the decline in crime rates in the 1990s. In 1996, the more restrictive Temporary Assistance for Needy Families program replaced the Aid to Families with Dependent Children program, limiting recipients to five years of benefits, capping federal welfare spending, and providing block grants to states, some of which changed their welfare systems to provide recipients with stronger incentives to work or return to school. These reforms might have subverted earlier efforts to shore up the legitimacy of the economic system with social welfare, but their long-term effects are still unclear (LaFree, 1998b).

Unemployment and Crime

Unemployment is related to crime in complex ways. Holding a job is necessary to commit some crimes, such as embezzlement, so higher unemployment rates might reduce certain offenses. Some employed workers "moonlight" in crime by doubling up, some use a job as a front to commit crime (for example, a storeowner who is also a professional fence), and others use legitimate income as a stake for a crime (for example, a drug deal). More unemployment might increase moonlighters' criminal activity, but it could also reduce crime by those who use their jobs as fronts or for stakes to finance crimes. Some people are committed to crime as a way of life and would not work even if jobs were available, so higher unemployment rates would not affect their criminal activity.

There might be a difference in criminal activity between people who are employed or temporarily unemployed, and people who have been out of work for a long time or have stopped looking for a job. Even more important than finding a job is keeping a job over time. Work binds people to legitimate institutions and gives them a "stake in conformity" that they do not want to jeopardize by involvement in crime. Criminals have poorer work records and higher unemployment rates than nonoffenders, but more and better job opportunities lead some offenders to choose legitimate sources of income over illegal ones. People who hold unattractive jobs that are boring, pay poorly, and offer little room for advancement might think they have little to lose if they are arrested, so finding a job to which they feel committed is more important than simply having some job.

People without jobs are especially likely to commit the kinds of crime that lead to imprisonment (Viscusi, 1986; Austin and Irwin, 1990). One survey found that a third of state prison inmates had been unemployed during the month prior to being arrested for the offense for which they were incarcerated, an unemployment rate much higher than the rate for the general population (Beck et al., 1993). Offenders who are even slightly more successful at work seem to commit fewer crimes than offenders who are less successful in the labor force (Petersilia, Greenwood, and Lavin, 1977; Freeman, 1987; Tauchen, Witte, and Griesinger, 1993). Unemployment prior to imprisonment is also a strong predictor of the rate at which inmates will return to crime after their release (Greenwood, 1982). Ex-convicts who find steadier employment and earn more money during the post-release period commit fewer crimes and have lower arrest rates (Rossi, Berk, and Lenihan, 1980; Anderson, Schumacker, and Anderson, 1991).

Structural changes in the economy, such as the relocation of manufacturing jobs to suburban areas or third world countries and the decline in the demand for unskilled workers, in combination with the concentration of poverty in inner-city areas, have threatened to create a permanent underclass of unemployed African Americans. Discrimination in hiring and pay poses a formidable barrier to upward mobility for this underclass and reduces its attachment to the labor force. Persistent adult unemployment generates crime by making it harder to establish stable households that exercise social control over children and adolescents. Lack of attractive jobs also gives young people an incentive to commit income-generating crimes, such as theft and the sale of drugs (McGahey, 1986; Duster, 1987; Sampson and Wilson, 1995).

Not only does the labor market affect criminal behavior, but criminal behavior reciprocally influences the labor market (Thornberry and Christenson, 1984). Convicted offenders, and even arrestees who have not been convicted, encounter barriers to employment. This leads to joblessness, job instability, and low earnings, all of which further increase the risk of criminal activity (Finn and Fontaine, 1985; Sampson and Laub, 1993; Bushway, 1998; Fagan and Freeman, 1999). Time spent in prison is time not devoted to developing the skills and experiences that lead to greater monetary rewards from legitimate jobs; often that time is used to meet accomplices and refine techniques in order to increase the rewards of crime relative to those of legitimate work.

Rising crime rates that lead to more incarceration can reduce a society's overall unemployment rate by disproportionately removing from the economy those most likely to be jobless at any given time: the unskilled, the uneducated, substance abusers, and disadvantaged minorities. The release of large numbers of inmates, especially into a weak economy, can push unemployment rates up, perhaps producing an upsurge in crime rates.

Researchers have found a positive, though not always substantial, relationship between unemployment rates and crime rates. In a review of the evidence, Freeman (1983: 106) concluded as follows: "There is a cyclical pattern to the crime rate, with crime rising over the cycle with unemployment—but only weakly, so that changes in crime rates are dominated by other factors." Later, he wrote that "although the rate of unemployment drifted upward from the 1950s to the 1990s, even the largest estimated effects of unemployment on crime suggest that it contributed little to the rising trend in crime" (Freeman, 1995: 171). When crime rates respond to changes in unemployment rates, they do so slowly because government and union benefits mute the impact of losing a job, and because deprivation does not immediately lead to criminal motivation (Chiricos, 1987; Land, Cantor, and Russell, 1995). Unemployment rates are more closely associated with property crime rates than with violent crime rates. One study found that the unemployment rate had no meaningful impact on the homicide rate, but did have statistically significant effects on robbery and burglary rates (Devine, Sheley, and Smith, 1988).

Figure 9.7 shows that the nation's unemployment rate declined substantially in the 1990s, from 7.5 percent in 1992 to 4.2 percent in 1999. The unemployment rate began to fall one year after the crime rate had started its descent, then paralleled the decline in crime rates for the remainder of the decade. This suggests that the improving employment situation reinforced the downward trend in crime rates, even if it did not cause the initial decline. However, the years from 1960 to 1992 include periods during which unemployment rates fell but crime rates did not. For example, the unemployment rate dropped from 5.7 percent in 1963 to 3.5 percent in 1969, but rates of all four indicator crimes climbed faster over those years than at any other time since World War II.

Because young black males commit indicator crimes out of proportion to their numbers in the population, their unemployment rate is worth examining separately. Keep in mind that in the 1990s changes in that unemployment rate might have been affected by increasing rates of incarceration and school enrollment. Figure 9.8 (p. 174) shows that after 1992, unemployment rates fell for black males between 16 and 19 years old, black males 20 and older, whites males between 16 and 19, and white males 20 and older. The movement from unemployed to employed status was greatest for the young black male group: The unemployment rate for this group was 11.2 percentage points lower in 1999 than in 1992, compared to declines of 6.8 for older black males, 5.9 for young white males, and 3.4 for older white males. This improvement in the economic situation of young black males suggests that the down-

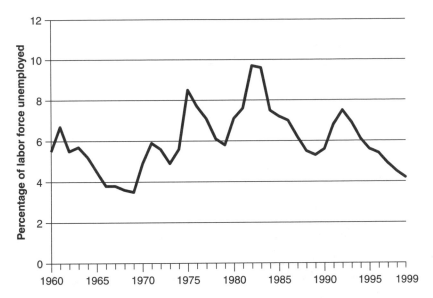

FIGURE 9.7   Percentage of Labor Force Unemployed, 1960–1999

Source: U.S. Department of Labor (Online: www.bls/gov/cps/cpsaat1.pdf [October 19, 2001])

ward trend in crime rates in the 1990s was reinforced, if not initially caused, by a substantial reduction in the unemployment rate of a demographic group that contributes disproportionately to high rates of the four indicator crimes.

Income and Crime

Crime rates are associated with measures of absolute economic position, such as hourly wages, annual income, and the proportion of the population living in poverty. One study of twenty-six Manhattan neighborhoods found that homicide rates were higher where there was more extreme poverty. Income inequality was only weakly associated with homicide rates (Messner and Tardiff, 1986). An analysis of national data for the 1967–1998 period found that increases in the proportion of young people living in poverty were associated with increases in juvenile homicide arrests (Messner, Raffalovich, and McMillan, 2001).

Figure 9.9 (p. 175) shows that the proportions of blacks and whites living below the poverty level decreased from 1993 to 1999, declines that paralleled the drop in the four crime indicators (though they did

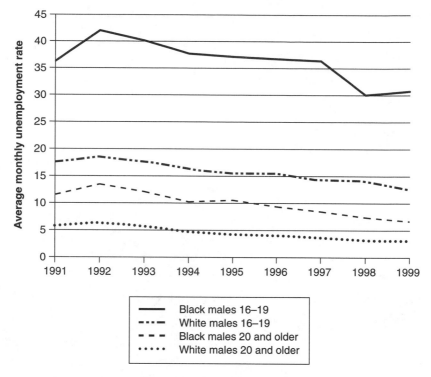

FIGURE 9.8   Average Monthly Unemployment Rates, 1991–1999

Source: U.S. Department of Labor (Online: data.bls.gov/servlet/SurveyOutputServlet [November 11, 2001])

not begin until shortly after crime rates had started to fall). Over this time, the poverty rate for whites fell from 12.2 to 9.8 percent (a 19.7 percent decline), while the poverty rate for blacks fell even more sharply from 33.1 to 23.6 percent (a 28.7 percent decline). By raising a significant proportion of blacks above the poverty level, the economic prosperity of the 1990s apparently contributed to the overall decline in crime rates. However, the rapid growth in the prison population during the decade disproportionately affected blacks, and might have depressed that group's poverty rate because people behind bars were not counted as poverty-stricken.

People who think they can make more money from crime than from a legitimate job, and particularly those who perceive the largest gap between the two sources of income, are especially likely to engage

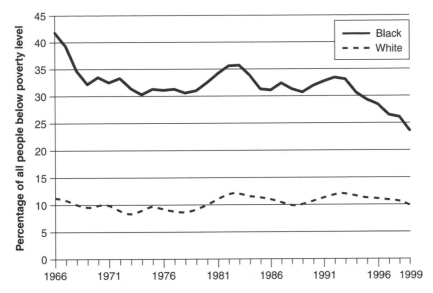

FIGURE 9.9   Percentage of All People below Poverty Level, 1966–1999

Source: U.S. Census Bureau (Online: www.census.gov/hhes/poverty/histpov/hstpov2. html [October 19, 2001])

in criminal behavior (Viscusi, 1986). Boston's crime rates rose from 1980 to 1989, and over that time the proportion of the city's young people who said they could earn more on the street than from a legitimate job rose from 41 to 63 percent. The proportion of young people who reported that they had several chances every day to make money from crime doubled (Freeman, 1992).

The actual, rather than perceived, earnings from crime are uncertain, and little is known about how illicit income varies over time and from place to place. Wilson and Abrahamse (1992) claim that earnings from crime are modest and are less than offenders can make from legitimate work, with the exception of motor vehicle theft. They also suggest that offenders often exaggerate their income from crime. In contrast, Freeman (1992, 1995; Fagan and Freeman, 1999) argues that adolescents can earn substantially higher hourly wages from crime than from legitimate work. Drug dealing seems to be the most lucrative criminal activity. Adolescents' decisions to commit or avoid crime are apparently sensitive to both legal and illegal wages. One study concluded that legitimate work must pay $30 an hour before youths will abandon crime (Huff, 1996).

Looking at National Longitudinal Survey of Youth data for respondents between the ages of 14 and 22 who were no longer enrolled in school, Grogger (2000) found that 95 percent of both those who did and those who did not derive income from crime had held legitimate jobs, suggesting that lack of employment opportunities was not strongly associated with involvement in crime. Furthermore, youths who had not made any money from crime earned hourly wages 15 percent higher, and worked 17 percent more hours each year, than youths who had made some money from crime. Grogger suggested that wage differentials between blacks and whites and between the young and the old could explain variations in crime rates among those groups.

According to Fagan and Freeman (1999), decreases in legitimate earnings and desirable jobs for males with few skills characterized the period from the mid-1970s to the early 1990s, contributing to the increase in crime rates over that time. Bureau of Labor Statistics (2000: 31) data reveal that the median hourly wages of 16- to 24-year-old males, a demographic group that contributes significantly to the nation's crime rate, fell by 22 percent between 1979 and 1996, from $8.39 to $6.53. Nearly two-thirds of that decline occurred between 1979 and 1983 (see Figure 9.10). Grogger (1998, 2000) believes that this decline in wages made selling crack an appealing way for young men to earn money and gave them little incentive to seek legitimate work, and that it explains the 18 percent increase in arrests for the group between 1979 and 1988.

During the 1990s, increasing wages and expanding work opportunities might have contributed to falling crime rates by attracting poten-

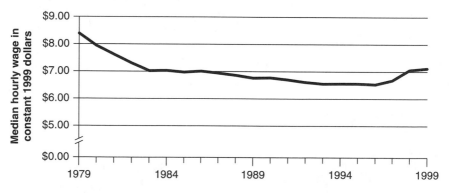

FIGURE 9.10   Median Hourly Wage, Males 16 to 24, 1979–1999

Source: U.S. Department of Labor (Online: www.bls.gov/pdf/cpswom99.pdf [June 5, 2001])

tial offenders to legitimate jobs and encouraging active offenders to commit fewer crimes and earn more money from legitimate work, or even abandon criminal careers altogether (Grogger, 2000). However, Figure 9.10 shows that the median hourly wages of the most crime-prone group, males between the ages of 16 and 24, changed little during the 1990s. The median hourly wage declined from $6.77 in 1990 to $6.53 in 1996, a 3.5 percent drop, then rose modestly to $7.12 in 1999, a 9 percent increase over 1996's wage. Because wages did not begin to rise until 1997, five years after crime rates had begun to fall, and because the increase in wages was quite modest, change in the median hourly wage for young males does not seem to explain the decline in the nation's crime rates.

Income Inequality, Inflation, and Crime

Robert K. Merton's (1968) strain or anomie theory distinguishes between culturally defined goals, such as wealth and power, and norms that define the socially acceptable means for reaching those goals, such as hard work at a legitimate job. A disjunction between means and goals can result from the socially structured incapacity of people to use the approved means to reach the cultural goals; racial discrimination that limits access to the institutionalized means for achieving success is one example of a socially structured incapacity. Strain, which is the frustration and sense of injustice that result from experiencing socially structured incapacities as low capabilities, can lead to criminal behavior aimed at achieving culturally approved goals through unacceptable means. Pressure to break the law is probably greatest for the lowest classes, because they are most distant from the goal of financial security and have the least access to the institutionalized means to achieve material success.

Research by Robert Agnew and his colleagues (1996: 698) shows that income-generating crime is related to "the central variable in classic strain theory—dissatisfaction with monetary status," whether that dissatisfaction is a result of objective or subjective monetary position. People with less education and lower incomes, which are measures of objective social class position, are less satisfied with their monetary situation. That dissatisfaction is associated with higher rates of criminal activity. Dissatisfaction with monetary status is also more common among people, regardless of their social class position, who desire but do not expect to make a lot of money. That sense of relative deprivation is also associated with greater criminal activity.

According to LaFree, crime rates are more strongly associated with measures of relative economic well-being, such as income inequality and inflation, than with measures of absolute economic well-being, such as the unemployment rate, the poverty rate, or hourly wages. The cross-national association between income inequality and homicide rates is particularly strong in nations that are more democratic, wealthier, and more densely populated—factors apparently linked to greater relative deprivation (Krahn, Hartnagel, and Gartrell, 1986). Cross-national research also shows that inequality generated by economic discrimination against certain groups, such as racial and ethnic minorities, is strongly associated with homicide rates (Messner, 1989). Within the United States, growing income inequality within both black and white racial groups is associated with increases in homicide, robbery, and burglary arrest rates for each group (LaFree and Drass, 1996; Messner, Raffalovich, and McMillan, 2001). Furthermore, crime rates are highest in cities where the difference between the incomes of the poor and the rich is greatest (Danziger and Wheeler, 1975; Blau and Blau, 1982; Sampson, 1985; Fowles and Merva, 1996).

LaFree's theory suggests that the decline in crime rates in the 1990s should have been preceded or accompanied by reductions in income inequality and inflation. Figure 9.11 shows the trend from 1967 to 1999 for the U.S. Census Bureau's Gini ratio, a widely used index of income inequality that measures the extent to which the distribution of the nation's household incomes deviates from a situation of absolute equality. If every household had the same income, the Gini ratio would be .000; if one household had all the income, the index would be 1.000. Household income inequality increased steadily from 1967 to 1999, with Gini ratios varying from .388 to .459 over that time. Income inequality grew substantially in the 1990s, with the Gini ratio rising from .428 in 1990 to .457 in 1999. Two years, 1995 and 1998, had small reductions in income inequality, but those reductions came several years after crime rates had begun to fall and therefore cannot explain the decline. Figure 9.11 offers no support for the argument that increasing economic legitimacy, as measured by declining income inequality, played a role in pushing crime rates down in the 1990s.

Because inflation most severely affects those living on low or fixed incomes, it is a measure of relative economic position that might be associated with crime rates. One study found that inflation was associated with rising rates of homicide, robbery, and burglary from 1957 to 1990 (LaFree and Drass, 1996). However, another study that uncovered statistically significant relationships between inflation and rates of homicide, robbery, and burglary for the 1948–1985 period found that those relationships disappeared once criminal opportunities and demographic

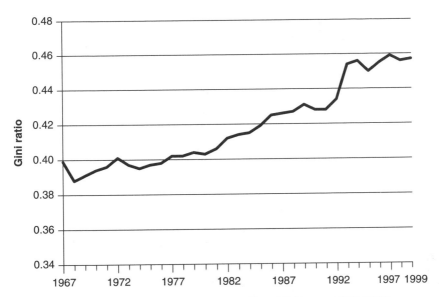

FIGURE 9.11   Household Income Inequality, All Races, 1967–1999

Source: U.S. Census Bureau (Online: www.census.gov/hhes/income/histinc/f04.html [October 18, 2001])

composition of the population were taken into account (Devine, Sheley, and Smith, 1988). Figure 9.12 (p. 180) shows that inflation, as measured by annual percentage changes in the Consumer Price Index, started to decrease a year before crime rates began to fall in the early 1990s, then continued to drop and remained at low levels throughout the decade. Low and declining inflation improved the relative economic well-being of certain groups, but it is unclear what impact this had on crime rates. The elderly, one group that is especially likely to be living on fixed incomes, benefitted from less inflation. However, because older people commit very little crime, their improved standard of living probably had no meaningful effect on the crime rate. Whether welfare recipients, another group living on fixed incomes, responded to the decline in inflation by committing less crime is a question requiring more research.

Crime and the Political System

A decline in the legitimacy of the political system could increase the motivation to commit crime and erode the formal and informal controls

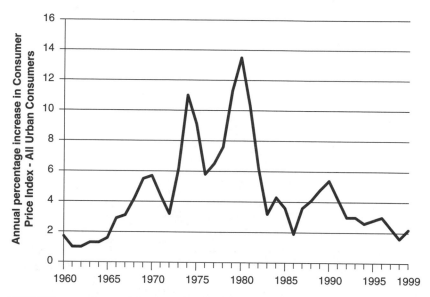

FIGURE 9.12   Annual Percentage Increase in Consumer Price Index, 1960–1999

Source: U.S. Department of Labor (Online: ftp://ftp.bls.gov/pub/special.requests/cpi/cpiai.txt [October 18, 2001])

that prevent crime. People are less apt to support the law, both in their own behavior and in their control of others' actions, if they do not believe that the government is worthy of their respect. LaFree claims that political legitimacy was diminished by the civil rights movement, anti-Vietnam War protests, and the feminist movement, all of which attacked injustices that the government had allowed to persist. The 1972 Watergate burglary, which led to President Richard Nixon's resignation in 1974, further eroded trust in the political system.

LaFree presents survey data that show that the proportion of people in the United States who trusted their government to do what was right remained steady at historically low levels from 1986 to 1996. The only year since 1958 with a lower level of political trust was 1974. The percentage of people who believed that government officials were crooked remained high and steady at near-record levels between 1988 and 1996. Figure 9.13, based on CBS/*New York Times* polls, reveals that political trust was considerably greater in the 1986–1991 period than in the 1993–1998 period when crime rates were dropping. Trust declined

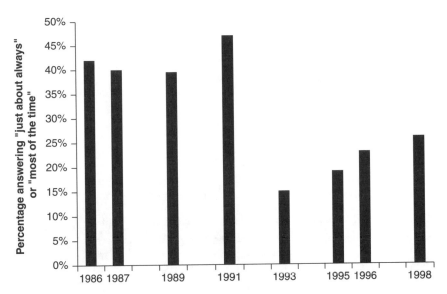

FIGURE 9.13   "How Much of the Time Do You Think You Can Trust the Government in Washington to Do What is Right?", 1986–1998*

*Averages were used for 1989, 1995, and 1998, in which two polls were conducted.

Source: Based on data from CBS/*New York Times* polls, 1986–1998. (Online: lib3.tufts. edu:2260/poll/1pext.dll?f-templates&fn=main-h.htm [October 25, 2001])

precipitously from 1991 to 1993, just as crime rates were starting to fall, then rose somewhat until 1998. This slight increase in trust might have contributed to the decrease in crime rates, but the absolute level of trust during the period of the decline in crime rates was much lower than it had been in the years prior to the decline. Overall, these survey results do not support the argument that increased political legitimacy led to lower crime rates.

LaFree proposes that the number of civil cases filed in U.S. District Courts reflects political legitimacy because such litigation challenges the way that the political system is treating people and can thus erode trust in government. He shows that the total number of civil cases filed rose sharply in the late 1960s and the 1970s, leveled off in the 1980s, then increased from 1990 to 1994. Because the population of the country grew from 1990 to 1999, a better measure than the absolute number of case filings, which LaFree uses, is the number of case filings per 100,000 people. Figure 9.14 shows that the number of case filings per capita increased slightly from 1991 to 1996, then decreased somewhat from 1996

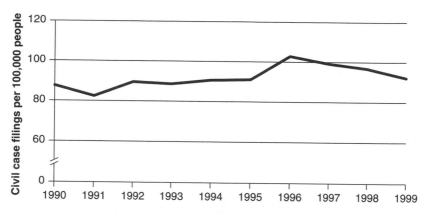

FIGURE 9.14 Civil Case Filings in U.S. District Courts, 1990–1999

Sources: U.S. Census Bureau, *Statistical Abstract of the United States, 1996 and 2001* (Online: www.census.gov/prod/2/gen/96statab/law.pdf [March 25, 2002]); Federal Judiciary Homepage (Online: www.uscourts.gov/judbus2000/tables/s07sep00.pdf [October 19, 2001])

to 1999. The growth in case filings until 1996 is the opposite of what LaFree's theory proposes, because it indicates that political legitimacy decreased during a time when crime rates were falling. The very small reduction in case filings per capita after 1996 is consistent with LaFree's theory, but it came five years after crime rates had started to drop, and so cannot account for the decline.

Another indicator of political legitimacy is the proportion of eligible voters who go to the polls on Election Day, with greater turnout indicating greater legitimacy. LaFree treats this issue briefly, comparing the 78 percent turnout in the 1964 presidential election to the 70 percent turnout in 1988 as evidence of declining political legitimacy. He does not mention that in 1971 the voting age was reduced from 21 to 18, bringing into the electorate a large number of younger voters who were especially likely to stay home on Election Day. Turnouts in national elections from 1988 to 2000 do not indicate that political legitimacy increased in a way that can explain the decline in crime rates. The proportion of all eligible voters who were registered to vote shows no pattern of increasing political participation over this time, either in presidential elections (66.6 percent in 1988, 68.2 percent in 1992, 65.9 percent in 1996, and 63.9 percent in 2000), or in off-year congressional elections (62.2 percent in 1990, 62.0 percent in 1994, and 62.1 percent in 1998). There was also no increase in the proportion of registered voters who actually went to the polls in presidential contests (57.4 percent in 1988, 61.3 percent in 1992, 54.2 percent in 1996, and 54.7 in 2000), or in off-year congressional elections (45.0 percent in 1990, 44.6 percent in 1994, and 41.9 percent in 1998) (U.S. Census Bureau, 2002). In sum, voter turnout did not change in a way consistent with the theory that increased political legitimacy caused crime rates to drop in the 1990s.

LaFree argues that collective action, such as the civil rights movement and the antiwar protests that challenged the political status quo from about 1959 to 1970, was uncommon in the 1990s, implying that this "settling down" reflected greater political legitimacy. However, his data show that this settling down began in the early 1970s, and that there was little collective action after 1980, raising the question of why it took so long for crime rates to begin to fall.

According to LaFree (1998a: 152), to "shore up political institutions, American society funded major increases in criminal justice spending." He acknowledges that this policy change was more than just a response to a decline in institutional legitimacy. Political leaders probably did not decide, consciously or otherwise, that decreasing public trust in government should be remedied with more spending on the police and the prisons. LaFree suggests that the increase in incarceration might have contributed to the decline in crime rates in the 1990s, but he asks at what cost that result was achieved, and claims that the decline was "surprisingly modest" compared to the impact that the increased spending on prisons should have had (LaFree, 1998a: 169).

Crime and Religion

Neither LaFree nor the *New York Times* explored the possibility that the decline in crime rates in the 1990s might have been associated with changes in the institution of religion. Increases in membership in organized religion, attendance at religious services, or faith in religious precepts could have reduced criminal activity by providing more of the socialization and social control also offered by families and schools.

Most research on religion and crime has focused on juvenile delinquency. Because some delinquent acts are status offenses, such as underage drinking and truancy, rather than criminal offenses, this body of research is not as pertinent to the question of why the four crime indicators fell as it might be. The two most commonly used measures of religiosity, or religious commitment, are salience (the importance of religion in a person's life) and attendance (the regularity with which a person goes to religious services). Researchers have also measured religiosity by denominational affiliation, the role of prayer and the study of sacred texts in a person's life, and participation in various religious activities (Johnson et al., 2000).

A review of forty studies of the religiosity–delinquency relationship concluded that three-fourths of them had found that greater religiosity led to less delinquency, and only one had found that greater religiosity led to more delinquency. The other studies showed either mixed effects or no effects at all. The studies that used the best research methods were the ones most likely to find that greater religiosity was associated with less delinquency. Every study that used four or more measures of religiosity and evaluated the reliability of its measures found that the most religious youths engaged in the least delinquency (Johnson et al., 2000).

Even though religious activities expose people to moral proscriptions and make real the threat of sanctions by "close monitoring and sanctioning of waywardness" (Evans et al., 1995: 210), religion is but one of several institutional influences on law-violating behavior. Several researchers have concluded that nonreligious processes of social control, especially those involving the family, have more impact than religious processes of social control on involvement in delinquency and crime (Elifson, Petersen, and Hadaway, 1983; Cochran, Wood, and Arneklev, 1994; Benda and Corwyn, 1997).

The Gallup Index of Leading Religious Indicators, which is the sum of responses to eight questions, has been used to gauge the strength of religion since 1941. This index would yield the maximum score of 1,000 if all respondents in the national survey

- Believed in God
- Stated a religious preference
- Belonged to a church or synagogue
- Attended religious services in the previous week
- Considered religion a very important part of their lives
- Had great confidence in organized religion
- Believed that religion answers problems
- Gave a high rating to the clergy's ethical standards

Scores on this index fell from 1961 to 1978, fluctuated and declined gradually from 1978 to 1993, then increased unevenly from 1993 to 1998. The 1998 score of 678 was the highest recorded since 1981, but still well below the scores of the 1960s. In the 1990s, as in earlier decades, most of the variation in the index was due to fluctuations in three items that measure the legitimacy of the religious institution: confidence in organized religion, rating of the clergy's ethical standards, and the belief that religion is relevant to dealing with everyday problems. These three items lost support in the 1980s but gained support after 1993. For example, the proportion of people with a high degree of confidence in organized religion fell from 64 percent in 1981 to 53 percent in 1993, then rose to 58 percent in 1999.

The increase in the legitimacy of organized religion from 1993 to 1999 parallels the decline in crime rates during those years. Because crime rates began to fall two years before the index of religious indicators did, the increase in religious legitimacy did not cause the initial decline in crime rates. However, it might have contributed to the continuation of the decline by enhancing the socialization and social control processes that prevent crime. Changes in religiosity warrant more attention as an influence on fluctuating crime rates than they received from criminologists and the news media in the 1990s.

Crime and Community

Criminologists have long considered the local community to be an important influence on criminal behavior. Robert J. Sampson (1995) proposes that crime might be prevented by fostering community-based prenatal and child care programs, investing in housing and deconcentrating inner-city poverty, and improving municipal health and public safety services. He also focuses on community in the sense of a stable group of people living in one location and interacting to meet common goals and needs. He suggests that crime might be reduced by strengthening informal controls over youths and increasing participation in voluntary organizations and collective action against crime and disorder. In a *Times* article, Elliott Currie attributes the decline in crime rates in the 1990s to innovative community programs that usually involve "collaborations between police and juvenile probation officers to reduce curfew violations, alternative schools for troubled young people, street-savvy mentoring programs and early intervention with high-risk infants" (April 12, 1998, sec. 2: 37).

Community structure is associated with crime rates, but "much of the effort to alter the structure of communities in order to reduce crime has not been noticeably successful or sustainable" (Hope, 1995: 23).

Measures aimed at reducing social disorder sometimes decrease fear of crime, but rarely reduce serious crime itself (Brown and Wycoff, 1987; Williams and Pate, 1987). Neighborhood Watch programs, urban patrol groups, and other crime-fighting voluntary organizations often fail to attract many residents of high-crime communities; even when implemented, these programs have little impact (Kenney, 1987; Rosenbaum, 1988). Voluntary organizations that emphasize broad social and economic changes in the community, rather than focusing narrowly on crime prevention, are more effective in reducing crime (Skogan, 1988; Hope, 1995).

During the 1990s, the *New York Times* occasionally quoted community leaders who claimed credit for the reduction in crime rates that the police said they had produced. An article that focused on the apparent success of aggressive policing in reducing crime in Manhattan's East Village quoted local leaders, merchants, and residents who noted that the decline began before Mayor Giuliani took office. They said that the renovation of apartment buildings had changed the appearance of the neighborhood, the opening of restaurants and clubs had created a lively night life, and the conversion of vacant lots once frequented by drug dealers into community gardens had improved the area. One resident remarked, "I think at one point we all decided that enough was enough and something had to be done. The police have been cooperative, but we had to take the initiative" (cited in January 3, 1995: B4). In other articles, community leaders pointed to programs they had developed to ameliorate such crime-producing conditions as joblessness and dropping out of school.

In 1997, the *Times* presented an in-depth discussion of Sampson, Raudenbush, and Earls's (1997) study of 343 Chicago neighborhoods. These researchers concluded that the strong community ties associated with lower levels of truancy, graffiti painting, and hanging out on street corners were not necessarily the result of strong personal or kin relationships; instead, community ties were strongest where the most residents owned homes and had lived in the area for a long time. An important predictor of a community's level of violence was *collective efficacy*, which Sampson described as "a shared vision, if you will, a fusion of a shared willingness of residents to intervene and social trust, a sense of engagement and ownership of public space" (cited in August 17, 1997: 27). The *Times* suggested that this research weakened the theory that crime was primarily the result of poverty, unemployment, single-parent households, and racial discrimination. Sampson noted that poverty and joblessness made it harder to develop and sustain collective efficacy. However, he saw William Julius Wilson's theory that the troubles of poor black families in northern cities were due to the loss of factory jobs as too narrow and incapable of explaining the variations in crime rates among Chicago's black neighborhoods that he and his colleagues had uncovered.

A common theme in the *Times* toward the end of the 1990s was the idea that community leaders and voluntary organizations needed to work hand-in-hand with the local police to reduce crime. Reporter Bob Herbert wrote in an op-ed piece that "[b]ig-city residents fed up with the violence that has plagued their lives and stolen so many of their children are exhibiting a greater willingness to become involved in anti-crime initiatives, and to work both directly and indirectly with the police" (October 2, 1997: A19). According to Chuck Wexler of the Police Executive Research Forum, "What is significant is when you have an ad hoc community group in Kansas City, or the ministers' Ten-Point Coalition in Boston standing shoulder to shoulder with the police in a particular neighborhood, say this isn't simply a police problem, this is a community problem. That is what is most effective" (cited in October 2, 1997: A19). Referring to community members who were involved in such efforts as "the forgotten heroes in this war against crime," Jack Levin interpreted Boston's success in fighting youth violence as follows:

> You can't evaluate in any quantitative way the contribution of the community vs. the police vs. demographics vs. locking people up. But my sense is that in Boston it is the community members who have made the biggest difference. The clergy is doing an outstanding job. They provide spiritual guidance, but they also supervise and monitor and guide these kids who otherwise would be raising themselves after school. (cited in October 2, 1997: A19)

In a *Times* op-ed piece, sociologists Orlando Patterson and Christopher Winship described the principles of Boston's approach as follows:

> First, inner-city violence should be dealt with primarily as a crime problem, rather than as a symptom of poverty, poor schools, broken families and the like. Second, there is agreement that only a small percentage of youths are at the core of the problem and that the community can help to identify them. Third, the community leadership should have an informal say in the decision to arrest certain teenagers (for instance, in cases of first offenses or when there are extenuating circumstances). Finally, if the police behave badly, they bear the full brunt of responsibility. (March 3, 1999: A17)

A pilot program using this model was initiated in 1999 in the Bedford-Stuyvesant area of Brooklyn to convince parolees and probationers suspected of gang violence to find jobs or get job training. Gang members were offered help in accomplishing these goals, and warned that if they were arrested or violated the conditions of their parole or probation, they would be punished as severely as possible, even for minor offenses (October 13, 1999: B8).

One place where local residents and law-enforcement officials have collaborated is Jacksonville, Florida. Prosecutor Harry Shorstein held weekly meetings with representatives of the police, the school board, the state child protective service organization, local hospitals, and a psychologist to share information on children between the ages of 6 and 15 who had committed crimes or gotten into serious trouble at school. Parents of the most troublesome children were urged to sign a contract placing their child under the supervision of Shorstein's office for one year, in lieu of court action. The children were required to attend school, provided with extra tutoring, and taught to control their anger; their parents had to attend parenting classes; and the family was assigned a volunteer mentor who could visit the home to monitor the child. Warrants were sometimes issued against parents who did not keep their children in school, though Shorstein tried to get parents to resolve problems before issuing warrants. Junior high school students were taken to court to see a trial and to jail to be lectured by young inmates on the hard life behind bars. Older adolescents who had been convicted in a criminal court were kept in a wing of the county jail apart from adult inmates, rather than sent to a state prison. There they received schooling, sex and drug education, and counseling. Juveniles who completed Shorstein's program without bad conduct reports had their criminal convictions withheld from their records, and therefore did not have to report the convictions to prospective employers. This strategy apparently had an impact, because juvenile crime decreased earlier and more substantially in Jacksonville than elsewhere in the country. Criminologist David Rasmussen attributed this success to the "interrelatedness" of the approach: "The whole, I suspect, is much greater than the sum of its parts" (cited in October 4, 1997: A7).

There are no studies that show that the communities that had the largest increases in the number of voluntary organizations or citizen participation in such organizations during the 1990s were also the ones that experienced the biggest declines in crime rates. In fact, some researchers have found that the high-crime communities most in need of such changes are the very ones where they are least likely to occur. The apparent successes in Boston and Jacksonville do suggest that community collaboration with law enforcement might reduce crime rates.

Conclusion

There is little evidence that crime rates fell in the 1990s because of increases in the legitimacy of the family, the economic system, or the political system.

Five of the six indicators examined in this chapter showed a continuation during the 1990s of a long-term decline in family legitimacy: Out-of-wedlock births increased, unmarried-couple households with children under 15 became more common, the proportion of married women with young children who worked in the paid labor force increased, the proportion of children living with both parents dropped, and the percentage of 3- and 4-year-olds enrolled in school grew. The only indication of an increase in family legitimacy was the continuation of a decline in the divorce rate that began in the early 1980s, and which might have contributed to lower age-specific crime rates for those who entered their crime-prone years in the 1990s.

There is also little reason to think that an increase in the legitimacy of the economic system caused the initial decline in crime rates, though some of the data suggest that economic factors might have reinforced the downward trend once it began. Confidence in big business and organized labor grew, but not until several years after crime rates had begun to fall. The unemployment rate first declined in 1993, one year later than the first decline in crime rates, and this could have contributed to the continued reduction in crime rates. However, other time periods have had similar reductions in unemployment rates without experiencing declining crime rates. The poverty rate began to fall shortly after crime rates had started to drop, perhaps reinforcing the downward trend in crime rates. Median hourly wages for young males improved, but again only several years after crime rates had started to fall. Income inequality continued to increase in the 1990s, contrary to what LaFree's theory suggests. Inflation diminished just before crime rates started to decline, but more research is needed to determine if this change affected the involvement in crime of people with low and fixed incomes.

Changes in political legitimacy cannot account for the decline in crime rates. Neither trust in the political system nor attitudes toward government officials changed in the 1990s in ways that can explain falling crime rates. Civil case filings actually increased until 1996, contrary to LaFree's theory, then declined slightly from 1996 to 1999, well after crime rates had begun to fall. Measures of voter registration and turnout also provide no support for the idea that political legitimacy increased in the 1990s.

Changes in religion, communities, and voluntary organizations might be associated with the decline in crime rates. The Gallup Index of Leading Religious Indicators reveals that religiosity increased after 1993, suggesting that it might have reinforced the downward trend in crime rates that began two years earlier. There is no evidence of any increase during the 1990s in the number of voluntary organizations or participation in such organizations that might account for the decline in crime rates, but this possibility warrants further study.

10 Why Did Crime Rates Fall in the 1990s?

Whatever caused crime rates to fall in the 1990s saved tens of thousands of lives and millions of dollars' worth of property. Knowledge of what caused the decline could lead to the development of measures to reduce rates even more, or at least keep them at the comparatively low levels that prevailed at the end of the millennium. An understanding of what caused rates to drop could also be used to predict future trends and prepare for, or even avert, impending increases in crime.

A daily reader of the *New York Times* might have concluded that the decline in the New York City's crime rate in the 1990s was unique. However, the rest of the country, especially its largest cities, also experienced falling crime rates, though reductions elsewhere began a little later and were a bit smaller than those in the nation's biggest city. Even without New York City's contribution, and even without the contribution of all cities with more than one million people, the nation's crime rates would have fallen in impressive fashion. That decline was not due to a decrease in the reporting of crime to the police, nor to police manipulation of crime statistics. The rise and fall of crime rates also cannot be explained by natural cycles. Such fluctuations simply alert criminologists to the need to investigate and understand the factors that cause rates to change.

Murder, robbery, and motor vehicle theft rates fell in tandem after 1991. Burglary rates also dropped, but that decline was a continuation of a trend that had started a decade earlier. The parallel decline in all four rates suggests that some common forces pushed them all down. Different factors could have accounted for the decline in each crime rate, but it seems unlikely that, for instance, more effective gun-control measures reduced murders, more intensive police patrols cut robberies, more use of dead-bolt locks curbed burglaries, and more installation of car-alarm systems decreased motor vehicle thefts, and that all such effects happened to occur at the same time. However, changes specific to each indicator crime might have reinforced downward trends that were primarily the result of broad changes affecting all four crimes.

Political leaders and law-enforcement officials are less interested in understanding the reasons that crime rates fall than in claiming personal credit for any decline. When rates rise, they typically point the finger at others or blame social forces beyond their control. New York City's situation in the mid-1990s was unusual because NYPD Commissioner Bratton effectively used the news media to tout the success of his crime-prevention policies, rather than defer to Mayor Giuliani, who expected to get credit for making the city safer. The clash between Bratton and Giuliani was precipitated by their narrow focus on the role of the police in cutting crime rates, a parochial perspective that characterizes political discourse in times of falling crime rates, and one that contrasts with criminology's emphasis on the use of evidence to assess the relative contribution of multiple factors to changes in crime rates.

Regression analysis is a statistical tool for measuring the relative impact of several independent variables (such as the number of police officers per capita, incarceration rates, and unemployment rates) on a dependent variable (such as the crime rate). Research using regression analysis has been cited throughout this book, but the method could not be used to determine the precise contribution of each independent variable to the decline in crime rates. What appears to be a single independent variable is sometimes actually a series of variables, not all of which are easily quantified. For example, a regression analysis to determine what has caused crime rates to fall should include an independent variable for the police. The most easily quantified variable is the number of officers per capita, but that measure is not associated with crime rates. Directed patrols do seem to have an impact on crime, but there are no statistical measures of how that type of policing varies from department to department. Other independent variables that apparently affect crime rates but defy easy measurement are age-specific rates of criminal behavior (as opposed to age-specific rates of arrest), the number of firearms in the hands of crime-prone segments of the population, and patterns of drug use. One problem with regression analysis is that the simplification of independent variables can obscure their impact on the dependent variable. For example, the influence of the age structure on crime rates has been tested by using the proportion of the population between the ages of 15 and 24, but that measure does not reveal how many people are at the high or low end of that age range, nor does it provide any information on the age distribution of the rest of the population.

The Police

The per capita size of a city's police force does not affect its crime rate, nor do the number of patrol cars or foot patrols. Community policing has no demonstrated impact on crime rates, though the strategic deployment of police resources against specific targets can curb crime under some circumstances. The perception of an increased threat of being stopped or arrested might reduce serious crime by deterring facilitating offenses, such as the unlicensed carrying of firearms or the possession and sale of drugs. New York City's decline in firearm homicides and firearm robberies in the mid-1990s could have been due, at least in part, to the quality-of-life initiative, which raised the risk that people carrying guns would be stopped by the police for minor infractions such as turnstile jumping or drinking alcoholic beverages in public. However, cities other than New York where the police did not deal aggressively with quality-of-life offenses also saw their crime rates drop.

The risk of arrest for those who committed indicator crimes did not increase much in the 1990s, suggesting that greater police effectiveness was not the reason that the prison population expanded. Increasing police attention to drug and firearm offenses in the 1990s might have deterred murders and robberies, but it is doubtful that such measures contributed to the declines in burglaries and motor vehicle thefts. The economic boom of the 1990s could have strengthened any deterrent effect resulting from directed patrols and problem-oriented policing if potential offenders were more easily dissuaded from committing crime because they weighed the costs of arrest against the benefits of legitimate work differently than they would have at a time when confidence in the economy was less, jobs scarcer, and wages lower.

The Prisons

The courts became harsher in their sentencing in the 1990s, sending a growing proportion of offenders to prison and imposing longer terms of confinement. Parole boards became less willing to release inmates, and some jurisdictions eliminated parole altogether. These changes led to a burgeoning prison population and rising correctional costs, but they also contributed to a substantial reduction in crime rates.

Applying the low-end estimate of elasticity to the number of crimes averted by the decline in crime rates during the 1990s shows that at least 10,800 murders, 2,176,000 robberies, 738,000 burglaries, and 748,000 motor vehicle thefts were prevented over the course of the decade by the incarceration of additional offenders. The offense rates of the additional prisoners that would have produced such reductions were two to eight crimes per year, well below the twelve to twenty-five range of offense rates derived from prisoner self-report surveys and arrest data. This is consistent with the assumption that criminals still on the street commit fewer crimes than inmates did when they were free. Unlike some of the other explanations for the decline in crime rates, such as drug patrols or gun-control laws, the increase in the incarceration rate can account for the decreases in all four crime indicators.

The increasing threat of imprisonment probably contributed to a growing unwillingness of young people to become or remain drug users and dealers. Ethnographic research indicates that in the years before crime rates fell, crack was increasingly seen as a drug with devastating consequences for sellers and users, their families, and their communities. The costs associated with imprisonment for the sale and possession of crack might have been even more important than the physiological effects of the drug or the systemic impact of the drug trade in causing young people to turn away from crack.

Incarceration interacts with other factors to affect crime rates. Imprisonment might be most effective in preventing crime when unemployment rates are low, as they were throughout much of the 1990s, because the threat of being locked up is probably a more effective deterrent when jobs are readily available. There is evidence that arrest for domestic violence is a more effective deterrent for employed men than for unemployed ones, probably because the costs of crime relative to its benefits are greatest when the economic situation is most favorable (Berk et al., 1992; Pate and Hamilton, 1992; Sherman, 1992b, 1992c). Incarceration might also have a greater impact on crime rates in a full-employment economy because more tax revenue is available for building prisons and housing prisoners. Complicating the incarceration-crime-unemployment relationship is the possibility that a high rate of incarceration keeps unemployment rates lower than they would be otherwise by removing from the labor force many of those who traditionally have been both the most likely to be out of work and the most likely to commit indicator crimes: young, uneducated, unskilled, minority-group males (Currie, 1999).

Drugs

The waxing and waning of drug epidemics is a function of changing tastes among users who seek new sources of stimulation as old ones lose their appeal. Drug use is also influenced by police aggressiveness in dealing with certain drugs, the penalties enacted by legislatures and meted out by the courts, and the willingness of parole boards to release inmates. Criminal justice measures can deter the sale and use of drugs by raising the cost of continued participation in the drug trade. The shift of many youths from crack to marijuana around 1990 was probably influenced more by stringent law-enforcement measures aimed specifically at crack than by the violence, AIDS, and overdoses associated with the drug. The strength of the drug–crime relationship varies by age, with the association between drug use and the commission of index offenses being stronger for adolescents than adults (Menard, Mihalic, and Huizinga, 2001). This might be because youths are more likely to lack the financial resources available to older drug users, and therefore must rely more on property crimes to pay for drugs. Demographic change that results in a larger number of people between the ages of 15 and 24 could thus increase the overall crime rate, even if the total amount of drug use in the population remains the same, because a larger number of youthful drug users will generate more crime. Shifts in the population that increase the relative size of older age groups would reduce the overall crime rate, because older drug users are less likely to commit crimes.

From about 1984 to 1991, participants in the crack trade were responsible for a high proportion of the murders and robberies in the nation's largest cities, more because of the systemic effects of the trade than because of the psychopharmacological or economic-compulsive aspects of crack use. The shift from a highly competitive, freelance, open-air crack trade to a more tightly organized, business-like, indoor trade reduced violent crime because dealers became less apt to fight over turf and more reluctant to jeopardize their profits by attracting police attention. The possession and use of firearms became less necessary in the more settled crack trade, contributing to the reduction in murders and robberies, as well as a drop in the proportion of those crimes committed with guns. Because firearms are rarely used by burglars and motor vehicle thieves, changes in the possession and use of firearms resulting from reorganization of the crack market had little or no impact on those property crimes. Because the declines in burglary and motor vehicle theft rates paralleled the decreases in murder and robbery rates, factors other than changes in the crack trade must also have contributed to the drop in crime rates in the 1990s.

Stronger institutions can reduce crime rates indirectly by curbing the use of drugs associated with crime. The greater availability of jobs might dissuade marginally committed users from continuing to consume drugs. In addition, young people who otherwise would have entered a drug subculture may be attracted to legitimate jobs. Increases in the strength of the family, the political system, and religion can attach people to groups with conventional standards that dissuade them from beginning or continuing to use drugs. Evidence indicates that changes in the economy and religion in the 1990s might have reduced drug use and the crime associated with it, but there is little reason to think that changes in the family or the political system had such effects.

Firearms

Changes in the possession, carrying, and use of firearms in the 1990s cannot explain the falling rates of burglary and motor vehicle theft, but might account for some of the decline in homicide and robbery rates. Studies done in several cities suggest that intensive police patrols focused on suspicious people and places can reduce violent crime, but the precise means by which they do so is unclear. Even though gun-control laws that target crime-prone groups, ban handgun sales, and license gun dealers prevent some violent crimes, potential offenders who are denied the right to buy guns from retail outlets often find them from other sources. Because some potential offenders who cannot buy guns legitimately are also unable to obtain them from illicit sources, laws such as the Brady Act might have reinforced the downward trend in murder and robbery rates in the 1990s.

Because guns can be stolen or purchased cheaply from illicit sources, economic prosperity probably has little direct effect on firearm ownership by crime-prone groups, but economic conditions might affect gun ownership indirectly. A booming economy that allocates more resources for the criminal justice system could reduce firearm ownership by incarcerating for longer terms a larger number of serious offenders, taking people off the street who are especially likely to own, carry, and use guns. More jobs that offer high wages and opportunities for advancement could attract young people who otherwise would have become drug dealers or users. If the drug subculture they would have become part of involves systemic violence, the opportunity for legitimate employment could indirectly reduce murders and robberies by decreasing the number of armed drug dealers and users.

Age Structure

Shrinkage in the relative size of the 15- to 24-year-old age group accounted for a modest portion of the decline in crime rates from 1990 to 1999. The small decrease in the relative size of that crime-prone age group slightly reduced the number of potential recruits to the crack trade, possibly curbing drug-related violence to some degree. In theory, this drop in the relative size of the crime-prone age group could have pushed crime rates higher by reducing the overall risk of incarceration: Youthful offenders are less apt than older ones to be imprisoned because the law treats them as juveniles and they have not yet accumulated a sufficiently serious criminal record to warrant a prison term. However, the dramatic upsurge in incarceration that began in 1973 and continued unabated throughout the 1990s overwhelmed any tendency for the small shrinkage in the crime-prone age group to increase crime rates by reducing the overall incapacitative and deterrent effects of incarceration.

Institutions and Community

Most evidence contradicts the claim that crime rates fell in the 1990s because of increases in the legitimacy of the family and the political system. Changes in the legitimacy of the economic system and religion may well have reinforced the downward trend in crime rates, but they apparently did not initiate it.

The only indicator of family legitimacy possibly associated with falling crime rates is the post-1980 drop in divorce rates, which could have improved socialization, social control, and protection by families and could have reduced the age-specific offense rates of children born in the 1980s who entered their crime-prone years in the 1990s. Such an effect could have reinforced the decline in crime rates, but it came too late to account for the initial decline from 1991 to 1992. The legitimacy of the family could be associated with the age structure of the population in the following way: During periods of low family legitimacy, low birth rates might prevail, reducing the size of the crime-prone age group years later and thereby depressing the overall crime rate at that time. In recent decades, family legitimacy has probably been undermined by the high rate of incarceration, which makes effective child-rearing more difficult by taking parents away from their children, possibly leading to higher crime rates when those children enter their crime-prone years. Crack use by parents could also have weakened the socialization, social control, and protection of children, though eventually it led the children and siblings of users to develop anti-crack attitudes and refrain from drug use or opt for marijuana, which is associated with a lower level of criminal behavior.

Confidence in the economic system grew and unemployment and poverty rates fell soon after crime rates started to decline, suggesting that even though an improving economy did not cause the initial decline in crime rates, it probably reinforced the downward trend. Improvement in the economy probably strengthened families in which parents found jobs, encouraged young people to seek conventional work rather than commit crimes or sell drugs, and changed youths' attitudes. However, increasing income inequality and minimal change in the hourly wages of young males indicate that in the 1990s the economic picture did not improve for everyone, especially disadvantaged groups with traditionally high crime rates. The impact of the low and declining level of inflation on criminal behavior by welfare recipients is unclear, but any impact of inflation on the elderly (the other major group living on fixed incomes) did not affect the overall crime rate much.

According to LaFree's theory, the legitimacy of the political system should have increased in the 1990s as crime rates fell. In fact, political trust and attitudes toward government officials did not improve, registration to vote and voter turnout did not increase, and the small change in civil case filings had no apparent effect on crime rates.

Two factors not incorporated in LaFree's theory are religiosity and community. The legitimacy of religion began to increase shortly after crime rates started to fall, suggesting that increased religiosity might have contributed to the continued decline in rates, though it did not initiate it. There is no compelling evidence that citizen participation in crime-fighting voluntary organizations increased in the 1990s, or that such a change could account for the decline in crime rates even if it had occurred. A few case studies do suggest that community collaboration with the police might prevent crime.

Understanding the Causes of the Decline in Crime Rates

This study began with a question: What caused the unprecedented decline in crime rates during the 1990s? Because of delays in conducting and publishing scholarly research, I turned to the *New York Times* for explanations. Some were offered by criminologists, and others by law-enforcement officials, political officeholders, and community leaders. Hypotheses about why crime rates had fallen were then assessed using published research and available police and government data.

How did the explanations of the drop in crime rates presented in the *Times* measure up against the evidence? The paper's repeated attribution of the reduction in rates to measures taken by the New York Police Department is not supported by research. The emphasis on this explanation was probably the result of the skillful use of the press by Commissioner Bratton and Mayor Giuliani to achieve their personal and organizational goals. The *Times* underestimated the impact of the rising rate of incarceration, rarely mentioning the possibility that the expansion in the inmate population had curbed crime through incapacitation and deterrence. More frequently expressed was the view that if crime rates were declining, the inmate population should be shrinking. The *Times* also gave limited attention to the possible effect on crime rates of declining unemployment and growing confidence in the economic system. These factors were rarely cited until crime rates had been falling for six or seven years.

The strongest aspect of the *Times*'s explanation of the decline in crime rates was its emphasis on changes in drug use and the drug market. In-depth consideration of criminologists' research on this issue was nicely supplemented with interview material from community leaders, local residents, and drug users. In contrast, the paper's discussion of the effects of shifts in the age structure was weak. By relying on a few criminologists who warned of an impending increase in crime rates that would result from growth of the crime-prone age group, rather than showing how changes in the age structure had already contributed modestly to the decline in crime rates, the *Times* conveyed the message that rather than be pleased that they were safer, people should instead be worrying that they would soon be in grave danger. Contrary to the criminologists' prediction that crime rates would rise substantially after 1995, rates had not increased by mid-2001. The discussion of the age–crime relationship in the *Times* rarely mentioned the rate at which people of any given age committed crime, emphasizing instead how many people of different ages there were in the population. Both age-specific crime rates and the relative size of the various age groups affect the overall crime rate.

On the basis of the evidence examined in this book, I believe that the rising rate of incarceration was probably the most important reason that crime rates fell after 1991. The expansion of the inmate population certainly incurred exorbitant costs, both in terms of its disastrous impact on the lives of offenders and their families and in terms of the huge expenditure of tax revenue on prison construction and the custodial care of inmates. The incarceration rate is, however, the only factor explored here that changed in the expected direction before the downward trend in crime rates began, and the only one that a substantial body of research has shown to influence crime rates. Indeed, it would be quite surprising if the imprisonment of half a million more prisoners in 1999 than in 1990 had not affected crime rates.

Systemic changes in the crack market and the shift of drug users from crack to marijuana also account for some of the decline in crime rates. These changes could have partly been the result of police anti-drug measures, but more important were the harsher sentences mandated by legislatures and imposed by the courts. Drug use and drug markets were also affected by factors other than the criminal justice system, including the self-limiting nature of violence in the crack trade and the attraction of potential users and dealers to the legitimate jobs that were increasingly available.

Rising confidence in the economic system and an improving employment picture, and perhaps the small growth in young men's wages and decreasing inflation, contributed to the drop in crime rates, though they did not initiate the decline. Economic improvement worked in combination with a rising risk of imprisonment to convince members of crime-prone demographic groups to choose legitimate work over criminal sources of income.

Other changes that apparently had modest effects on the downward trend in crime rates were shifts in the age structure, the long-term decline in the divorce rate, the increase in religiosity, and perhaps a decrease in the carrying and use of firearms by young, minority-group males living in large cities. Change in the relative size of different age groups contributed modestly to the reduction in crime, but the decline in the rates at which all age groups committed crime was more important. That decline was apparently due to the incapacitative and deterrent effects of the rising rate of incarceration, changes in drug use and the drug market, and improvements in the economy. Increased religiosity might have reinforced the downward trend in crime rates, but more research is needed to determine its precise impact. Direct evidence that fewer members of crime-prone demographic groups were carrying and using firearms is sparse, but the rapid decline in handgun homicides among such groups and the reduced incentive to carry guns once the crack market had stabilized suggest that such a change could have reduced homicides and robberies, though not burglaries and motor vehicle thefts.

The policy implications of these conclusions is not obvious. People in the United States were certainly safer in 1999 than in 1990. About 34,000 people who were alive at the end of 1999 would have been killed during the decade had homicide rates not fallen. This increased safety has, however, come at a cost: Years of offenders' lives have been wasted behind bars at great financial cost to taxpayers, and members of inmates' families have suffered, perhaps in ways that increased their own chances of committing crime. Few question the advantages of a low unemployment rate, but policies to achieve and maintain such a rate are less clear. Drug use patterns vary over time, but little is known about which policies are most effective in reducing drug use, or, more subtly, in shifting users from drugs more associated with crime to those less associated with crime. My hope is that this book contributes to an understanding of why crime rates declined in the 1990s, and that it will generate thoughtful discussion of why rates fell and how they can be kept down or further reduced.

APPENDIX

William Spelman's (2000a) method of determining the impact of incarceration on crime can be illustrated with the change in the murder rate from 1991 to 1992. Over this time the number of state and federal prisoners per 100,000 people rose from 313 to 332, a 6.1 percent increase. If an elasticity of −.2 is used, this growth in incarceration is expected to produce a −1.22 (= 6.1 × −.2) percent drop in the murder rate. Thus, the 1992 murder rate should be .988 (= 1 − .012) of what it was in 1991, based solely on the effect of the growth in incarceration. Next, the impact on the actual murder rate of all factors other than the growth in the incarceration rate is calculated by dividing the change in the murder rate by the effect of incarceration on that rate. From 1991 to 1992, the murder rate per 100,000 people fell from 9.8 to 9.3, a 5.1 percent decline. In other words, the 1992 rate was .949 (= 1 − .051) of 1991's rate. Dividing .949 (the change in the murder rate) by .988 (the effect of the change in the incarceration rate on the murder rate) produces a figure of .961. This figure means that had the 1991–1992 expansion in the prison population not taken place, the murder rate in 1992 would have been 96.1 percent of what it was in 1991. In other words, the murder rate would have decreased by 3.9 percent from 1991 to 1992 even if the incarceration rate had not changed. Finally, the annual estimates (such as .961) of the effects of all nonprison factors on changes in murder rates are multiplied by each other to arrive at an estimate of what the murder rate would have been at the end of a period of time had there been no expansion in the prison population.

The first column in Table A.1 shows the effect of all nonprison factors on changes in rates of the indicator crimes for the 1990s. These numbers are derived by multiplying the net effects of nonprison factors for each year in the decade. The second column is the net effect of changing incarceration rates on the crime rates; this is 1 minus the value in the first column. The third column shows the actual change in per capita crime rates from 1990 to 1999. The figures in the fourth column are calculated by subtracting the percentage change in the crime rate attributable to changing incarceration (the second column) from the percentage change in the actual crime rate (the third column), and then dividing the difference by the percentage change in the actual crime rate (the third column).

TABLE A.1   Estimated Changes in Indicator Crime Rates as a Result of Changes in Incarceration Rates, 1990–1999

	Effect of nonprison factors	Effect of prison	Change in crime rate	% of rate change due to prison
Elasticity = –.2				
Murder	73.1%	26.9%	–39.4%	31.7%
Robbery	71.9%	28.1%	–41.6%	32.4%
Burglary	67.3%	32.7%	–37.7%	13.3%
Motor vehicle theft	74.5%	25.5%	–36.0%	29.1%
Elasticity = –.4				
Murder	81.7%	18.3%	–39.4%	53.5%
Robbery	80.4%	19.6%	–41.6%	52.8%
Burglary	75.2%	24.8%	–37.7%	34.3%
Motor vehicle theft	83.2%	16.8%	–36.0%	53.4%

Sources: Based on methods used in William Spelman, "The Limited Importance of Prison Expansion," in Alfred Blumstein and Joel Wallman, eds., *The Crime Drop in America.* Cambridge, UK: Cambridge University Press, 2000, pp. 104–108; and data from Kathleen Maguire and Ann L. Pastore, eds., *Sourcebook of Criminal Justice Statistics 2000.* (Online: www.albany.edu/sourcebook [February 2, 2001])

BIBLIOGRAPHY

Abrahamse, Allan. *The Coming Crime Wave of Violence in California*. Santa Monica, CA: Rand, 1997.

Agnew, Robert, et al. "A New Test of Classic Strain Theory," *Justice Quarterly* 13 (December 1996), 475–499.

Andenaes, Johannes. *Punishment and Deterrence*. Ann Arbor: University of Michigan Press, 1974.

Anderson, Dennis B., Randall E. Schumacker, and Sara L. Anderson. "Releasee Characteristics and Parole," *Journal of Offender Rehabilitation* 17 (1991), 133–145.

Austin, James, and John Irwin. *Who Goes to Prison?* San Francisco: National Council on Crime and Delinquency, 1990.

———, et al. "The Use of Incarceration in the United States," *Criminologist* (May/June 2001), 14–16.

Baumer, Eric. "Poverty, Crack, and Crime: A Cross-City Analysis," *Journal of Research in Crime and Delinquency* 31 (August 1994), 311–327.

———, et al. "The Influence of Crack Cocaine on Robbery, Burglary, and Homicide Rates: A Cross-City, Longitudinal Analysis," *Journal of Research in Crime and Delinquency* 35 (August 1998), 316–340.

Baumgartner, Frank R., and Bryan D. Jones. *Agendas and Instability in American Politics*. Chicago: University of Chicago Press, 1993.

Bayley, David H. *Police for the Future*. New York: Oxford University Press, 1994.

Beck, Allen, et al. *Survey of State Prison Inmates 1991*. Washington, DC: U.S. Department of Justice, 1993.

Benda, Brent B., and Robert Flynn Corwyn. "Religion and Delinquency: The Relationship after Considering Family and Peer Influences," *Journal for the Scientific Study of Religion* 36 (March 1997), 81–92.

Berk, Richard A., and Phyllis J. Newton. "Does Arrest Really Deter Wife Battery? An Effort to Replicate the Findings of the Minneapolis Spouse Abuse Experiment," *American Sociological Review* 50 (April 1985), 253–262.

———, et al. "A Bayesian Analysis of the Colorado Springs Spouse Abuse Experiment," *Journal of Criminal Law and Criminology* 83 (Spring 1992), 170–200.

Berkowitz, Leonard, and Anthony LePage. "Weapons as Aggression-Eliciting Stimuli," *Journal of Personality and Social Psychology* 7 (1967), 202–207.

Bernard, Thomas J., and R. Richard Ritti. "The Philadelphia Birth Cohort and Selective Incapacitation," *Journal of Research in Crime and Delinquency* 28 (February 1991), 33–54.

Bjerregaard, Beth, and Allan J. Lizotte. "Gun Ownership and Gang Membership," *Journal of Criminal Law and Criminology* 86 (1995), 37–58.

Black, Dan, and Daniel Nagin. "Do 'Right to Carry' Laws Reduce Violent Crime?" *Journal of Legal Studies* 27 (1998), 209–219.

Blau, Judith, and Peter Blau. "The Cost of Inequality: Metropolitan Structure and Violent Crime," *American Sociological Review* 47 (February 1982), 114–129.

Block, Michael K. *An Economic Analysis of Theft with Special Emphasis on Household Decisions under Uncertainty.* Ph.D. Dissertation, Department of Economics. Stanford, CA: Stanford University, 1972.

Blumstein, Alfred. "Disaggregating the Violence Trends," in Alfred Blumstein and Joel Wallman, eds., *The Crime Drop in America.* Cambridge, UK: Cambridge University Press, 2000, pp. 13–44.

———. "Prisons," in James Q. Wilson and Joan Petersilia, eds., *Crime.* San Francisco: ICS Press, 1995a, pp. 387–419.

———. "Violence by Young People: Why the Deadly Nexus," *National Institute of Justice Journal* (August 1995b), 2–9.

———, and Allen J. Beck, "Population Growth in U.S. Prisons, 1980–1996," in Michael Tonry and Joan Petersilia, eds., *Prisons,* vol. 26 of *Crime and Justice: A Review of Research.* Chicago: University of Chicago Press, 1999, pp. 17–61.

———, David P. Farrington, and Soumyo Moitra. "Delinquency Careers: Innocents, Desisters, and Persisters," in Michael Tonry and Norval Morris, eds., *Crime and Justice: An Annual Review of Research,* vol. 6. Chicago: University of Chicago Press, 1985, pp. 187–219.

———, and Richard Rosenfeld. "Explaining Recent Trends in U.S. Homicide Rates," *Journal of Criminal Law and Criminology* 88 (Summer 1998), 1175–1216.

Bouza, Tony. "NYPD Blues: Good, Lucky, or Both?" *Law Enforcement News* (January 31, 1997), 8–10.

Bowers, William J., and J. H. Hirsch. "The Impact of Foot Patrol Staffing on Crime and Disorder in Boston: An Unmet Promise," *American Journal of Police* 6 (1987), 17–44.

Boydstun, John E. *San Diego Field Interrogation: Final Report.* Washington, DC: Police Foundation, 1975.

Boyum, David. *Reflections on Economic Theory and Drug Enforcement.* Ph.D. Dissertation. Cambridge, MA: Harvard University, 1992.

———, and Mark A. R. Kleiman. "Alcohol and Other Drugs," in James Q. Wilson and Joan Petersilia, eds., *Crime.* San Francisco: ICS Press, 1995, pp. 295–326.

Braga, Anthony A., et al. "Problem-Oriented Policing, Deterrence, and Youth Violence: An Evaluation of Boston's Operation Ceasefire," *Journal of Research in Crime and Delinquency* 38 (August 2001), 195–225.

———, et al. "Problem-Oriented Policing in Violent Crime Places: A Randomized Controlled Experiment," *Criminology* 37 (August 1999), 541–580.

Bratton, William, and W. Andrews. "A Good Police State," *New York Daily News,* May 2, 1999, p. 44.

———, and George L. Kelling. "Putting Police Officers Back on the Beat," *Boston Sunday Globe,* February 14, 1993, p. A2.

————, with Peter Knobler. *Turnaround: How America's Top Cop Reversed the Crime Epidemic.* New York: Random House, 1998.

Brown, Lee P., and Mary Ann Wycoff. "Policing Houston: Reducing Fear and Improving Service," *Crime and Delinquency* 33 (January 1987), 71–89.

Brownstein, Henry H. *The Rise and Fall of a Violent Crime Wave: Crack Cocaine and the Social Construction of a Crime Problem.* Guilderland, NY: Harrow and Heston, 1996.

Bureau of Labor Statistics. *Highlights of Women's Earnings in 1999.* Washington, DC: U.S. Department of Labor, May 2000. (Online: www.bls.gov/pdf/cpswom99/pdf [June 5, 2001])

Bushway, Shawn D. "The Impact of an Arrest on the Job Stability of Young White American Men," *Journal of Research in Crime and Delinquency* 35 (November 1998), 454–479.

Cappell, Charles L., and Gresham Sykes. "Prison Commitments, Crime, and Unemployment: A Theoretical and Empirical Specification for the United States, 1933–1985," *Journal of Quantitative Criminology* 7 (1991), 155–199.

Centers for Disease Control and Prevention. *Fatal Firearm Injuries in the United States, 1962–1994.* Atlanta: Centers for Disease Control and Prevention, 1997.

————. *Nonfatal and Fatal Firearm-Related Injuries—United States, 1993–1997.* Atlanta: Centers for Disease Control and Prevention, November 19, 1999. (Online: www.cdc.gov/mmwr/preview/mmwrhtml/mm4845a1.htm [May 11, 2001])

Chaiken, Jan M., and Marcia R. Chaiken. "Drugs and Predatory Crime," in Michael Tonry and James Q. Wilson, eds., *Drugs and Crime,* vol. 13 of *Crime and Justice: A Review of Research.* Chicago: University of Chicago Press, 1990, pp. 203–239.

Chiricos, Theodore G. "Rates of Crime and Unemployment: An Analysis of Aggregate Research Evidence," *Social Problems* 34 (April 1987), 187–211.

Clark, Gerald. "What Happens When the Police Strike," *New York Times,* November 16, 1969, sec. 6, pp. 45, 176–185, 187, 194–195.

Cochran, John K., Peter B. Wood, and Bruce J. Arneklev. "Is the Religiosity-Delinquency Relationship Spurious? A Test of Arousal and Social Control Theories," *Journal of Research in Crime and Delinquency* 31 (February 1994), 92–123.

Cohen, Jacqueline. *Incapacitating Criminals: Recent Research Findings.* Washington, DC: National Institute of Justice, U.S. Department of Justice, December 1983a.

————. "Incapacitation as a Strategy for Crime Control: Possibilities and Pitfalls," in Michael Tonry and Norval Morris, eds., *Crime and Justice: An Annual Review of Research,* vol. 5. Chicago: University of Chicago Press, 1983b, pp. 1–84.

Cohen, Lawrence E., and Kenneth C. Land. "Age Structure and Crime: Symmetry versus Asymmetry and the Projection of Crime Rates through the 1990s," *American Sociological Review* 52 (April 1987), 170–183.

Cook, Philip J. "The Influence of Gun Availability on Violent Crime Patterns," in Michael Tonry and Norval Morris, eds., *Crime and Justice: An Annual Review of Research,* vol. 4. Chicago: University of Chicago Press, 1983, pp. 49–89.

———. "Reducing Injury and Death Rates in Robbery," *Policy Analysis* 6 (1980), 21–45.

———, and Jens Ludwig. *Gun Violence: The Real Costs.* New York: Oxford University Press, 2000.

Cosgrove, Colleen A., and Mary Ann Wycoff. "Investigations in the Community Policing Context," in Corina Sole Brito and Tracy Allan, eds., *Problem Oriented Policing: Crime-Specific Problems, Critical Issues and Making POP Work,* vol. 2. Washington, DC: Police Executive Research Forum, 1999, pp. 151–176.

Cullen, Francis T., Bonnie S. Fisher, and Brandon K. Applegate. "Public Opinion about Punishment and Corrections," in Michael Tonry, ed., *Crime and Justice: A Review of Research,* vol. 27. Chicago: University of Chicago Press, 2000, pp. 1–79.

Currie, Elliott. *Crime and Punishment in America.* New York: Holt, 1998.

———. "Reflections on Crime and Criminology at the Millennium" *Western Criminological Review* 2 (1999). (Online: wcr.sonoma.edu/v2n1/currie.html [December 17, 2001])

Curtis, Richard. "The Improbable Transformation of Inner-City Neighborhoods: Crime, Violence, Drugs, and Youth in the 1990s," *Journal of Criminal Law and Criminology* 88 (Summer 1998), 1233–1276.

Danziger, Sheldon, and David Wheeler. "The Economics of Crime: Punishment or Income Redistribution," *Review of Social Economy* 33 (October 1975), 113–131.

Decker, Scott, and Barbara Salert. "Predicting the Career Criminal: An Empirical Test of the Greenwood Scale," *Journal of Criminal Law and Criminology* 77 (Spring 1986), 215–236.

———, Susan Pennel, and Ann Caldwell. *Illegal Firearms: Access and Use by Arrestees.* Washington, DC: U.S. Department of Justice, 1997.

DeFronzo, James. "Economic Assistance to Impoverished Americans: Relationship to Incidence of Crime," *Criminology* 21 (February 1983), 119–136.

Devine, Joel A., Joseph F. Sheley, and M. Dwayne Smith. "Macroeconomic and Social-Control Policy Influences on Crime Rate Changes, 1948–1985," *American Sociological Review* 53 (June 1988), 407–420.

DiIulio, John J., Jr., and Anne Morrison Piehl. "Does Prison Pay: The Stormy National Debate over the Cost-Effectiveness of Imprisonment," *Brookings Review* (Fall 1991), 28–35.

Donohue, John J., III, and Steven D. Levitt. "Legalized Abortion and Crime," John M. Olin Program in Law and Economics Working Paper No. 177. Palo Alto, CA.: Stanford Law School, April 2000. (Online: papers.ssrn.com/paper. taf?abstract_id=174508 [September 20, 2000])

———, and Peter Siegelman. "Allocating Resources among Prisons and Social Programs in the Battle against Crime," *Journal of Legal Studies* 27 (January 1998), 1–43.

Downs, Anthony. "Up and Down with Ecology—The 'Issue-Attention Cycle,' " *Public Interest* 28 (1972), 38–50.

Dunford, Franklyn W., David Huizinga, and Delbert S. Elliott. "The Role of Arrest in Domestic Assault: The Omaha Police Experiment," *Criminology* 28 (May 1990), 183–206.

Dunworth, Terence. *National Evaluation of the Youth Firearms Violence Initiative.* Washington, DC: U.S. Department of Justice, November 2000.

DuPont, Robert L., and Mark H. Greene. "The Dynamics of a Heroin Addiction Epidemic," *Science* 181 (1973), 716–722.

Duster, Troy. "Crime, Youth Unemployment, and the Black Underclass," *Crime and Delinquency* 33 (April 1987), 300–316.

Eck, John E., and Edward R. Maguire. "Have Changes in Policing Reduced Violent Crime? An Assessment of the Evidence," in Alfred Blumstein and Joel Wallman, eds., *The Crime Drop in America.* Cambridge, UK: Cambridge University Press, 2000, pp. 207–265.

———, and William Spelman. *Problem-Solving: Problem-Oriented Policing in Newport News.* Washington, DC: Police Executive Research Forum, 1987.

Elifson, Kirk W., David M. Petersen, and C. Kirk Hadaway. "Religiosity and Delinquency: A Contextual Analysis," *Criminology* 21 (November 1983), 505–527.

Esbensen, Finn-Aage. "Foot Patrols: Of What Value?" *American Journal of Police* 6 (1987), 45–65.

Evans, T. David, et al. "Religion and Crime Reexamined: The Impact of Religion, Secular Controls, and Social Ecology on Adult Criminality," *Criminology* 33 (May 1995), 195–224.

Fagan, Jeffrey, and Richard B. Freeman. "Crime and Work," in Michael Tonry, ed., *Crime and Justice: A Review of Research,* vol. 25. Chicago: University of Chicago Press, 1999, pp. 225–290.

———, and Deanna L. Wilkinson. "Guns, Youth Violence, and Social Identity in Inner Cities," in Michael Tonry and Mark H. Moore, eds., *Youth Violence,* vol. 24 of *Crime and Justice: A Review of Research.* Chicago: University of Chicago Press, 1998, pp. 105–188.

———, Franklin E. Zimring, and June Kim. "Declining Homicide in New York City: A Tale of Two Trends," *Journal of Criminal Law and Criminology* 88 (Summer 1998), 1277–1323.

Federal Bureau of Investigation. *Crime in the United States: Uniform Crime Reports.* Washington, DC: U.S. Department of Justice, 1991–2000.

Ferdinand, Theodore N. "Demographic Shifts and Criminality: An Inquiry," *British Journal of Criminology* 10 (April 1970), 169–175.

Fiala, Robert, and Gary LaFree. "Cross-National Determinants of Child Homicide," *American Sociological Review* 53 (June 1988), 432–455.

Finn, R. H., and Patricia A. Fontaine. "The Association between Selected Characteristics and Perceived Employability of Offenders," *Criminal Justice and Behavior* 12 (September 1985), 353–365.

Fowles, Richard, and Mary Merva. "Wage Inequality and Criminal Activity: An Extreme Bounds Analysis for the United States, 1975–1990," *Criminology* 34 (May 1996), 163–182.

Freeman, Richard B. "Crime and the Economic Status of Disadvantaged Young Men," in George E. Peterson and Wayne Vroman, eds., *Urban Labor Markets and Job Opportunities*. Washington, DC: Urban Institute, 1992.

———. "Crime and Unemployment," in James Q. Wilson, ed., *Crime and Public Policy*. San Francisco: ICS Press, 1983, pp. 89–106.

———. "The Labor Market," in James Q. Wilson and Joan Petersilia, eds., *Crime*. San Francisco: ICS Press, 1995, pp. 171–191.

———. "The Relation of Criminal Activity to Black Youth Employment," *Review of Black Political Economy* 16 (Summer/Fall 1987), 99–107.

Gallup Organization, The. (Online: www.gallup.com/poll/indicators [April 27, 2001])

Gartner, Rosemary, and Robert Nash Parker. "Cross-National Evidence on Homicide and the Age Structure of the Population," *Social Forces* 69 (December 1990), 351–371.

Gifford, Lea S., et al. *Background Checks for Firearm Transfers, 1999*. Washington, DC: U.S. Department of Justice, June 2000.

Gitlin, Todd. *The Whole World Is Watching: Mass Media in the Making and Unmaking of the New Left*. Berkeley: University of California Press, 1980.

Gladwell, Malcolm. *The Tipping Point: How Little Things Can Make a Big Difference*. Boston: Little, Brown, 2000.

Goldstein, Paul J. "The Drugs/Violence Nexus: A Tripartite Conceptual Framework," *Journal of Drug Issues* 14 (1985), 493–506.

———, et al. "Crack and Homicide in New York City: A Case Study in the Epidemiology of Violence," in Craig Reinarman and Harry G. Levine, eds., *Crack in America: Demon Drugs and Social Justice*. Berkeley: University of California Press, 1997, pp. 113–130.

Golub, Andrew Lang, and Bruce D. Johnson. *Crack's Decline: Some Surprises across U.S. Cities*. Washington, DC: U.S. Department of Justice, July 1997.

Gottfredson, Michael R., and Travis Hirschi. *A General Theory of Crime*. Stanford, CA: Stanford University Press, 1990.

Gove, Walter R., Michael Hughes, and Michael Geerken. "Are Uniform Crime Reports a Valid Indicator of Index Crimes? An Affirmative Answer with Minor Qualifications," *Criminology* 23 (August 1985), 451–501.

Greenberg, David F., and Ronald C. Kessler. "The Effect of Arrests on Crime: A Multivariate Panel Analysis," *Social Forces* 60 (March 1982), 771–790.

———, Ronald C. Kessler, and Colin Loftin. "The Effect of Police Employment on Crime," *Criminology* 21 (August 1983), 375–394.

Greene, Judith A. "Zero Tolerance: A Case Study of Police Policies and Practices in New York City," *Crime and Delinquency* 45 (April 1999), 171–187.

Greenfeld, Lawrence A. *Alcohol and Crime: An Analysis of National Data on the Prevalence of Alcohol Involvement in Crime*. Washington, DC: U.S. Department of Justice, April 1998.

Greenwood, Peter W. "Controlling the Crime Rate through Imprisonment," in James Q. Wilson, ed., *Crime and Public Policy*. San Francisco: ICS Press, 1983, pp. 251–269.

———. "Selective Incapacitation: A Method of Using Our Prisons More Effectively," *NIJ Reports* (January 1984), 4–7.

———, with Allan Abrahamse. *Selective Incapacitation*. Santa Monica, CA: Rand, 1982.

Grogger, Jeff. "An Economic Model of Recent Trends in Violence," in Alfred Blumstein and Joel Wallman, eds., *The Crime Drop in America*. Cambridge, UK: Cambridge University Press, 2000, pp. 266–287.

———. "Market Wages and Youth Crime," *Journal of Labor Economics* 16 (October 1998), 756–791.

Harcourt, Bernard E. *Illusion of Order: The False Promise of Broken Windows Policing*. Cambridge, MA: Harvard University Press, 2001.

Hickman, Matthew J., and Brian A. Reaves. *Community Policing in Local Police Departments, 1997 and 1999*. Washington, DC: U.S. Department of Justice, February 2001.

Hirschel, J. David, and Ira W. Hutchison III. "Female Spouse Abuse and the Police Response: The Charlotte, North Carolina Experiment," *Journal of Criminal Law and Criminology* 83 (Spring 1992), 73–119.

Hirschi, Travis. *Causes of Delinquency*. Berkeley: University of California Press, 1969.

Hope, Tim. "Community Crime Prevention," in Michael Tonry and David P. Farrington, eds., *Building a Safer Society: Strategic Approaches to Crime Prevention*, vol. 19 of *Crime and Justice: A Review of Research*. Chicago: University of Chicago Press, 1995, pp. 21–89.

Huff, C. Ronald. "The Criminal Behavior of Gang Members and Nongang At-Risk Youth," in C. Ronald Huff, ed., *Gangs in America*, 2nd ed. Thousand Oaks, CA: Sage, 1996, pp. 75–102.

Hyatt, Raymond, and William Rhodes. *Price and Purity of Cocaine: The Relationship to Emergency Room Visits and Deaths, and to Drug Use among Arrestees*. Washington, DC: Office of National Drug Control Policy, 1992.

Jacob, Herbert, and Michael J. Rich. "The Effects of the Police on Crime: A Second Look," *Law and Society Review* 15 (1981), 109–115.

Jencks, Christopher. "Behind the Numbers—Is Violent Crime Increasing?" *American Prospect* (Winter 1991), 98–109.

Joanes, Ana. "Does the New York City Police Department Deserve Credit for the Decline in New York City's Homicide Rates? A Cross-City Comparison of Policing Strategies and Homicide Rates," *Columbia Journal of Law and Social Problems* 33 (2000), 265–311.

Johnson, Bruce D., Andrew Golub, and Eloise Dunlap. "The Rise and Decline of Hard Drugs, Drug Markets, and Violence in Inner-City New York," in Alfred Blumstein and Joel Wallman, eds., *The Crime Drop in America*. Cambridge, UK: Cambridge University Press, 2000, pp. 164–206.

———, Andrew Golub, and Jeffrey Fagan. "Careers in Crack, Drug Use, Drug Distribution, and Nondrug Criminality," *Crime and Delinquency* 41 (July 1995), 275–295.

———, Ansley Hamid, and Harry Sanabria. "Emerging Models of Crack Distribution," in T. Mieczkowski, ed., *Drugs, Crime, and Social Policy: Research, Issues, and Concerns*. Boston: Allyn and Bacon, 1992, pp. 56–78.

———, et al. "Drug Abuse in the Inner City: Impact on Hard-Drug Users and the Community," in Michael Tonry and James Q. Wilson, eds., *Drugs and Crime*, vol. 13 of *Crime and Justice: A Review of Research.* Chicago: University of Chicago Press, 1990, pp. 9–67.

Johnson, Byron R., et al. "A Systematic Review of the Religiosity and Delinquency Literature," *Journal of Contemporary Criminal Justice* 16 (February 2000), 32–52.

Karmen, Andrew. *New York Murder Mystery: The True Story behind the Crime Crash of the 1990s.* New York: New York University Press, 2000.

Katz, Charles M., Vincent J. Webb, and David R. Schaefer. "An Assessment of the Impact of Quality-of-Life Policing on Crime and Disorder," *Justice Quarterly* 18 (December 2001), 825–876.

Katz, Jack. *Seductions of Crime: Moral and Sensual Attractions in Doing Evil.* New York: Basic Books, 1988.

Kelling, George L., and William J. Bratton. "Declining Crime Rates: Insiders' Views of the New York City Story," *Journal of Criminal Law and Criminology* 88 (Summer 1998), 1217–1231.

———, et al. *The Kansas City Preventive Patrol Experiment: A Summary Report.* Washington, DC: Police Foundation, 1974.

———, et al. *The Newark Foot Patrol Experiment.* Washington, DC: Police Foundation, 1981.

Kennedy, David M. "Pulling Levers: Getting Deterrence Right," *National Institute of Justice Journal* (July 1998), 2–8.

Kenney, Dennis Jay. *Crime, Fear, and the New York City Subways: The Role of Citizen Action.* New York: Praeger, 1987.

Kleck, Gary. *Targeting Guns: Firearms and Their Control.* New York: Aldine de Gruyter, 1997.

———, and E. Britt Patterson. "The Impact of Gun Control and Gun Ownership Levels on Violence Rates," *Journal of Quantitative Criminology* 9 (1993), 249–288.

Kleiman, Mark A. R. "Crackdowns: The Effects of Intensive Enforcement on Retail Heroin Dealing," in Marcia R. Chaiken, ed., *Street Level Drug Enforcement: Examining the Issues.* Washington, DC: National Institute of Justice, 1988.

Krahn, Harvey, Timothy F. Hartnagel, and John W. Gartrell. "Income Inequality and Homicide Rates: Cross-National Data and Criminological Theories," *Criminology* 24 (May 1986), 269–295.

Lab, Steven P. *Crime Prevention: Approaches, Practices and Evaluations,* 3rd ed. Cincinnati, OH: Anderson Publishing, 1997.

LaFree, Gary. *Losing Legitimacy: Street Crime and the Decline of Social Institutions in America.* Boulder, CO: Westview, 1998a.

———. "Social Institutions and the Crime 'Bust' of the 1990s," *Journal of Criminal Law and Criminology* 88 (Summer 1998b), 1325–1368.

———, and Kriss A. Drass. "The Effect of Changes in Intraracial Income Inequality and Educational Attainment on Changes in Arrest Rates for African-Americans and Whites, 1957 to 1990," *American Sociological Review* 61 (August 1996), 614–634.

Land, Kenneth C., David Cantor, and Steven T. Russell. "Unemployment and Crime Rate Fluctuations in the Post-World War II United States: Statistical

Time-Series Properties and Alternative Models," in John Hagan and Ruth D. Peterson, eds., *Crime and Inequality*. Stanford, CA: Stanford University Press, 1995, pp. 55–79.

Larson, Richard C. "What Happened to Patrol Operations in Kansas City," *Evaluation* 3 (1976), 117–123.

Levitt, Steven D. "The Effect of Prison Population Size on Crime Rates: Evidence from Prison Overcrowding Litigation," *Quarterly Journal of Economics* 111 (1996), 319–351.

———. "The Limited Role of Changing Age Structure in Explaining Aggregate Crime Rates," *Criminology* 37 (August 1999), 581–597.

———. "Using Electoral Cycles in Police Hiring to Estimate the Effect of Police on Crime," *American Economic Review* 87 (June 1997), 270–290.

LH Research. *A Survey of Experiences, Perceptions, and Apprehensions about Guns among Young People in America*. Cambridge, MA: Harvard University, School of Public Health, 1993.

Lipton, Douglas S., and Bruce D. Johnson. "Smack, Crack, and Score: Two Decades of NIDA-Funded Drugs and Crime Research at NDRI 1974–1994," *Substance Use and Misuse* 33 (1998), 1779–1815.

———, Robert Martinson, and Judith Wilks. *The Effectiveness of Correctional Treatment: A Survey of Treatment Evaluation Studies*. New York: Praeger, 1975.

Lizotte, Allan J., et al. "Patterns of Adolescent Firearms Ownership and Use," *Justice Quarterly* 11 (1994), 51–73.

Loeber, Rolf, and David P. Farrington, eds. *Serious and Violent Juvenile Offenders: Risk Factors and Successful Interventions*. Thousand Oaks, CA: Sage, 1998.

Loftin, Colin, and David McDowall. "The Police, Crime and Economic Theory: An Assessment," *American Sociological Review* 47 (June 1982), 393–401.

Logan, Charles H. "Arrest Rates and Deterrence," *Social Science Quarterly* 56 (December 1975), 376–389.

Lott, John, and David B. Mustard. "Crime, Deterrence, and Right-to-Carry Concealed Handguns," *Journal of Legal Studies* 26 (1997), 1–68.

Ludwig, Jens. "Concealed-Gun-Carrying Laws and Violent Crime: Evidence from State Panel Data," *International Review of Law and Economics* 18 (1998), 239–254.

———. "Gun Self-Defense and Deterrence," in Michael Tonry, ed., *Crime and Justice: A Review of Research*, vol. 27. Chicago: University of Chicago Press, 2000, pp. 363–417.

Makinen, Tuija, and Hannu Takala. "The 1976 Police Strike in Finland," *Scandinavian Studies in Criminology* 7 (1980), 87–106.

Martinson, Robert. "What Works?—Questions and Answers about Prison Reform," *Public Interest* 35 (Spring 1974), 22–54.

Marvell, Thomas B., and Carlisle E. Moody, Jr. "Age Structure and Crime Rates: The Conflicting Evidence," *Journal of Quantitative Criminology* 7 (1991), 237–273.

———, and Carlisle E. Moody, Jr. "The Impact of Enhanced Prison Terms for Felonies Committed with Guns," *Criminology* 33 (May 1995), 247–281.

————, and Carlisle E. Moody, Jr. "The Impact of Out-of-State Prison Population on State Homicide Rates: Displacement and Free-Rider Effects," *Criminology* 36 (August 1998), 513–535.

————, and Carlisle E. Moody, Jr. "The Impact of Prison Growth on Homicide," *Homicide Studies* 1 (August 1997), 205–233.

————, and Carlisle E. Moody, Jr. "Prison Population Growth and Crime Reduction," *Journal of Quantitative Criminology* 10 (1994), 109–140.

————, and Carlisle E. Moody, Jr. "Specification Problems, Police Levels, and Crime Rates," *Criminology* 34 (November 1996), 609–646.

McGahey, Richard M. "Economic Conditions, Neighborhood Organization, and Urban Crime," in Albert J. Reiss, Jr. and Michael Tonry, eds., *Communities and Crime*, vol. 8 of *Crime and Justice: A Review of Research*. Chicago: University of Chicago Press, 1986, pp. 231–270.

McGarrell, Edmund, Steven Chermak, and Alexander Weiss. *Reducing Firearms Violence through Directed Police Patrol: Final Report on the Evaluation of the Indianapolis Police Department's Direct Patrol Project*. Indianapolis, IN: Crime Control Policy Center, 1999.

————, et al. "Reducing Firearms Violence through Directed Police Patrol," *Criminology and Public Policy* 1 (November 2001), 119–148.

McGuire, William J., and Richard G. Sheehan. "Relationships between Crime Rates and Incarceration Rates: Further Analysis," *Journal of Research in Crime and Delinquency* 20 (1983), 73–85.

McNamara, Joseph D. "Preface," in George L. Kelling et al., *The Kansas City Preventive Patrol Experiment: A Summary Report*. Washington, DC: The Police Foundation, 1974, pp. iii–iv.

Menard, Scott, Sharon Mihalic, and David Huizinga. "Drugs and Crime Revisited," *Justice Quarterly* 18 (June 2001), 269–299.

Merton, Robert K. "Social Structure and Anomie," in *Social Theory and Social Structure*, 1968 enlarged ed. New York: Free Press, 1968, pp. 185–214.

Messner, Steven F. "Economic Discrimination and Societal Homicide Rates: Further Evidence on the Cost of Inequality," *American Sociological Review* 54 (August 1989), 597–611.

————, Lawrence E. Raffalovich, and Richard McMillan. "Economic Deprivation and Changes in Homicide Arrest Rates for White and Black Youths, 1967–1998: A National Time-Series Analysis," *Criminology* 39 (August 2001), 591–613.

————, and Kenneth Tardiff. "Economic Inequality and Levels of Homicide: An Analysis of Urban Neighborhoods," *Criminology* 24 (May 1986), 297–317.

Monkkonen, Eric H. *Murder in New York City*. Berkeley: University of California Press, 2001.

O'Brien, Robert M. *Crime and Victimization Data*. Thousand Oaks, CA: Sage, 1985.

Office of National Drug Control Policy. *National Drug Control Strategy: 2001 Annual Report*. Washington, DC: U.S. Government Printing Office, 2001.

Ousey, Graham C., and Matthew R. Lee. "Examining the Conditional Nature of the Illicit Drug Market-Homicide Relationship: A Partial Test of the Theory of Contingent Causation," *Criminology* 40 (February 2002), 73–102.

Parenti, Christian. *Lockdown America: Police and Prisons in an Age of Crisis.* London: Verso, 2000.

Parker, Robert Nash, and Randi S. Cartmill. "Alcohol and Homicide in the United States 1934–1995—or One Reason Why U.S. Rates of Violence May Be Going Down," *Journal of Criminal Law and Criminology* 88 (Summer 1998), 1369–1398.

Pate, Antony M., and Edwin E. Hamilton. "Formal and Informal Deterrents to Domestic Violence: The Dade County Spouse Assault Experiment," *American Sociological Review* 57 (October 1992), 691–697.

Petersilia, Joan, Peter W. Greenwood, and Marvin Lavin. *Criminal Careers of Habitual Felons.* Santa Monica, CA: Rand, 1977.

Pfuhl, Erdwin H., Jr. "Police Strikes and Conventional Crime: A Look at the Data," *Criminology* 21 (November 1983), 489–503.

Piehl, Anne Morrison, and John J. DiIulio, Jr. " 'Does Prison Pay?' Revisited: Returning to the Crime Scene," *Brookings Review* (Winter 1995), 21–25.

President's Commission on Law Enforcement and Administration of Justice. *The Challenge of Crime in a Free Society.* Washington, DC: U.S. Government Printing Office, 1967.

Reaves, Brain A., and Andrew L. Goldberg. *Law Enforcement Management and Administrative Statistics, 1997: Data for Individual State and Local Agencies with 100 or More Officers.* Washington, DC: U.S. Bureau of Justice Statistics, 1999.

Reinarman, Craig, and Harry G. Levine. "The Crack Attack: Politics and Media in the Crack Scare," in Craig Reinarman and Harry G. Levine, eds., *Crack in America: Demon Drugs and Social Justice.* Berkeley: University of California Press, 1997, pp. 18–51.

Rennison, Callie Marie. *Criminal Victimization 2000: Changes 1999–2000 with Trends 1993–2000.* Washington, DC: U.S. Department of Justice, June 2001.

Reppetto, Thomas A. *Residential Crime.* Cambridge, MA: Ballinger, 1974.

Reuter, Peter, et al. *Drug Use and Drug Programs in the Washington Metropolitan Area.* Santa Monica, CA: Rand, 1988.

Rosenbaum, Dennis P. "Community Crime Prevention: A Review and Synthesis of the Literature," *Justice Quarterly* 5 (September 1988), 323–395.

Rosenfeld, Richard. "Patterns in Adult Homicide: 1980–1995," in Alfred Blumstein and Joel Wallman, eds., *The Crime Drop in America.* Cambridge, UK: Cambridge University Press, 2000, pp. 130–163.

Rossi, Peter H., Richard A. Berk, and Kenneth J. Lenihan. *Money, Work, and Crime: Experimental Evidence.* New York: Academic Press, 1980.

Roth, Jeffrey A., and Joseph F. Ryan. *The COPS Program after 4 Years—National Evaluation.* Washington, DC: U.S. Department of Justice, August 2000.

Sampson, Robert J. "The Community," in James Q. Wilson and Joan Petersilia, eds., *Crime.* San Francisco: ICS Press, 1995, pp. 193–216.

———. "Structural Sources of Variation in Race-Age-Specific Rates of Offending across Major U.S. Cities," *Criminology* 23 (November 1985), 647–673.

———, and Jacqueline Cohen. "Deterrent Effects of the Police on Crime: A Replication and Theoretical Extension," *Law and Society Review* 22 (1988), 163–189.

————, and John Laub. *Crime in the Making: Pathways and Turning Points through Life*. Cambridge, MA: Harvard University Press, 1993.

————, and Stephen W. Raudenbush. *Disorder in Urban Neighborhoods—Does It Lead to Crime?* Washington, DC: U.S. Department of Justice, February 2001.

————, and Stephen W. Raudenbush. "Systematic Social Observation of Public Spaces: A New Look at Disorder in Urban Neighborhoods," *American Journal of Sociology* 105 (November 1999), 603–651.

————, Stephen W. Raudenbush, and Felton Earls. "Neighborhoods and Violent Crime: A Multilevel Study of Collective Efficacy," *Science* 277 (August 15, 1997), 918–924.

————, and William Julius Wilson. "Toward a Theory of Race, Crime, and Urban Inequality," in John Hagan and Ruth D. Peterson, eds., *Crime and Inequality*. Stanford, CA: Stanford University Press, 1995, pp. 37–54.

Shannon, Lyle W., with Judith L. McKim. *Criminal Career Continuity: Its Social Context*. New York: Human Sciences Press, 1988.

Sheley, Joseph F., and James D. Wright. *In the Line of Fire: Youth, Guns, and Violence in Urban America*. New York: Aldine de Gruyter, 1995.

Sherman, Lawrence W. "Attacking Crime: Police and Crime Control," in Michael Tonry and Norval Morris, eds., *Modern Policing*, vol. 15 of *Crime and Justice: A Review of Research*. Chicago: University of Chicago Press, 1992a, pp. 159–230.

————. "Defiance, Deterrence, and Irrelevance: A Theory of the Criminal Sanction," *Journal of Research in Crime and Delinquency* 30 (1993), 445–473.

————. "The Influence of Criminology on Criminal Law: Evaluating Arrests for Misdemeanor Domestic Violence," *Journal of Criminal Law and Criminology* 83 (Spring 1992b), 1–45.

————. "The Police," in James Q. Wilson and Joan Petersilia, eds., *Crime*. San Francisco: ICS Press, 1995, pp. 327–348.

————. "Police Crackdowns: Initial and Residual Deterrence," in Michael Tonry and Norval Morris, eds., *Crime and Justice: A Review of Research*, vol. 12. Chicago: University of Chicago Press, 1990, pp. 1–48.

————. *Policing Domestic Violence: Experiments and Dilemmas*. New York: Free Press, 1992c.

————. "Policing for Crime Prevention," in *Preventing Crime: What Works, What Doesn't, What's Promising—A Report to the Attorney General of the United States*. Washington, DC: U.S. Department of Justice, Office of Justice Programs, 1997, pp. 8-1–8-58.

————, and Richard A. Berk. "The Specific Deterrent Effects of Arrest for Domestic Assault," *American Sociological Review* 49 (April 1984), 261–272.

————, and Dennis P. Rogan. "Effects of Gun Seizures on Gun Violence: Hot Spot Patrol in Kansas City," *Justice Quarterly* 12 (1995), 673–694.

————, James W. Shaw, and Dennis P. Rogan. *The Kansas City Gun Experiment*. Washington, DC: U.S. Department of Justice, January 1995.

————, and David Weisburd. "General Deterrent Effects of Police Patrol in Crime 'Hot Spots': A Randomized, Controlled Trial," *Justice Quarterly* 12 (1995), 625–648.

———, et al. "From Initial Deterrence to Long-Term Escalation: Short-Custody Arrest for Poverty Ghetto Domestic Violence," *Criminology* 29 (November 1991), 821–850.

Shover, Neal. *Great Pretenders: Pursuits and Careers of Persistent Thieves.* Boulder, CO: Westview, 1996.

Silverman, Eli B. *NYPD Battles Crime: Innovative Strategies in Policing.* Boston: Northeastern University Press, 1999.

Skogan, Wesley G. "Community Organizations and Crime," in Michael Tonry and Norval Morris, eds., *Crime and Justice: A Review of Research*, vol. 10. Chicago: University of Chicago Press, 1988, pp. 39–78.

———. *Disorder and Decline: Crime and the Spiral of Decay in American Neighborhoods.* Berkeley: University of California Press, 1990.

———, and Susan M. Hartnett. *Community Policing, Chicago Style.* New York: Oxford University Press, 1997.

Skolnick, Jerome H., and David H. Bayley. "Theme and Variation in Community Policing," in Michael Tonry and Norval Morris, eds., *Crime and Justice: A Review of Research*, vol. 10. Chicago: University of Chicago Press, 1988, pp. 1–37.

Skorneck, Carolyn. "683,000 Women Raped in 1990, New Government Study Finds," *Boston Globe*, April 24, 1992, pp. 1, 32.

Smith, Tom W. "A Call for a Truce in the DGU War," *Journal of Criminal Law and Criminology* 87 (Summer 1997), 1462–1469.

Spelman, William. *Criminal Incapacitation.* New York: Plenum, 1994.

———. "The Limited Importance of Prison Expansion," in Alfred Blumstein and Joel Wallman, eds., *The Crime Drop in America.* Cambridge, UK: Cambridge University Press, 2000a, pp. 97–129.

———. "What Recent Studies Do (and Don't) Tell Us about Imprisonment and Crime," in Michael Tonry, ed., *Crime and Justice: A Review of Research*, vol. 27. Chicago: University of Chicago Press, 2000b, pp. 419–494.

Steffensmeier, Darrell J., and Miles D. Harer. "Did Crime Rise or Fall during the Reagan Presidency? The Effects of an 'Aging' U.S. Population on the Nation's Crime Rate," *Journal of Research in Crime and Delinquency* 28 (August 1991), 330–359.

———, and Miles D. Harer. "Is the Crime Rate Really Falling? An 'Aging' U.S. Population and Its Impact on the Nation's Crime Rate, 1980–1984," *Journal of Research in Crime and Delinquency* 24 (February 1987), 23–48.

———, and Miles D. Harer. "Making Sense of Recent U.S. Crime Trends, 1980 to 1996/1998: Age Composition Effects and Other Explanations," *Journal of Research in Crime and Delinquency* 36 (August 1999), 235–274.

Tauchen, Helen, Ann Dryden Witte, and Harriet Griesinger. "Criminal Deterrence: Revisiting the Issue with a Birth Cohort," National Bureau of Economic Research Working Paper 4277, February 1993.

Taylor, Ralph B. *Breaking Away from Broken Windows: Baltimore Neighborhoods and the Nationwide Fight against Crime, Grime, Fear, and Decline.* Boulder, CO: Westview, 2001.

Taylor, Robert W., Eric J. Fritsch, and Tory J. Caeti. "Core Challenges Facing Community Policing: The Emperor *Still* Has No Clothes," *ACJS Today* (May/June 1998), 1, 3–5.

Thornberry, Terence P., and R. L. Christenson. "Unemployment and Criminal Involvement: An Investigation of Reciprocal Causal Structures," *American Sociological Review* 49 (June 1984), 398–411.

———, et al. "The Role of Juvenile Gangs in Facilitating Delinquent Behavior," *Journal of Research in Crime and Delinquency* 30 (1993), 55–87.

Tillman, Robert. "The Size of the 'fCriminal Population': The Prevalence and Incidence of Adult Arrest," *Criminology* 25 (August 1987), 561–579.

Tittle, Charles R., and Alan R. Rowe. "Certainty of Arrest and Crime Rates: A Further Test of the Deterrence Hypothesis," *Social Forces* 52 (June 1974), 455–462.

Tonry, Michael. *Malign Neglect: Race, Crime, and Punishment in America.* New York: Oxford University Press, 1995.

Tracy, Paul E., Jr., Marvin E. Wolfgang, and Robert M. Figlio. *Delinquency Careers in Two Birth Cohorts.* New York: Plenum, 1990.

Trojanowicz, Robert. *An Evaluation of the Neighborhood Foot Patrol Program in Flint, Michigan.* East Lansing: Michigan State University, 1983.

U.S. Census Bureau. (Online: www.census.gov/prod/2002pubs/01statab/election. pdf [March 20, 2002])

U.S. Department of Agriculture. (Online: www.ers.usda.gov/briefing/ consumption/data/webtablexls [March 1, 2001])

Viscusi, W. Kip. "Market Incentives for Criminal Behavior," in Richard B. Freeman and Harry Holzer, eds., *The Black Youth Employment Crisis.* Chicago: University of Chicago Press for National Bureau of Economic Research, 1986, pp. 301–346.

Visher, Christy A. "The Rand Inmate Survey: A Reanalysis," in Alfred Blumstein et al., eds., *Criminal Careers and "Career Criminals",* vol. 2. Washington, DC: National Academy Press, 1986, pp. 161–211.

von Hirsch, Andrew. "Selective Incapacitation: A Critique," *NIJ Reports* (January 1984), 5–8.

Welch, Michael, Melissa Fenwick, and Meredith Roberts. "Primary Definitions of Crime and Moral Panic: A Content Analysis of Experts' Quotes in Feature Newspaper Articles on Crime," *Journal of Research in Crime and Delinquency* 34 (November 1997), 474–494.

———, Melissa Fenwick, and Meredith Roberts. "State Managers, Intellectuals, and the Media: A Content Analysis of Ideology in Experts' Quotes in Feature Newspaper Articles on Crime," *Justice Quarterly* 15 (June 1998), 219–241.

Williams, Hubert, and Antony M. Pate. "Returning to First Principles: Reducing the Fear of Crime in Newark," *Crime and Delinquency* 33 (January 1987), 53–70.

Wilson, James Q., and Allan Abrahamse. "Does Crime Pay?" *Justice Quarterly* 9 (September 1992), 359–377.

———, and Barbara Boland. "Crime," in William Gorham and Nathan Glaser, eds., *The Urban Predicament.* Washington, DC: Urban Institute, 1976, pp. 179–230.

———, and Barbara Boland. "The Effect of the Police on Crime," *Law and Society Review* 12 (1978), 367–390.

————, and George L. Kelling. "Broken Windows: The Police and Neighborhood Safety," *Atlantic Monthly* 249 (March 1982), 29–38.

Wintemute, Garen. "Guns and Gun Violence," in Alfred Blumstein and Joel Wallman, eds., *The Crime Drop in America.* Cambridge, UK: Cambridge University Press, 2000, pp. 45–96.

————, et al. "Effectiveness of Expanded Criteria for Denial of Firearm Purchase." Paper presented at the annual meeting of the American Society of Criminology, Toronto, 1999.

————, et al. "Prior Misdemeanor Convictions as a Risk Factor for Later Violent and Firearm-Related Criminal Activity among Authorized Purchasers of Handguns," *Journal of the American Medical Association* 280 (1998), 2083–2087.

Wolfgang, Marvin E. *Patterns in Criminal Homicide.* Philadelphia: University of Pennsylvania Press, 1958.

————, Robert M. Figlio, and Thorsten Sellin. *Delinquency in a Birth Cohort.* Chicago: University of Chicago Press, 1972.

Wright, James D., and Peter H. Rossi. *Armed and Considered Dangerous: A Survey of Felons and Their Firearms.* New York: Aldine de Gruyter, 1986.

Wright, Mona A., Garen J. Wintemute, and Frederick A. Rivara. "Effectiveness of Denial of Handgun Purchase to Persons Believed to Be at High Risk for Firearm Violence," *American Journal of Public Health* 89 (1999), 88–90.

Wright, Richard T., and Scott H. Decker. *Burglars on the Job: Streetlife and Residential Break-ins.* Boston: Northeastern University Press, 1994.

Wycoff, Mary Ann. *Community Policing Strategies.* Washington, DC: U.S. Department of Justice, November 1995.

Yu, Jiang, and Allen E. Liska. "The Certainty of Punishment: A Reference Group Effect and Its Functional Form," *Criminology* 31 (August 1993), 447–464.

Zedlewski, Edwin. *Making Confinement Decisions.* Washington, DC: National Institute of Justice, 1987.

Zimring, Franklin E. "Is Gun Control Likely to Reduce Violent Killings?" *University of Chicago Law Review* 35 (1968), 721–737.

————, and Gordon Hawkins. *Crime Is Not the Problem: Lethal Violence in America.* New York: Oxford University Press, 1997.

NAME INDEX

SUBJECT INDEX